"SPECIAL EDITION" DESTROYING THE HOMELAND

OH, SAY CAN YOU SEE?

THE FALL OF AMERICA. HOW DID WE GET HERE?

JOHN E. SURAJ PERSAD

BOOK DEDICATION

Chief Master Sergeant
Johnny Wedderburn, Sr.
December 10, 1939 - August 18, 2015

To my brother-in-law Johnny Wedderburn Sr., deceased (USAF Ret. Chief Master Sergeant). Thank you for three decades of decorated service to the nation during combat and peacetime operations and for your family's unwavering support of the mission. You exemplified the virtues of service, respect, wisdom, family, honesty, work ethic, and kindness, which have been carried forward in the family. Our many social discussions have been inspirational and also a great source of first-hand history from differing perspectives on the evolution of the American landscape. For these reasons, among many more, I find it necessary to dedicate this book to your memory. Our conversations about this book would have been great. Obviously, you were needed elsewhere and called for higher service. Catch you on the flip side, Chief. "Hot Dog Mister." My Air Force brother. Carry On Chief..

Acknowledgment

All praise to God, the creator, for allowing me to raise my voice in the continued defense of my country through the dissemination of information. Many paths, one God.

To my children, I am incredibly proud of you and your families. Continue the traditions and teachings that have strengthened our family. The love and caring you show us daily as we age and for including us in the combined responsibility of passing down our values to the grandchildren is noted and a blessing for us. The integrity of the family unit is paramount.

A special thanks to my wife Gerarda (CDR, USPHS. Ret, Frm. U.S. Army) for her love, support, and strength. You set an excellent example of resilience and strength of character for the family to follow, especially as a cancer survivor. We couldn't survive without you. We all follow your lead and "failure is not an option" ethos. Love you forever.

To Idalis, Joseph, and Anthony, the oldest grandchildren, continue to learn about the value of family, respect, and traditions and strive to be the best in all you do. Never be satisfied with mediocrity. Chart your own path in life and dream big. Let nothing or anyone hold you back from being successful or changing your trajectory. Love you.

Adriano and Danilo, my youngest grandchildren, inspire and give me immense joy. I will avidly assist in your development as humanly possible. Time with you both is one of our greatest blessings. I Love you very much.

To all Americans serving the nation who place their lives on the line to protect and secure us at home and abroad, I express my gratitude to you and your families and pray for your continued safety. God bless.

Thank you to my friends, family, discussion groups, and acquaintances who have assisted me in researching and getting information firsthand. I couldn't have pulled it off without you. Special thanks to the students who helped with the many surveys.

To all the veterans from the Miami and Asheville VA hospitals whom I spoke to and who offered their heartfelt concerns about the state of our nation and their displeasure with policies, leadership, and society's support for terrorism, I can only provide this book as a way to speak up and give them a voice. Thank you for your service.

To the IDF (Israeli Defense Force) men and women who defend their nation with the warrior spirit, our support and respect are with you and the State of Israel. "WARRIOR ON." The Islamist fight is on our doorstep. Good must triumph over evil, and you must wipe out the architects and supporters of evil.

To those American warriors from all branches who have made the journey ahead of us, I salute you and wish you peace and rest. Old soldiers never die; we just get called to higher service.

To my "Undisclosed" friends still serving, I recognize you and your work for the nation. Thank you for the many discussions on foreign policy and race issues in America. Your accomplishments and years of military, intelligence, political, and community service give me a reason to pause and respect greatness.

To those professional associates still fighting on the front line to keep us safe at home, I appreciate your candor and perceptions on American policies, government, Islamism, and national security. Your input is much appreciated. Thank you for your belief in this nation we call home. God bless.

A special thanks to all the First Responders, especially Law Enforcement, who place their lives in harm's way daily to protect us from criminal elements and harm. Your sacrifices and those of your families are appreciated.

To the victims of the horrific act of political violence and assassination attempt on former President Trump at the rally in Pennsylvania, I send my prayers of hope for our nation.

ABOUT THE AUTHOR

The author is of East Indian descent and was born in England to Jamaican and Guyanese East Indian immigrants. His father served in the RAF (Royal Air Force) during WW2, and his mother trained as a nurse in England. John is a neoconservative with a diverse background and was educated in the British and American systems. He lived in Jamaica after leaving England and attended Clarendon College in Chapelton (a mountain community in the central region). His education includes the Cambridge University Examinations, a Bachelor's degree in Technical Management, a Post-Baculerate certification as a Paralegal, a Master's in International Policy and Practice from The George Washington University, Elliott School of International Affairs, and numerous professional military and government schools. His academic tracks heavily concentrate on Transnational Security, Strategic Leadership, Aviation, and International Policy.

John is a former Commissioned Warrant Officer (CW3) in the United States Army Aviation Corps, a graduate of the U.S. Army Warrant Officer Career College, U.S. Army Aviation Flight Academy, U.S. Army Intelligence School, U.S. Army Combat Readiness Center, and holds Federal Aviation Administration (FAA) certifications as a Flight Engineer (FE), Commercial Pilot (CP), and Airline Transport

Pilot (ATP). He is also dual-rated as an aviator in Helicopters and Airplanes. He holds occupational certification as an Aviation Safety Officer and Aircraft Accident Investigator, Intelligence Aircraft Pilot, Rotor Wing Reconnaissance Pilot, Electronic Warfare Officer, Information System Security Officer, and Flight Operations Officer.

During his career, he has been deployed for many operations worldwide, and in his last assignment, he supported multiple operations in Europe and Asia. Upon completing his service, he changed careers and went to UPS Airlines as a commercial pilot, flying the DC8, B757, and B767-300ER platforms internationally. After 9/11, John volunteered for training at the Federal Law Enforcement Training Center (FLETC) to be a Deputized Federal Aviation Law Enforcement Officer assigned under the Department of Homeland Security. John is a disabled American veteran who is extremely thankful and proud of his service to the United States Army. He is currently retired from flying, and his writings and podcasts bring to light perspectives of an immigrant coming to his adopted country, embracing the nation's core values, assimilating while being true to his heritage, and fully engaging in the American dream.

John continues to serve today as a security and leadership consultant, volunteers as a training advisor to the Boone Police Department in N.C. and other agencies and advises several foreign clients on strategic leadership, corporate security, and risk management. John is a member of the Rotary Club and the Military Officers Association of America, where he and his wife assist veterans in various capacities. John is happily retired with his wife Gerarda,

MSSW, LCSW, QCSW (U.S. Army Frm., CDR. USPHS. Ret), whom he met during their early Army careers. John often jokes, *"The Army gave me a life and issued me a wife."* They have two professional sons, Anthony (MBA. USA. Frm) and Omar (J.D. MSBS.), their immediate families, and a close nephew, Saheed (USA. Ret), in their circle of influence. Together, John and Gerarda have five grandchildren, and they hang their hats between North Carolina, Florida, and Europe. Living the American Dream.

AUTHOR'S NEOCONSERVATIVE BELIEF FRAMEWORK

Neoconservatism is a socio-political and intellectual movement that originated in the United States during the second half of the 20th century. The phrase "neoconservative" derives from the phrase "new conservatism," which can be interpreted as a departure from the traditional conservative principles. Neoconservatism emerged as a prominent foreign policy ideology in the late 20th and early 21st centuries, showcasing a set of policy preferences and conceptual frameworks with a holistic cognizance.

The salient characteristics of evolved neoconservatism encompass the following but are not limited to:

1). Neoconservatives support a strong and active foreign policy that involves intervention. Their ideology advocates for the utilization of military power to advance American interests second to diplomatic missions, disseminate democracy, and confront perceived menaces to national security head-on. This approach is occasionally denoted as "democratic globalism" or "Wilsonianism," deriving inspiration from Woodrow Wilson's concept of advocating democracy globally while incorporating some concepts of Nationalism.

2). Neoconservatives advocate prioritizing democracy and promoting human rights protection as fundamental components of U.S. foreign policy. They hold the belief that fostering democratic governance worldwide enhances global stability and is in political alignment with American principles.

3). Neoconservatives frequently exhibit skepticism toward international organizations and treaties, favoring unilateral or coalition actions that prioritize American interests first (nationalism lite). They might perceive international institutions, such as the U.N., as obstacles to decisive action.

4). Exceptionalism is frequently embraced by neoconservatives, who assert that the United States has a distinct role and obligation in advancing freedom and democracy on a global scale, but I stand fast on the premise that we must do so without infringing on the sovereignty of others or inserting ourselves in their self-governing.

5). Advocacy for a Robust Military ties in with Neoconservative principles that typically endorse allocating ample resources and establishing a formidable military. They contend that a robust defense is indispensable for safeguarding national interests and upholding global stability. The concept of "peace through strength" is reinforced but relegated to the background secondary to comprehensive diplomatic practices.

6). Neoconservatives express apprehension regarding appeasement, which they view as a form of weakness or capitulation when confronted with threats. They stress the importance of diplomatically operating from a position of strength, intelligence, and assertiveness when engaging opponents, especially those of Eastern ideologies, which view appeasement as a weakness and a green light to push their agenda. This also includes the Chinese and Russian leadership. Many opportunities have been missed.

NOTE: It is crucial to acknowledge that although neo-conservatism has exerted significant influence on the formation of U.S. foreign policy, it is not a uniform or homogeneous ideology. Those of us who adhere to this ideology may hold varying views on particular policy matters, and the movement has undergone evolutionary changes over the years, especially in the Bush presidency era. In contrast to traditional conservatives, neoconservatives exhibit a greater inclination toward a holistic approach to identifying root issues and scrutinizing cultural affairs and mass media contributions. This includes, but is not limited to, music, art, literature, theater, film, and, more recently, television and the Internet. It is based on the grounds that these mediums serve as vehicles through which a society forms and manifests its values and self-definition. Some social scientists argue that Western society, especially American society, lacks moral principles, direction, and values. It's postulated that Western culture is morally corrupt, citing violent and sexually explicit films, television programs, and video games that indoctrinate the easily influenced as the cause.

Previously considered vulgar and inappropriate conduct are now acceptable practices and widely acknowledged as customary, and the average information consumer accepts this. It would be hard-pressed for any American resident to disagree with this neo-conservative theory, as the current landscape and America's visible decline into immorality, anarchy, lawlessness, and judicial corruption support the arguments presented. I would also offer the observation that culturally, Asians, Spanish, Africans, and African Americans are much more attuned to conservative values and beliefs, religion, and traditions. I propose another argument that President Trump falls under this Neo-Conservative umbrella. American interests first, as it should be: protection of our national identity, deterrence through strength, strong national defense, sound, balanced economic and trade policy, a one-nation, one-people policy, and the preservation of constitutional rights to include our Judeo-Christian belief system. Those policies seem very neoconservative to me, doing what is best for the nation and our security. Interestingly enough, one doesn't have to be a Democrat or Republican to practice some variation of this belief framework. Political affiliation only means that one has a different approach to accomplishing the most basic centric goals of any government, such as prosperity and safety for the nation and citizenry. Political parties are destructive to the well-being of a nation if polarization, corrupted power, and racial division occur and run amuck within a nation.

AUTHORS NOTE

a) Knowledge allows us to use our full reasoning abilities and incorporate logic to become informed information consumers. It prevents ignorance and stupidity.

b). Accurate information is elusive in today's world of spin and deception. We must qualify information to avoid being quagmired in the mindless game of political zombies and social deception. Research platforms that should be representative of both sides are absent. One of the widely used sources in colleges, Google Scholar, is nothing more than a left-wing medium for spreading liberal socialist works and propaganda material. Remember, Garbage in, Garbage out.

c). Disregarding the differences in Eastern and Western ideology is a colossal mistake American diplomats and lawmakers continuously repeat. Ignoring old-world customs and forcing American contemporary beliefs upon the "old world" is damaging to East-West relations and the difference between showing strength, compassion, and weakness.

d). If only respect, tolerance, and good fellowship towards one another could be returned to our society, most of the world's issues would be solved.

e). Politics must never define us; we must define politics and how it is used to benefit our nation collectively. Never use politics to divide but unite and further a nation's interests.

f). Society is rife with hypocrisy. Many of our politicians in power today run on a concept of inclusivity but squash and demonize any voice or action that differs from their party narratives. "Freedom of speech" now means "Freedom to express views only if the views align with liberal democratic socialist messaging." How's that for diversity and inclusivity? How is that for democracy? Which party doctrine and leader is destroying democracy? Why are the leftist activists always involved in rioting and disruption tactics? Look at France in July 2024. These questions we must ask ourselves.

g). The DEI (Diversity, Equity, Inclusion) framework pushed by the liberal democratic socialist machine is propagating our nation's divide, racial hatred, and cultural exclusion at all levels of society. How is this a good thing? In many professional circles, the general consensus on the meaning of DEI is (Didn't Earn It). This undermines the credibility and perceptions accompanying the well-deserved achievement of minorities. Any policy that places one group ahead of another because of race or sexual orientation is discriminatory in nature. It doesn't matter how you look at it. Taking meritocracy out of the selection equation encourages mediocracy and acceptance of minimum effort standards in society as a norm. If this prevails, good luck with having the "Best of the Best" as your doctor, Lawyer, commercial pilot, military officer, scientist, engineer, and other such positions requiring a high level of proficiency and competition to ensure excellence in the field.

TERMINOLOGY

Liberal International World Order: The Biden administration has used this as an ideological reference for its policies, incorporating Liberalism, Globalism, Progressives, and Socialism within its ideology. This is a continuation of Obama's policies.

Multiculturalism: This encompasses various interpretations in the fields of sociology, politics, and philosophy. In sociology and common parlance, it is a synonym for "ethnic pluralism." On a global level, such occurrences can arise from the unlawful movement of people between various jurisdictions worldwide, as observed in Europe and the United States. Multiculturalism centers around the strategies societies adopt to address cultural and religious disparities while maintaining their distinctiveness from the dominant nation. Noncompliance with the customs and fundamental values of the host country is a significant issue in Europe. It is frequently linked to concepts such as "identity politics," "the politics of difference," and "the politics of recognition."(www.researchomatic.com/ multicultural-diversity-82756.html)

Liberal Democratic Socialist Machine/Complex: Liberal socialism is a political ideology that combines the principles of liberalism with socialism (Democratic Socialism Meaning & Definition | Good Party. https://goodparty.org/political-terms/democratic-socialism). Democratic socialism is a political ideology on the left side of the political spectrum that advocates for a combination of political democracy and a socially owned economy. It places importance on economic democracy, workplace democracy, and workers' self-management within the framework of a socialist, decentralized planned, or democratic centrally planned socialist economy. Democratic socialists contend that capitalism is fundamentally incongruous with the principles of liberty, egalitarianism, and cohesion, asserting that the actualization of a socialist society is the sole means to attain these ideals. This amalgamation of ideologies has assimilated the progressives and globalists into its ranks while also drawing the support of fringe factions advocating for Fascist and Marxist ideology. They constitute what I term the Liberal Democratic Socialist Machine, and the integration of supportive mainstream media, social media, and social advocacy groups, including universities, is known collectively as the Complex. It is essential to *note that Islamist and Communist factions (Iran, China, and Russia actors) have infiltrated these groups to piggyback and push their disruptive ideologies for their own gain.

Gender Confusion: This refers to the Transgender and Transsexual groups, more commonly referred to as the constantly evolving LGBTQ+, LGBTQIA, LBGTQIA+, and LBGTQIA2s+ community. The latest evolved term 2SLGBTQIA+ is an acronym that means: 2 Spirit, Lesbian, Gay, Bisexual, Transgender, Queer, Questioning, Intersex, Asexual,+ Pansexual, + Agender,+ Gender Queer, + Bigender, + Gender Variant, and + Pangender. By the time this book is published, this acronym will probably be outdated and, of course, offend someone. It is sad that their "cry for help" is being exploited by the Democratic Party voter pandering schemes to secure a loyal base.

Zombie Electorate: The majority of our nation's uninformed electorate consists of a combination of individuals from Generation Z and Generation Y, as well as those who have been influenced by Socialism, Islamism, Liberalism, and Globalism and who have "by choice" decided to remain misinformed. They demonstrate a lack of concern for civic knowledge, patriotic service, personal responsibility, and accountability for their actions. There is a direct correlation between the Zombie electorate and those that are targeted by the Liberal Democrat Socialist disinformation strategy to disseminate false flag narratives. Almost all their information on society, politics, and their minuscule bubble is provided by social media, the likes of TikTok. The art of personal research of facts, speaking from a position of knowledge, and applying analysis and common sense is nonexistent today. The liberal democratic socialist media complex actually reinforces this, as it keeps impressionable in a society controlled and dancing to their every drumbeat. Mental slavery comes in many shapes and colors. Those nonconformists who drop out of lock-step with this liberal-socialist mindset and those who start thinking for themselves are immediately demonized, socially disgraced, and labeled as traitors, racists, Uncle Tom's, and fascists in an attempt to render them socially irrelevant so their message won't take hold (African American Conservatives). Countering the opposing narrative with smear campaigns is their Modi operandi.

Military Industrial Complex/Defense Industrial Complex/Military Industrial Congressional Complex: The military-industrial complex refers to the intricate connection between a nation's military and the defense industry corporations responsible for providing it with the necessary resources and equipment. The United States Military-Industrial Complex (MIC), or Defense Industrial Complex, is of immense magnitude and significantly influences foreign policy. It also includes the members of Congress who support the complex and advocate for benefits for their state. This complex drives foreign policy and generates enormous wealth.

Islamist: Refers to an individual or collective that employs Islamic symbols and traditions to advance their radicalized sociopolitical goals. The term "Islamic" pertains explicitly to aspects of Islam as a religious belief rather than a sociopolitical organization.

Islamism: This is a religious-political ideology. Islamists, known as "al-Islamiyyun," seek to implement their interpretation of Islam in society. Most belong to "al-harakat al-Islamiyyah," Islamic institutions or social mobilization movements. Islamists promote sharia, pan-Islamic political unity, Islamic states, and rejection of non-Muslim influences, particularly Western or universal economic, military, political, social, or cultural influences.

Sharia Law: This set of religious laws is an integral part of the Islamic tradition. It is derived from the scriptures of Islam, specifically the Quran and the Hadith. Human rights groups assert that certain traditional sharia practices entail significant transgressions against fundamental human rights, gender equality, and freedom of expression, leading to criticism of countries governed by sharia. In multiple instances, the European Court of Human Rights in

Strasbourg has determined that Sharia law is "inconsistent with the fundamental tenets of democracy."

Media Complex: The Political Media Complex (PMC) refers to the interconnected relationships between a state's political and ruling classes and its media industry. They collaborate with the Military Industrial Complex, the Financial Industrial Complex, and weaponized agencies to influence societal changes, shape party narratives, and determine party policies. It may also include other interest groups, like social activists, and all forms of social media and written publications. PMC is a term used negatively to describe the cooperation among governments, politicians, and the media industry aimed at carrying out the government's agenda and disseminating propaganda.

Economic or Financial Industrial Complex: The U.S. dollar is currently encountering challenges such as increasing tensions with China, the rise of digital currencies, emerging protectionist measures, and the importance of currency dominance in America's goal to establish a global order based on free markets and democracy, as well as supporting the growth of a more interconnected global economy. The financial complex comprises major organizations and banks that generate financing, investments, and economic pressures to support the development of US markets and the expansion of trade worldwide. It is utilized in financial statecraft, which involves using economic strategies to influence international capital flows. Economic statecraft is at play for strategic outcomes to be realized.

Famous Quotes

"If Fascism comes to America, it will come in the name of Liberalism." - Ronald Reagan.

"For other nations, utopia is a blessed past never to be recovered; for Americans, it is just beyond the horizon." – Henry A. Kissinger.

"Let us resolve to be masters, not the victims, of our history, controlling our own destiny without giving way to blind suspicions and emotions." – John F. Kennedy.

"Aggression unopposed becomes a contagious disease." – Jimmy Carter.

"It is by a thorough knowledge of the whole subject that [people] are enabled to judge correctly of the past and to give a proper direction to the future." – James Monroe

"While men inhabiting different parts of this vast continent cannot be expected to hold the same opinions, they can unite in a common objective and sustain common principles." - Franklin Pierce.

"The worst things in history have happened when people stop thinking for themselves, especially when they allow themselves to be influenced by negative people. That's what gives rise to dictators. Avoid that at all costs. Stop it first on a personal level, and you will have contributed to world sanity as well as your own." - President Donald Trump.

The Mexican contingent: They said, "No way," sir; I said, "Way," said - President Donald Trump.

TABLE OF CONTENTS

PART I

INTRODUCTION AND HISTORICAL REVIEW

CHAPTER 1

DESTROYING THE HOMELAND, AN OVERVIEW

America is being destroyed from within. Will you, the electorate, just sit there in your "Cone of ignorance and misinformation bliss" and allow this heinous act to be perpetrated on our beloved homeland? This book will challenge your ability to use common sense analysis, not be "Zombie Electorates," and make sound sociopolitical decisions for the continued safety and welfare of our beloved nation. In other words, it means being "Informed, responsible Americans" who think independently rather than being politically brainwashed. In 2024, you are observing an unprecedented version of America, where the extent of a nation's decline due to four years of inadequate and corrupt governance is becoming evident. This is even more apparent when examining the circumstances and gross negligence surrounding the failed assassination attempt on a former president and opposition frontrunner in the upcoming general elections. I present an unabashed neoconservative perspective on the current events unfolding in our country, including the deteriorating state of governance, pervasive government corruption, agency weaponization, foreign affairs failure, escalating immorality, racial segregation, deliberate undermining of the African American culture, the potential for civil war and global conflict, the erosion of our democratic system, the emergence of a monocratic government, the transformation of our social fabric, and the observable impact on our voting demographics in America due to irregular migration and open borders. Quite a troubling list, isn't it? It is flabbergasting to observe how such a significant number of Americans are either unable or unwilling to perceive the extensive damage taking place in our nation and the erosion of societal norms, including the deceptive disenfranchising of the African American culture over several decades. In this second book, I present numerous contentious and thought-provoking inquiries for the reader to ponder and reflect upon, intending to challenge your norms and hopefully think outside the constructed narratives in society. Awaken America before it is too late!

Most topics and areas covered interrelate on some level, so overlapping concepts, views, and information are unavoidable. Currently, the United States is engaged in a complex and interconnected conflict that spans both domestic and international arenas, involving political, ideological, and religious forces. The failures in these three domains are the driving force behind our military conflicts. The resolution of these conflicts will determine whether America can maintain its position as the "Land of the Free" and "One Nation under God" while remaining loyal to its inherent Judeo-Christian values and established traditions. The United States faces the potential loss of its individuality and international reputation as a champion of fairness, tranquility, and democratic values in governance. In my opinion, most of this is driven by the economic and power ambitions of the deep state, including the military-industrial complex and the liberal democratic new world order. The mechanism used to brainwash the American electorate is the democratic media complex, which coordinates with the

3

deep state in pushing a concerted narrative for consumption. In today's America, where the liberal democratic socialist machine controls most of the research outlets, i.e., Google Scholar and AI, it is increasingly difficult to get unbiased research material, and most universities' research papers are heavily liberal-slanted.

Conservative views are similar to being Jewish on campus; it's just not tolerated by academia or the students. It is essential to remember, now more than ever, that free and impartial media from state control is the counterbalance to entrenched deep-state indoctrination. Without this counterbalance, the information is skewed, and the people are misled on a mass scale, as is occurring today. The global arena and our domestic governance issues are not as black and white as you are led to believe by the politicians and media complex. However, a tangled web of deceit and power struggles exists, with the American people caught between the shadow power elitists behind America's leadership and the people's vision for our nation. American foreign policy affects the world, and the reasoning and analysis behind formulating our policies (Global/domestic) are essential to understand, as our national survival and global positioning depend on them.

National identity is a critical conversation that needs to be addressed in America. It concerns preserving national core values as we witness the steady decline of national identities in many European countries due to irregular migration and their unwillingness to assimilate within the host nation. This is not a manufactured talking point. I urge you to watch foreign YouTube news station coverage and

Asian news feeds as the catastrophe in Europe from open borders and liberal policies becomes clear. The CDC (Center for Disease Control) released data on February 02, 2024, indicating that in September of the previous year, the number of migrant encounters at the southern border exceeded the number of births in the United States. This statistic indicates that the Liberal Democratic Socialist Party is making progress towards substituting Americans and our fundamental principles with illegal immigrants who do not share our values and lack the intention to integrate and contribute to the growth of our nation under a unified flag. In essence, they are effectively altering the demographics of America prematurely. On the domestic front, our homeland is being destroyed; it is absolutely mindboggling the destructive forces acting on our society. America has never been so divided in my time.

In three (3) short years (2021-2024), the United States has transcended from prosperity and relative calm to rapidly descending into a cauldron of racial hatred, racial division, political discord, declining values and beliefs, exploding crime, civil disturbances, public property destruction, population demographic manipulation, vote pandering, political persecution, judicial and government corruption, failure to protect the homeland, federal government overreach, and political alignment of states in the union against the federal government. Now, the possibility of a looming civil war is entirely possible. What is happening in our nation reads like an apocalyptic novel; you couldn't make it up if you tried. Therefore, in order to avoid this situation, it is imperative that we restore efficient governance and strong leadership, reunite the nation under one flag, and implement strategic long-term planning while also adjusting our trajectory and mitigating the harmful influences that are eroding our democratic procedures. An actively involved and well-informed voting population with a strong President and effective governance practices will be crucial in achieving this monumental task.

(1). Is the American electorate prepared to tolerate the erosion and compromise of constitutional safeguards and institutions and the destruction of our democratic process? The blatant attack on the democratically chosen Republican Presidential candidate through the weaponization of the State and Federal judicial systems (Courts/DA), Federal Justice and Intelligence agencies (FBI, CIA, NSA), and the corruption of the election process? Additionally, independent media organizations are used as party surrogates to push misinformation to indoctrinate the electorate and propagate censorship of free speech. Furthermore, do we comprehend the national security threats that the Biden administration is exposing the country to through its lack of leadership in the geopolitical arena and insecure borders? Do we suffer from intellectual blindness? Open your eyes and take note of the travesties that are taking place both in the United States and around the world.

(2). The inquiries that ensue are whether the United States of America's foreign policies and interference throughout the last century have contributed to the current state of global alliances and insecurity and whether it is necessary to reconcile with Islamic nations and the international community as the Democratic complex advocates.

(3). Have our American domestic policies, identity politics, and toxic politicking created our rapid social decay, racial hatred, cultural divisions and isolation, and transformation of our social construct to the point where a civil war might be on the horizon to save our nation?

(4). Is the United States able to maintain its government integrity, domestic stability, hegemony, and competitive advantage globally while combating the destabilizing forces of Socialism, Libertarianism, Environmental Activism, the World International Order, Migratory Multiculturalism, Islamism, and existing destructive global doctrine and alliances?

(5). Given the modification of military doctrine, the prioritization of diversity, equity, and inclusion (DEI) indoctrination over combat effectiveness, and the depletion of assets (e.g., equipment abandoned in Afghanistan and arsenals emptied to assist Ukraine), does it compromise our ability to project strength in the "peace through strength" equation and maintain dominance over the Great Power competitors?

(6). Are we Americans ready to acknowledge the internal catalysts that push the U.S. towards war and the need for a divided world alliance and a designated "bad guy" to sustain the operation and economics of our deep state and the Military Industrial Complex?

My Core Belief: At the outset, to avoid confusion on where I stand politically, globally, and socially, let me declare my modified belief system steeped in neoconservatism while adopting a blend of nationalist and Globalist doctrine, which I ascribe to. I believe in (a). Placing America first, (b). Judeo-Christian values and belief system, (c). Projecting Peace through Strength, (d). Global Shared Hegemony, and (e). A global partner in encouraging economic wealth through multilateral trade and international security alliances, making obsolete the global power divisions of the Cold War era. It is imperative for American policies to undergo a transformation in order to establish a new direction toward national economic prowess, leadership, and the establishment of a fresh global order that encourages "dialogue before bullets."

The necessity for global progress is evident, as the previous East/West and European alliances have demonstrated their propensity for causing significant harm and hindering peaceful and economically sustainable coexistence. Without effective leadership and unity, the only foreseeable outcome is mutual destruction. We as a nation must address the current issues by utilizing the existing facts and the most recent emerging trends. Irrespective of my beliefs, the book leans towards identifying destructive policies, regardless of the political party. Instead, it is grounded in a well-defined belief system that is backed by factual evidence and current events publicly displayed in society. The book highlights the threats to our democracy and the potential for the United States to be drawn into a global conflict and, worse, domestic civil war. As highlighted in my previous book, I will reiterate that uncritically adhering to party ideologies is deleterious to the democratic process. The guiding principles should be based on objective facts and impartial analysis, prioritizing the citizens' interests and considering the nation's overall improvement.

The writings incorporate perspectives and interpretations of fact-based information influenced by my multicultural heritage, variegated socialization experiences, religious exposure (Christian, Islamic, and Hindu), academic background, and professional assessment. A number of the concerns that have been delineated are often avoided for fear of social exclusion and liberal demonization. Consequently, I am convinced that these matters merit investigation and significantly affect the future well-being of our familial unit and our country, "One Nation Under God!" It is essential to consider and analyze different perspectives in order to fully grasp the complexities of the issues at hand. This is a crucial element in being a democratic society. Failing to embrace diverse perspectives and suppressing contrary opinions will condemn us to a state of ignorance, which is obviously prevalent in contemporary American society. The current political landscape in America is marked by deliberate efforts from the Democratic Socialist Liberal faction to suppress speech and viewpoints that deviate from the established norms. These actions bear resemblance to the principles of socialism and communism. We must refrain from being a shallow electorate and peel back the layers of deception in the proverbial onion to see the true endgame of the liberal democratic socialist complex.

In the words of an annoyingly famous sitcom star, "Steven Urkel," of the '90s show Family Matters, I pose this question on behalf of America in that irksome nasal voice: **"Did I do that?"** It could be argued that America's political doctrine, ideology, prejudices of the ruling class, and foreign policy from the 1900s to the present are responsible for the precarious state our world is in. This was and still is an underlying premise of the Obama-Biden Democratic party doctrine. We must question if American values, Judeo-Christian beliefs, patriotism, religious and cultural tolerance, citizen safety, and global leadership are a thing of the past, or are they worth advocating for - for future generations? Think these realities through carefully, as it really doesn't matter what side of the aisle you're on; this radicalization of America is not what true Democrats or Republicans yearn for. We are way past party politics now, I'm afraid. If the overt nightly news bias, our demonstrated failure to govern domestically and globally, loss of values in society, racial discord, increase in criminality, Islamist indoctrination, government corruption, racial discord, crime, illegal immigrant crisis, national security threat(open border), political persecution of opponents, and democratic socialism masked as liberalism, which is destroying the foundations of our nation, don't scare the daylights out of you, then, in that case, the transformation to your psyche has already begun. One disturbing factor that bewilders me is President Biden's democrat Party administration popularity among some, in spite of the global geopolitical quagmire and instability they have created, the lack of confidence by allies in American leadership, and the decline of domestic social norms and issues of morality to date; many still support their failed policies. Are we as a nation not paying attention to the facts that are presenting themselves? Hopefully, you will make a qualified and informed decision for the next election and move forward to securing our national integrity and survival. I suggest engaging in common sense analysis.

Take away all the election rhetoric and objectively examine the policies, facts, and successes, as I have done to make your own assumptions. Explore the double standards in the public witch-hunt by our judicial system, the overt protection of one side, and the concerted government and media attack of the other political party to eliminate the political opponent chosen by the people, all directed by the sitting democrat administration. This is echoed by both sides of the aisle, as it is too apparent to sweep under the rug or spin. Imagine individual state officials taking it upon themselves to try and destroy the people's choice for the next president because they presume to know best. These so-called protectors of democracy all conclude that "we the people" cannot be left with such an essential task as choosing our next President; they must do it for us. I wonder what definition of democracy the Democratic Party ascribes to? This is, of course, denied by those in the bubble of deniability, or is it a planned action on their behalf? What cannot be debated is the anarchical state of our nation, the drive to create a one-party dominant rule, extreme political polarization, and the systematic attack on our constitutional rights as we are currently engulfed in that reality. There is a lot to unpack in our nation, lots of deceit and misinformation by nefarious actors; objective reasoning is necessary to understand the truth.

Regardless of which side of the political spectrum you reside on, America's survival, safety, and welfare must always be our primary responsibilities, "America before Party always." With this objective of awakening our electorate, I will continue to pose many provocative questions throughout the book for contemplation. I hope it has the intended effect of arousing your curiosity and getting you, the reader, engaged and ready to protect the integrity of our way of life.

Regardless of our heritage, we only have one country, "America." Let us protect her.

SO HERE WE ARE, AMERICA

Without a doubt, the international community has once more entered a state of instability and unpredictability that is not conducive to promoting peaceful coexistence, proportional prosperity, or shrewd decision-making in the realms of politics, national security, foreign affairs, or domestic matters. It is safe to assert, based on the current United States domestic and foreign policy climate and the manner in which the United States exerts its influence, exercises governance, and weak power projection in the geopolitical sphere, it will not be well remembered in history, but as the years of political bloopers and blunders. It is simple to assign blame, as the majority of people do superficially, and to assign finger-pointing in contemporary literary works. Nevertheless, I contend that a more constructive approach to the comprehension process would be to reexamine historical events and gain insight into the mechanisms that shaped those convictions, the strategies employed, and the social and political foundations that likely led to our current predicament. Furthermore, the book will illuminate the entities or organizations that have wielded authority and exerted influence domestically and internationally. It can be contended that the very factors that propelled the Deep State, the Economic Complex, and the military-industrial complex during the 20th century continue to act in the present day to conduct business; their survival and growth are contingent on the United States designating a "Bad Guy Regime" and igniting geopolitical conflicts in the region. Some may argue, with hindsight, whether specific challenges could have been managed differently to avert the current state of bewilderment and our precarious position or whether such considerations are even relevant in the pursuit of progress. Assume for a moment that we acquire some positive insight from any of these perceived errors: Is it possible to prevent a national crisis or global war by learning from our past errors? By having our leaders modify their reasoning and approach to some of our domestic and foreign problems, we could be successful in averting an impending global and domestic crisis.

It is critical to acknowledge that the progress of the United States throughout the century and any subsequent actions were not undertaken in isolation since no nation operates in a vacuum. The circumstances surrounding any action must be considered before judgment is cast. A predominant action or development invariably prompted a specific action to be undertaken, regardless of its correctness, incorrectness, or indifference. An evolving example of this is unfolding before our eyes. Regrettably, Europe is rapidly running out of time to make a definitive choice regarding its commitment to open borders, multiculturalism, and globalism. By remaining passive, Europe risks the rapid extinction of its hard-earned Judeo-Christian values, freedoms, and identity. The deterioration of their societal framework has undergone a significant negative transformation, leading to the erosion of the distinct identities of individual nations. America must heed these mistakes, or else it will inevitably replicate the same course of action. It is surprising to me that the media outlets are not covering this angle, or is this the course of action favored by the ruling class liberal elitists?

If you watch the individual nations' news media and social media sites, you will see that a lot of turmoil is unfolding in Europe. Another perception that is pushed by the mainstream media and permeates our average society is that the majority of Arab Nations, former Soviet Bloc breakaway countries, Asia, and Russia are in shambles, and they have horrible lives. This couldn't be further from the truth. It may surprise some readers that compared to many different parts of the world, most American cities seem like a true third or fourth-world environment. At the time of writing this book, America still doesn't have a high-speed rail system or highly efficient public transportation system in large or even medium-sized cities. Most citizens cannot afford to have health insurance, most cities' infrastructure is in shambles, and the crime-related deaths in some cities supersede combat losses, to name just a few deficiencies. Misinformation and news censorship have been used over time to distract the population from our nation's deficiencies and push how great we have it in the United States versus other countries to prevent focus on our internal issues. America is great; we are a unique and successful experiment in democracy, and life can be exceptional. "BUT," we must keep developing and advancing our society and infrastructure, secure personal freedoms, and expand the capitalist form of the economic system to benefit all, lest we lose this nation forever.

AREAS OF DISCUSSION

(a) A fundamental comprehension of the origins of American foreign policy doctrine and the politics of the pre-Great War era is necessary to comprehend our nation's historical trajectory concerning previous socioeconomic policy motivators. This formative period will examine the belief systems of influential individuals in the American government during the 1900s and later, the prevailing cultural ideologies and philosophies, and the fundamental political and financial forces that shaped our foreign policy framework. The vast body of research on the theories underlying all political ideologies is duly recognized. On the contrary, I will adopt the inverse approach by initially scrutinizing the policies and results and associating them with an ideology. It is my conviction that America's foreign policy was, and still is, predominantly reactionary on purpose, shaped by the cultural "manifest destiny" beliefs of the elitist class, the economic imperative to expand American industry overseas, and a combination of internationalism, détente, and nationalistic policy—in other words, it produced its own "Americana brand," if you will, driven by economic greed. Evidently, it has not produced the most favorable outcomes, given that the underlying rationales for the policies were sometimes flawed to begin with. The best evaluator of policies is time, and the course of history speaks loudly. A comprehensive examination of significant events, ideologies, and figures that impacted our policies will allow us to grasp how they molded the United States foreign policy. By cultivating a cognizance of our political past, we may, with any luck, be better equipped to confront present-day challenges and navigate forthcoming developments. To the same extent, Americans need to look at where we are now in relation to where we have been and where we are headed as a nation to gauge our level of advancement socially and globally.

(b) After the introspection, we will address the central issue of America's survivability domestically and globally as a hemogenic leader, maintaining our Judeo-Christian value system, preserving our constitutional framework, and existing socially as one nation under a unified flag. The equality, sabotage, and social experiment involving African Americans will also be explored, as this group has been exploited for political gain.

(c) The United States is confronted with three existential challenges: ideological, political, and religious conflicts fueled by diverse factions both within the country and on an international scale. Furthermore, our military actions are intertwined in the political, religious, and ideological conflict, mandated to safeguard American hegemony and contend with the threat from the great powers. A thin line delineates these three conflicts; however, when considered collectively, they constitute a formidable menace to the survival of our nation in terms of national security. Each of these will be discussed to highlight its uniqueness and pertinence to national sovereignty and identity. We will also explore the biases and perceptions formed by media reporting and the information flow that is disseminated for public consumption to create our collective perceptions. "Control the Information, Control the People," and in essence, by controlling the narrative, it secures public approval and party power while silencing opposing voices.

(d). Hiding behind the banner of "protecting democracy," the Democratic Party elitists and shadow power complex presume to know what is best for our nation. They will destroy any aspiring leader, politician, or party that opposes their view. They have gone as far as inserting themselves in our democratic processes by engaging in election interference, voter fraud, and Department of Justice manipulation and removing the constitutional protection of the voting power of the "people" in choosing our next president. To those who may argue against the protection of voting rights, these rights are embedded in the Equal Protection Clause of the 14th Amendment and the Supreme Court's affirmation of the notion referenced in the writings by Justice Marshall and Rehnquist. Yes, I am referring to the state of our beloved America, not some communist state or banana republic. We must take heed of the state of our union. Anarchy has always been the tool of so-called social liberal activists and social disruptors intent on changing the world by burning it down. It is no wonder other nefarious actors piggyback on these organizations to accomplish their bidding.

CHAPTER 2
CRITICAL ISSUES FACING AMERICA

This chart offers an overview of the most critical issues, the corrupting ideology, and the political party supporting the problems.

ISSUES DESTROYING US. *DOMESTIC ISSUES- SOCIETAL DECLINE- GEOPOLITICS	DOMINANT IDEOLOGY *INFLUENCING POLICY AND SOCIAL ACTIVISM UNREST	POLITICAL PARTY *SPONSORED OR CONDONED	INFLUENCE ON SOCIETY *POS/ NEG
Racial Hatred-Cultural Segregation	Multicult./Liberal	Dem/Rep	Negative
Islamist Ideology, Terrorism Support / Pro-Sharia	Liberalism, Democratic Socialism - Islamism	Democrat	Negative
Anti-Christianity / Anti-Semitism / Anti-Israel	Liberalism-Democratic Socialism/Fascism	Democrat	Negative
Gov. Weaponization	Liberalism-Socialism	Democrat	Negative
Corruption / Accountability	Socialism-China Influenced	Democrat	Negative
Erosion Law & Order/Policing	Liberalism Globalism	Democrat	Negative
(+) Crimes in Society	Liberalism Socialism	Democrat	Negative
Riots-Violent Demonstration	Democratic Socialism	Democrat	Negative
Border Policy Disaster	Liberal International Order	Democrat	Negative
Border Transnational crime & Terrorism vulnerability	Globalism-Democratic Socialism-Lib. Int.	Democrat	Negative

	Order		
Erosion of Values & Beliefs	Liberalism Socialism	Dem/Rep	Negative
Conservative Censoring	Democratic Socialism	Democrat	Negative
(+) Immorality & Vulgarity	Liberalism Transsexualism	Democrat	Negative
Weaponizing Judicial System	Liberalism/Marxism	Democrat	Negative
Destroying U.S. Democratic Principles and Processes	Liberals / Socialism Communism Marxism	Democrat	Negative
Disastrous Foreign Policy	Liberal International Order	Dem/Rep	Negative
Polarized Politicking / Media	Liberalism-Socialism	Democrat	Negative
Declining U.S. Hegemony	Liberal International Order	Dem/Rep	Negative
(-) Competitive Advantage	Liberal International Order	Dem/Rep	Negative
Cultural Weaponization	Liberalism - Globalism	Democrat	Negative
Changing Social Construct	Liberalism - Globalism	Democrat	Negative
Foreign Indoctrination-China, Russia, Iranian proxies	Liberalism, Comm Socialism, Marxism	Dem/Rep	Negative

WHAT SHOULD KEEP AMERICANS UP AT NIGHT?

So, referencing the table above, here are the issues that keep most Americans and me up most nights, especially after a good dose of national and international news reporting. Perhaps you, the reader in general, share concerns about the increasing challenges of navigating society, the prospects for our families, the type of socialization our younger generation is experiencing, the increased exposure to amoral lifestyles in schools, the elimination of parent's rights to decide on what values are taught, the impending terrorist threat to the homeland, and the trajectory of our country as we edge closer to global nuclear conflict. Two increasingly unstable regions in particular that have me worried are the India, Pakistan, and China regions, as well as the Iran, Israel, and Syria regions. The geopolitical landscape for these two areas is rapidly evolving strategically. Iran is ready for a breakout to exert dominance in the region, secure Syria and Jordan, and strike a devastating blow to Israel. This would make them a regional powerhouse to influence the rest of the Arab nations. America is at its weakest state in terms of leadership and projecting strength. There is a time and place for everything to occupy its own space in society. Still, the lines are being blurred, cultural traditions are being ignored, societal boundaries have gone asunder, geopolitical trends are ignored, the art of effective diplomacy is dead, and family rights and decision-making regarding our children have been delegated by the government to school boards and politicians[1]. Our state of

---

[1] Wasserman, Gary, and Elliott Fullmer. *The basics of American politics.*

the union is weak, and America's global leadership is absent, reflected by the multiple conflicts and the increasingly tumultuous geopolitical landscape. When the cat is sleeping, the rats will play. America is the cat, in case you were wondering. Watch Iran and China flex before the elections in 2024.

WELL, WE'VE GOTTEN OURSELVES IN A PICKLE AMERICA

a). Do we possess an understanding of the milieu, history, ideology, and politics that the democratic elites have contributed to this catastrophic trajectory of the nation and the world? Do we comprehend the underlying principles of Internationalism, Nationalism, American Exceptionalism, Manifest Destiny, Détente, and Isolationism, and how each political philosophy influences America's geopolitical positioning in the future? It is important to note that any ideology that runs unchecked without a counterbalance can negatively affect societies.

b). Regarding foreign policy, domestic policies, national security, law and order, government corruption, and governance, the ineptitude of the current democratic party leadership is at trepidatious levels. Our current President's (Biden) cognitive decline leaves the United States vulnerable. With the volatile global arena and the great power competitor's aggressive stance, we are very close to an international conflict that could include battlefield-scale nuclear deployment. The events unfolding force us to ask, is there a long-term strategic plan our

Taylor & Francis, 2023.

leaders are following, or are we just **making it up** every four years as a new President tries to carve their place in history?

c). Maybe the contesting great-power nations of the world have reached critical mass. Is it again time for a global war to weed out the weaker of us, reform alliances, control territories and markets, dictate our global ideology, and allow the most powerful nations to chart the next century for our world, making similar mistakes of the past? Is our reign as a world leader truly over? What are the perceived trigger points for world leaders to engage in open warfare? What are the underlying issues why dialogue and some level of amicable cooperation cannot be achieved by GPC (great power competitor) leaders? Is this direct dialogue even being pursued, and if not, why not? A scary thought to ponder: a nation and world on a trajectory for a catastrophic human event, with the "leader of the free world" incapable of executing a compelling diplomatic mission, who displays cognitive decline, and where the foxes are running the hen house in our seat of power, is of grave concern to me, and should be to you, the electorate. Furthermore, what about the terrorist threat to our homeland? In a briefing to Congress for the second time, the FBI director, Christopher Wray, has expressed critical concern, verbalizing that the terrorist threat level to America is "at a whole other level" and "rival groups have been coming together." There are "blinking red lights everywhere," he expressed, including attack orders on the US homeland similar to Israel, something the intelligence agencies have not witnessed before. It seems to be a matter of when and not if it happens. What about China's increasing cyber threat presence? China's hackers have been positioning themselves to wreak havoc on American infrastructure and cause massive disruptions and possible collapse to the American homeland. China's attention is not solely directed toward political and military objectives but also financial, transportation, and energy industry objectives. We can see that low blows are not just a possibility in the event of a conflict; instead, low blows against civilians are part of China's plan to panic the citizenry. China has been capitalizing on the Biden open border policy to change the voter demographics in America, and state/nonstate bad actors have been using this opportunity to position themselves for any irregular warfare acts on the homeland, including sponsoring the fentanyl distribution chain by China. Analyzing these issues collectively should create dire concern in the readers' minds. I fear that the next attack on the homeland will be orchestrated over our southern border, using the cartel's network to inflict damage and have an avenue for escape. It would be naïve to think that hostile elements will not utilize this "golden tactical opportunity" to infiltrate the United States through its open borders and resettlement policies. The only ones in denial are our elected democrat party officials, or are they?

d). Unfortunately, we live in a society where our democratic party has weaponized government to push ideologies incongruent with American values and beliefs. Imagine we live in a society where the government is alarmingly concerned about the 2SLGBTQIA+ community's safety in schools and pushing transgenderism but totally disregards and often supports demonizing and exploiting the vulnerability of Jewish students in schools and the workplace while propagating pro-Islamist support at the highest levels of government. This demonstrates the focus of our party in power and what ideology is pushed in our educational institutions. Are we, as a Judeo-Christian society that embraces the freedoms, practices, and similar probity of other religions, satisfied with fringe elements in society dismantling baseline morals, values, the sanctity of life, and the indoctrination by cultural liberalism, socialism, Marxism, and radicalized Islamic doctrine? When do we say enough is enough?

e). To pertinent constituents of the **"apathetic younger generation"** and the **"by choice"** misinformed individuals, who together form the majority of our nation's uninformed **"Zombie Electorate."** Are you capable of comprehending your participation in the decline of our nation, or are you willing to fight for your nation's success, exercise your civic duty and responsibility to be a well-informed participant in democracy, understand the impact of issues on your future, and the significance of being a patriotic American? Or are you an ignominious mouthpiece for unsustainable Liberalism, Socialism, Islamism, and Antisemitism in a bid to destroy our democratic republic, our homeland?

f). How far is the pendulum going to swing concerning the resocialization of society and redefining acceptable behaviors regarding iniquitous deportment, public vulgarity, replacement of genetically defined genders in society with a warped version of sexual deviant gender identification predicated on personal preference and amoral practices, perverse indoctrination of our children in schools by transgenderism and sexually explicit material, and identity politics that construct racial hatred and intolerance in society?

g). American elitists and the shadow power complex have a comprehensive and long-term strategy in place, and the lack of awareness, information, and involvement in our government will ultimately contribute to our demise. Our democratic processes are being threatened, and election tampering is being supported by the Department of Justice (DOJ). Our social construct in the United States is being altered without our consent by the government and the liberal democratic socialist complex. Ponder the current narratives and trajectory concerning societal issues; no elucidation is necessary for the reader. Widely publicized in the media and congressional hearings, our nation lacks the moral fortitude to prevent drag queens from engaging in twerking in the presence of young children at school, conducting drag and transsexual-themed story-time readings that involve inappropriate sexual conditioning and insinuations through the stories, or prohibiting the distribution and access of explicit sexual literature in educational institutions and public libraries to our children. Those citizens and parents who oppose are vilified and labeled as homophobes, admonished by school board officials, destroyed by social media corroborators, or arrested. Similarly, we are unable to halt the widespread animadversion of religion and the promotion of alternative lifestyles as being normal that specifically target our children, beliefs, and societal constructs in general. I vehemently oppose institutions and "fame-seeking" "bandwagon hopping" mental health practitioners condoning sex reassignment and indoctrinating children with objectionable perspectives based on immorality, as defined by monotheist religions' basic belief structures and genetics. It goes against the limits set by parental authority and infringes on parental freedom to raise children in a manner befitting the individual's family value framework. This is an intrusion by the government, forcing ideologies upon the people that go against Judeo-Christian principles in favor of perversion, hiding in the civil rights space under the discrimination and acceptance banner. Might I point out that other major religions, Hinduism, true Islam, and Judaism, share similar if not identical moral belief structures as Christianity.

Rational adults will agree that political, transsexual, transgender, and Islamist indoctrination has no place in our early through high school education system in America. The focus here should be on STEM, Arts, History, Civics, and Literature to mold an academically well-endowed teenager ready to take on advanced study and become productive members of society. In a democratic society, this indoctrination and government overreach in our schools and homes should never be allowed to occur or be accepted. These controversial sexual orientations can be characterized as adult personal lifestyle choices mimicked by impressionable youngsters that their respective parents must address in concert with responsible mental health professionals referencing their belief structure and socialization, and not the school system or government overreach. The Democratic Party's view of expanded government has resulted in an erosion of parents' rights to decide on their family's belief structure and issues of morality. This manifests as increased unethical conduct, the embrace of deceitful ways of life, and the abandonment of our Judeo-Christian heritage. Will you embrace the "New World Order" ideology that is being overwhelmingly imposed upon America? Are you satisfied with the current course of society's warped evolution in America? If so, read no more; the point of rational reasoning has been breached for you.

h). Where, then, are the preservation of rights and freedoms of most conservative-minded Americans following a religious and/or moral compass, I ask? The democratic party's liberal socialist machine condones this infringement of rights to push and protect these behaviors for securing votes, regardless of the irreparable damage to our nation, and if opposed, will weaponize agencies and social activists to suppress said opposition and demonize individuals, as is witnessed in the current news cycles daily. Is this the version of freedom and rights Democrats profess to uphold? Monocracy or Autocracy in action, pick one.

i). How far will the left and alternative lifestyle groups go in discrediting or making irrelevant the virtues, beauty, rights, and the specialized importance of actual birth-designated "women" (xx Chromosomes) in society, with total disregard for the significance "real women" play in the continuation of human existence, nurturing of young, matriarchal family roles, leaders, and being a necessary psychological counterbalance to their male counterparts? Separate but equal responsibilities of Men and Women complement and secure the success of families, cities, societies, and our nation. Where are the voices of the "feminist" movement when the very core of being female and the strength and uniqueness of "feminism" are threatened? Sorry, there are no substitutions; imposters will not suffice. It's not debatable; nature got it right: we need each other for the survival and sanity of humanity. Two sexes, anything else, is an anomaly created by society and insecure personalities. "Dress up" and "role play" cannot determine sexual orientation; nature and, in turn, biology does. Sorry, a fact of creation that cannot be explained away. It is indisputable that every solitary natural creation is perfectly harmonized, has a metabolic, psychological, and evolutionary purpose, and complements the whole, which is the survival of humanity.

I prognosticate that the most crucial questions in contention are: how much longer are we, God-fearing Americans (all Races and Religions), going to stand aside and watch the erosion of our national values, beliefs, and the transformation of our social construct? When do we say enough is enough to the public displays of sexual vulgarity permeating society and attacks on our time-honored traditions based on the Judeo-Christian philosophy of family, respect, worship, sexuality, and marriage, which have preserved our moral existence, and delayed our nation's fall into licentious behavior and immorality? How much more Judicial corruption can the American Justice System sustain before the legal protections afforded under our constitution become irrelevant? How many more shocks of political and liberal-socialist activist-instigated cultural disseverment, racial hatred, and political discord can our society absorb before shattering our collective union as Americans and eventuating into civil war? How much more can the individual's rights be eroded and conservative voices silenced before concern and revolt set in? Maybe it is time for Americans to show their patriotism and the so-labeled "flyover states," which I prefer to call the "heartbeat of America," stand up and be accountable, or face the consequences of losing the country and way of life their forefathers and many legally welcomed immigrant Americans fought to preserve, and die for. The battle today is not of race or culture as some would have you believe, but an ideological battle for our constitutionally protected freedoms and the heartbeat of our American culture. "Live Free or Die" (New Hampshire State Motto, 1945)

Current Policy Trajectory: In my previous book, I explained how party politics is counterproductive and destroys our democratic processes; it is incredibly enlightening and worth the read. Politics should never be allowed to define and separate us as citizens, or all is lost. Our imprudence and lack of province as citizens are directly attributed to our decline as a nation. With all being said, please acknowledge that all is not lost; America is still the shining light in the fog, and we all have a duty to protect that premise. Let us, for the moment, suppose Americans fail to coalesce under one flag with foreign and domestic policy based on strategy, objectivity, and citizen-centricity. In that case, we are destined by our inaction to be defeated by liberalism and fundamentalists and dominated by the counteractions of our savvy adversaries, Putin, Xi Jinping, or the Ayatollah. Do we even have the truth about world events and the driving forces that promulgate these developments, considering the perfusion of biases and state control of our media outlets? Are we, as a people, willing to surrender our freedoms and submit the country to some liberal form of what I refer to as a "Zootopian ideology" of open borders, uniformed thought, classless society, floating morality, oligarchy, secularism, and cronyism versus meritocracy in our institutions? Might I remind the readers that the absence of these practices in our society to date has made us a world power and leader of democratic principles globally? Now, this is being challenged and eroded from within by the fringe ideological groups upheld by the liberal democratic socialist complex. It is unfathomable that our nation is flirting with civil war after only three years of overt exposure to this perverse ideology and corrupted governance. How many more years of this exposure can we absorb before imploding?

Seeking Knowledge: I cannot reiterate enough how vital the information-gathering process and weeding through false flag information campaigns are to our understanding of issues that impact our nation and family. Our sources are coerced and controlled by the State, which are the governing elitists that engage in deceptive politicking that influence politicians, media, and nations in the Western sphere. It is imperative that we, as Americans, get off our posteriors, become engaged in the welfare of our country, and seek accurate knowledge and information. It is inconceivable how many Americans are uninformed and ill-informed zombies, believing anything they hear without qualifying the source and content. These zombies have delegated thinking to others so they can be relieved of this burdenous task, and that is why there is so much

31

ignorance regarding domestic and foreign policies and destructive domestic issues that are allowed to take root in our country. Differences in political doctrine are anticipated and a vital part of our two-party political system in preventing radicalism on both sides of the spectrum. How is it then possible for an intelligent nation to ignore the destructive ideologies and immoral practices dismantling our solidarity as a nation and our societal and racial advancement towards equality, our deviation from Judeo-Christian values, the political weaponization of institutions and government attacks to silence political opponents in general elections, and the institutional and social indoctrination by Islamists. It should be deemed incomprehensible in a so-called developed nation. Don't you think?

I will make a very controversial assessment, one that I have held for many years, based on my diverse socialization, culture, education, and travels. Our current global and domestic climate lends immense credibility to these views. It is pretty self-evident that because we have not shown leadership, strength, and resolve as the leader of the free world, a vacuum has been created, and our hegemony is being challenged. In the case that America doesn't readjust and learn how to lead and respond objectively to this progressive threat and continue to apply feckless Western or American philosophy and methodology in policy and actions, then in that circumstance, we will lose and be subjected to a growth of terrorism and liberal/socialist ideology that will destroy and consume Western identity. Over time, the cost of containing this cancer to society and returning social order will bear a high human toll. To be blunt, we have sacrificed life (American treasure) and afforded operating space to these destructive ideologies through our indecisiveness and actions of political pandering over the years. Don't misinterpret the meaning of this statement as suggesting military action alone, as it speaks to my belief of a much more involved holistic approach to policy making, steeped in strategic objectivity, incorporating strength through deterrence, tactical diplomacy, human security, accountability, solidifying partner states alliance and development, standing firm on morals and values, and swift, decisive resolve in dealing with threats as they emerge domestically and globally. It also incorporates a psychological reasoning factor into our approach to solving East-West issues, referencing an Eastern "thinking" template when dealing with Eastern-based actors. The American public and our politicians need to readjust their thinking on warfare. Bluntly, war is hell on earth, extraordinarily destructive, and bloody. There is no politically correct or humane way to conduct warfare as we attempt to do. Swift and total annihilation of the enemy should be the objective, with measures taken to limit collateral damage when tactically beneficial to the overall mission accomplishment. Here is a novel idea: if we were to fight wars in their proper form, nations and humanity would heavily refrain from so quickly using this egregious modality (combat action) as a means to an end, which is generally geopolitical.

Questioning the Status Quo: It is essential to question the left-leaning party line indoctrination by global media, which spreads biased and manipulated information to shape Western perspectives on global events and nations' actions, ultimately categorizing international actors as either "Naughty" or "Nice." The expression "caveat emptor" is relevant more than ever in this case. As news and information consumers, are we being exposed to unbiased and accurate information, or are we being manipulated under a "false flag shadow government operation," intentionally guided toward a preconceived outcome to secure public acceptance of the ruling elite's covert governance? As a collective, we must seek information from a broad scope (all local and foreign news sources) to ascertain if the actions of major powers like China and Russia are antagonistic or reactionary in nature. Why is there not more extensive communication among senior leaders in these situations? The leaders in power should communicate directly rather than relying on administration heads who may be influenced by the shadow government. When conflict is on the table, diplomacy must be at its highest. Referencing current events, the Biden administration met with President Putin in Geneva for an abbreviated time in 2021. From then till now, there have been no other meetings of substance to date. With the antagonistic relationship between both nations, one would think that leaders would attempt to diffuse contentious points. Apparently, with no attempt from Biden and his public displays of "gaff," that was all the proof Putin needed to ascertain Biden's leadership ineptness and the administration's lack of resolve. Without effective dialogue and follow-up meetings to develop a positive relationship, he decided it was a good time to push boundaries with the U.S. leader, as actions confirmed that

Biden was ill-equipped mentally to perform with the big boys. Geopolitics is a game of high-power chess, not dominoes; it requires extensive intellectual acumen, political strategizing, and institutional, regional, global, economic, and military knowledge. In light of the egregious instances of bias and corruption prevalent in Western news coverage, it is not unpatriotic to inquire about the absence of aggressive diplomatic missions and raise such concerns regarding the noticeable lack of leader engagements in this high-stakes arena. In order to comprehend the forces at work in the global arena, it is critical to examine every angle, given that public opinion influences policy choices.

It is paramount to investigate why there is a preference for "Testosterone posturing" and "Military Action" over engaging in dialogue and diplomatic missions between the leaders of opposing parties. Conflict pays higher returns than peace to the shadow government's military-industrial complex and other aligned complexes. The pushed narratives surrounding high-profile leaders are often undermined by Western media, which refrains from giving opponents credibility or, in their minds, elevating the status of other leaders in the world and believing that talking to opposing leaders may enhance their credibility. It is wise to keep your opposition or competitor close. With that biased mindset and narrative pushed publicly, the meetings have already been sabotaged by the predetermined talking points and the atmosphere established. Boxing in or nationally shaming an adversary early on limits the negotiations and concessions available, as they, too, must appear strong for their nation. It is common knowledge that the military-industrial complex needs a geopolitical conflict or a designated adversary to maintain profitability by increasing production and securing contracts. This complex, including the Financial Industrial Complex, utilizes the Media Complex to promote the storyline globally. Conflict is ultimately advantageous for our economy in the long term. During prolonged periods of peace and absence of conflict, the Military-Industrial Complex (MIC) would experience its lowest financial state. Every negotiation of a contract, missile deployment, use of ammunition, development or replacement of a weapon system, and creation of armament results in billions of dollars of benefit for the complex. Additionally, numerous corporations act as subsidiaries, support the mission, and help shape the narrative.

Nations might and will have opposing views on geostrategy based on their interests. Still, I refuse to believe there isn't common ground to be attained, and I seriously doubt that warfare and bloodshed are the answer. Prudent individuals might question why there hasn't been any in-depth investigative reporting and public interviewing of world and military leaders at a point in time when the chance of a global conflict between great powers seems imminent. Where are the attempts at strategic tactical dialogue and transparency so that the people can see the efforts of our leadership? It will be the people who will be fighting and dying; we should have the benefit of hearing all sides before we are plunged into war. Sorry, as a former military officer, I have enough insight not to blindly trust the government officials and the state-sponsored media with my family and grandchildren's future. The people deserve to hear all sides, why all these defensive or aggressive actions are being taken, and what particular threats are being perceived by each leader requiring posturing for hostilities and retaliatory actions. Having all this information out in the open and hearing what is transpiring behind the curtain allows us to make the hard decisions with some level of confidence and puts the "behind-the-scene actors" on notice.

To any advocate of our current policy trajectory, I urge you to carefully consider the above statements: also, the prevailing social unrest characterized by crime, racial tension, sexual indecency, gender ambiguity, imminent conflict, radicalization, Anti-American sentiment, and Anti-Semitic sentiment among our seemingly irresponsible and coerced youth, which is currently evident across the entire nation, and ask yourselves if this is the "Rabbit Hole" you choose for the future of your family and country. Additionally, please take into account the support and influx of lethal synthetic drugs from China through illicit channels, underpinned by Mexico, to disrupt our nation and our porous border policies that give rise to numerous potential national security risks. Why has Biden not publicly confronted Xi Jinping on this issue at the state leadership level? When was the last occurrence since the Trump presidency when President Biden engaged in serious dialogue, from state leader to state leader, with President Putin or President Xi, especially with the increased military positioning and escalation toward major hostilities in play? My guess is the democrat puppet masters cannot Biden to embarrass the administration, as he is obviously not able to match wits with these leaders and force de-escalation effectively. If you may, observe the myriad of disastrous foreign and domestic issues stemming from this presidency, as well as the bipartisan leaks about the President's mental slippage. That is what the electorate gets for electing a mentally declining and incompetent leader to navigate America's posturing in a highly challenging and potentially explosive geopolitical landscape. The Presidency is a highly functioning position.

After considering all these factors, I encourage you to reassess your position. Even to those without expertise, it is clear that the psychological operations (psyops) warfare conducted by malicious individuals and adversarial financiers against the United States is remarkably successful. Mainly focus on the significant uprisings of individuals supporting Hamas, terrorism, and displaying antisemitic sentiments in our universities and cities with a prominent Islamic presence. Pose the appropriate inquiry: who, in your opinion, bears the responsibility for the indoctrination and contamination of our young people and future generations through the dissemination of pro-terrorist and anti-American ideology in the United States? Track the flow of funds, why these disruptive organizers are being funded by prominent democrat financiers, the likes of Soros, and then ask why America funds the same terrorist organizations overseas. Oh, the tangled web of deceit we operate under; it is mindboggling, to say the least. The seeds are being sown; it is essential to note that Eastern geopolitics adopts some short-term strategies that support its long-term generational strategy compared to the West's shorter-term plans, typically spanning 3-5 years. Now is the moment for America to awaken and reevaluate strategies.

Let us impartially identify the indisputable factors disrupting our nation: from the religious extremists employing terrorist methods to propagate their version of Islam, the repressive political systems promoting their agenda of control and supremacy, to the liberal/socialist movement, influenced and financed by proxy agents and covert foreign countries. We can deduce that their main objective is to instigate disagreement within American society, undermine the American political and legal system, and ultimately fragment our nation to undermine our constitution, laws, morals, and principles, thereby rendering the United States ineffectual on the global platform. The United States' response has been insufficient so far as it persistently attempts to appease these foreign nations and actors. The insufficiency of our responses and our lack of comprehension regarding the Eastern psychology that fuels terrorist warfare and Historical Hate have bolstered our enemies' ability to survive and act without fear of consequences. In actuality, the understanding of Middle Eastern mentality, as it relates to displaying strength and weakness, ideological expansion, tribalism, and intolerance of Western beliefs, is grossly misunderstood, and by miscalculating this, we in the West have emboldened and, in some cases, aggravated our prospects of separate but tolerated coexistence. If these concepts had been understood, then Europe would never have adopted the policy of multiculturalism and mass migration into its societies. Now, most European nations are scrambling to correct their mistakes and protect their national identities and society.

Chapter 3
A Historical Review

AMERICAS FORMATIVE FOREIGN AFFAIR YEARS

How did we start this trajectory? It has always been my belief that knowing where one comes from and the path traveled is necessary to determine one's destiny. The same applies to our nation in this circumstance. Through a critical analysis of the historical progression of political and cultural ideologies, alongside the external factors that have shaped U.S. policy, one can acquire a significant understanding of the guiding principles and events that have shaped American foreign policy. Policy and the prevailing ideologies of the differing periods have never remained constant; instead, they have been pragmatically modified in response to changing circumstances, such as the international environment, global economics, and evolving social perceptions of national interest. One can even say that U.S. foreign policy has been reaction-driven.

This approach and understanding can offer an enlightened perspective and course of action to positively impact the U.S. trajectory and avert an unprecedented catastrophic event. After this introspective process is concluded, our attention can shift over to the complex matters that are affecting the national and global landscape today, including (a) ideological warfare, (b) religious warfare, (c) leadership, (d) political power competition, and

(e) foreign and domestic policy. This analysis will additionally explore the ramifications of these issues in the United States within domestic and global contexts. In order to gain a good perspective, an examination of the potential ramifications of external and internal pressures on the United States is warranted while also considering the feasibility of modifying our philosophical approach if required. This objective can be attained through proficient leadership and clearly articulated foreign policy endeavors that foster worldwide well-being. Essentially, it pertains to acquiring knowledge derived from past errors, aiming to avoid their repetition in future initiatives. This writing posits the contention that the United States and the global community find themselves at various critical junctures that possess the potential to transform our existence significantly. Subsequent sections will expound upon this assertion in greater depth.

WHAT LENS WERE WE USING

The late 1800s to the early 1900s marks the beginning of our examination of the American political journey. During this time, ruling elites and industry leaders viewed the world and foreign policy through the lens of "Exceptionalism," which held that the United States was inherently more moral, intelligent, and forward-thinking than other nations. Consequently, given the considerable authority vested in us during that era, we were compelled to modify our conduct. It became incumbent upon us to disseminate our Christian internationalistic ideology and exert influence over the trajectory of historical events according to our dictates, even resorting to drastic measures such as overthrowing or supporting foreign governments. Additionally, a financial aspect was inherent in this ideology, as it aimed to promote the advancement of American industry, including the financial sector, through foreign policies that sought to acquire wealth and serve American interests, potentially at the expense of other nations. However, it is noteworthy to mention that European governments, particularly those of England, France, Spain, and Portugal, played a significant role in fostering change through their past colonial practices. It facilitated the emergence of three pivotal factors in the governance of nations throughout history: (1) The establishment of dependency, (2) The regulation of social and industrial progress, and (3) The suppression of democratic principles to uphold authority over the populace and deter resistance against the ruling elite. This shaping of the political landscape played into the ideology of the United States at the time. I subscribe to the argument that Colonialism, in contrast to certain scholarly writings, made a substantial contribution to the advancement of the New World in certain respects; this argument, however, is for another time.

In moving forward, it is necessary to understand the wielders of influence in our nation then and now, as well as other contributing ideologies. The power brokers, commonly known as the "Shadow Government," are exclusive collectives of influential individuals in various domains, including corporate influencers, lobbyist groups, financial elites (financial complex), the military-industrial complex, law enforcement, and covert intelligence agencies. These entities clandestinely exert influence over

American political doctrine and foreign policy through many avenues. Throughout the twentieth century and subsequent years, these prominent operators of control exerted considerable influence on the political and economic fabric of the nation, plying their trade discreetly. Nevertheless, the covert activities undertaken by these entities have elicited apprehensions regarding the transparency and responsibility of the democratic framework in the United States, as well as chariness from many of our democratically elected officials. Within the realm of American politics, a longstanding dichotomy has consistently emerged between the conceptualization of foreign policy and its subsequent execution. Within this interstice, the shadow government exerts its influence with impunity.

EARLY PLAYERS FORMING AMERICAN FOREIGN POLICY

The significance of the early actions of Secretary of State John Watson Foster and the law firm Sullivan & Cromwell (1879-Current) concerning American interventionism policy during the tenure of the Dulles brothers within the Dwight D. Eisenhower administration has been widely recognized by political historians and scholarly literature as the formative years for American foreign policy. Academic scholars have concurred with the notion that a Calvinist worldview shaped John and Allen Dulles under the influence of their mentors, namely their grandfather, John Foster, secretary of state for President Harrison, and their uncle Robert Lansing, who served as Secretary of State under President Wilson. The

43

aforementioned emerging ideology was widely implemented in the period following World War II, specifically during and after the Korean War; within the framework of an escalating conflict with the Soviet Union, the Eisenhower administration endeavored to impede the inclination of developing nations in the "Third World" to embrace the communist ideology.

Nevertheless, during the post-World War II era, characterized by heightened endeavors in international diplomacy to foster global collaboration, American authorities exhibited reluctance to deploy military personnel abroad. During this exploratory period, John Foster Dulles was appointed Secretary of State within the Eisenhower administration. Following this, the establishment of the Central Intelligence Agency (CIA) promptly ensued in response to the growing demand for systematic intelligence collection and information dissemination. Allen Dulles, who was employed at the prestigious law firm Sullivan & Cromwell, assumed the director role at the Central Intelligence Agency. The Dulles brothers continued their grandfather's legacy of becoming the first Secretary of State to participate in the annexation of a sovereign nation. Allen skillfully employed this organization to address perceived communist threats in developing nations effectively, employing clandestine military interventions, providing support to rebellions, and implementing strategies of economic statecraft. By doing so, they set a significant precedent for using "regime change" by any means necessary to pursue foreign policy objectives. The forthcoming chapters will analyze the influences exerted by the Dulles brothers, particularly emphasizing their involvement in Iran.

John Foster Dulles and Allen Dulles were instrumental in identifying and facilitating the establishment of the initial shadow government in the United States. Collectively, they revolutionized the United States' foreign policy in the 1950s, specifically during President Eisenhower's tenure. Here is a summary of their influence on foreign policy at that time, which has had long-lasting consequences for years.

John Foster Dulles (Secretary of State, 1953-1959): John Foster Dulles held the United States Secretary of State position during President Dwight D. Eisenhower's administration. Throughout his term, he played a crucial role in shaping the foreign policy of the Eisenhower administration, which later became widely recognized as the "Eisenhower Doctrine."

Eisenhower Doctrine: Dulles was a strong proponent of restraining the expansion of communism. The Eisenhower Doctrine, as expressed by Dulles in 1957, expanded upon the tenets of the Truman Doctrine and committed the United States to providing economic and military support to Middle Eastern nations resisting communist aggression. This was explicitly done to counterbalance the Russian presence in the area.

Brinkmanship: Dulles was renowned for his strategy of "brinkmanship," wherein he would exert pressure on adversaries, particularly the Soviet Union, to the point of potential conflict to secure diplomatic concessions. This approach was demonstrated in managing crises such as the Suez and Taiwan Strait. Dulles was instrumental in establishing regional alliances to contain communism. He played a crucial role in establishing SEATO (Southeast Asia Treaty Organization) and the CENTO (Central Treaty Organization), with the specific objective of halting the expansion of communism in Asia and the Middle East.

Allen Dulles (Director of Central Intelligence, 1953-1961) CIA: During President Eisenhower's administration, Allen Dulles held the position of Director of Central Intelligence. As the director of the CIA, he substantially impacted U.S. intelligence and covert activities throughout the Cold War. This profoundly impacted our Cold War doctrine, subsequently influencing our approach to isolating numerous nations that hold significance in today's geopolitical landscape. Our ideology at that time, steeped in arrogance and the brazen methodology of policy execution, created many enemies across the pond and the sands, creating this inherited hatred of America and its policies, even when advantageous to the greater good. This is very evident in our backyard, the Latin America and Caribbean (LAC) region, where inconsistent policy, interference in governance, military coups, and regime change have plagued the region under the hand of America through the CIA.

Covert Operations: Dulles masterminded and participated in various clandestine endeavors, such as the ousting of Iranian Prime Minister Mohammad Mossadegh in 1953 and the Guatemalan coup in 1954. These measures were implemented to counter the perceived influence of communism and safeguard the strategic interests of the United States. Arguably, the early interference in these nations has played a significant role in the instability observed in both regions.

U-2 Incident/Bay of Pigs: Allen Dulles was implicated in the U-2 Incident of 1960, wherein a United States reconnaissance aircraft was downed within Soviet airspace. The occurrence caused tension in U.S.-Soviet relations and resulted in humiliation for the Eisenhower administration. In reference to the Bay of Pigs Invasion, and despite Allen Dulles not currently being in office at the time of the invasion, he undoubtedly played an integral part in the initial planning phases of the operation. The unsuccessful incursion of Cuba in 1961 was intended to topple Fidel Castro's regime. It constituted a notable setback for U.S. diplomatic strategy in curbing the soviet expansion within the region. The efforts to remove Castro from power altogether were never pursued with great intensity after, which is a matter of contention with many Cuban Americans of that era.

The Dulles brothers' foreign policy was characterized by a persistent opposition to communism, a dedication to containment, and a readiness to employ covert methods to accomplish U.S. strategic goals. Although they achieved specific objectives, such as the containment of communism in particular areas, their endeavors were beset by formidable obstacles and setbacks, which further complicated international relations during the Cold War era. These policies and the strategies that were enacted were not long-term based or ideally suited for establishing global networks, cultivating alliances, and preserving extended hegemony internationally. These ideologies have remained deeply embedded in our diplomatic missions and foreign policy to this day. Many politicians still have the mentality that "Foreign policy and strategy doesn't convert to votes," so we end up with a foreign policy mindset based on "short-term, election cycle" returns.

ANNEXATION OF HAWAII 101

Like Grandfather, like Grandchildren: John Watson, who was later known as the first Secretary of State to successfully achieve the first conquest of a foreign nation, orchestrated the eventual overthrow of the Hawaiian Monarchy in January 1893. Citing American interests and taking control of Hawaii's economy began with pulling off this political takeover. This was done under the presidency of Benjamin Harrison, with discreet encouragement from the President himself. The secret "Committee of Safety," consisting of 13 Caucasian lawyers and businessmen, rebelled against the Hawaiian monarchy as directed. In response, U.S. troops were sent by the Secretary of State to support the rebels, who then established themselves as the new government. The United States promptly recognized this new government, aiming to annex Hawaii. However, in December 1893, during President Cleveland's term, the involvement of American troops in the coup was criticized as an abuse of power. Representatives of the queen royal faction also lodged disputes against the U.S. annexation of Hawaii. Senate hearings were held, but despite significant behind-the-scenes lobbying, Congress failed to restore the monarchy or annex Hawaii. It would take another five years before annexation finally occurred. During this time, Hawaii gained strategic importance to the United States after the sinking of the battleship Maine in Cuban waters. The pushed narrative in Washington was that the Japanese population in Hawaii could potentially pave the way for Japanese dominance in the Pacific.

As a result, President McKinley signed the resolution for annexation into law on July 7, 1898. It is worth noting that Sanford Dole, a lawyer and influential figure, was appointed as the governor of the newly established Territory of Hawaii. Interestingly enough, he was also James Dole's cousin, known as the "Pineapple King." Furthermore, their grandfather was a Christian missionary sent to convert the natives and promote the American system of land ownership and plantation society (Christian Internationalism). This led to significant land acquisitions by Anglo-American businessmen, resulting in the displacement of native Hawaiians. This remains a sore point with many native Hawaiians today. This acquisition can be viewed as a form of subtle imperialism driven by Christian internationalism, economics, and the misguided belief in manifest destiny, which was popular then.

SHADOW GOVERNMENT – DEEP STATE PLAYERS

The shadow government in America, Iran, becomes an enemy: As they evolved throughout history, this entity or group of individuals assumed numerous identities. They became indispensable as the United States expanded beyond its territorial limitations. The term "deep state" or "invisible government" refers to an organization or group of unelected officials, bureaucrats, military officers, intelligence agents, and corporate elites who wield economic and political influence and power inconspicuously, irrespective of the people's will or elected representatives. Assassinations, coups, election outcomes, and wars are allegedly planned and, through influence, executed by these organizations to advance their agenda, as in the early dealings with Persia/Iran, which "they" considered to be "in the best interest of the nation." They (shadow government) hold true that the average citizen cannot comprehend the magnitude of decisions needed to expand and secure the nation geopolitically, so the decision rests with them. This narcissistic viewpoint is alive and well today, as it guides policy promulgated by the unelected political and economic elitists in America.

In the early 1900s, the industrial sector of the United States experienced an unprecedented expansion, and large corporations amassed immense wealth and influence. Prominent individuals, the likes of John D. Rockefeller and J.P. Morgan, exerted political influence through their financial empires. One of the most widely used agencies was the law firm Sullivan & Cromwell, which facilitated numerous historically significant international transactions and supported the interests of prominent investors and the OCI (Overseas Consulting Inc.). The OCI was an alliance of eleven renowned engineering firms in America with the objective of enriching themselves and the United States at the expense of less developed countries; it became affiliated with Sullivan and Cromwell and later on the early rendition of the Central Intelligence Agency (CIA). This company desired to exploit Iran's untapped oil reserves in conjunction with the Dulles brothers (John Foster Dulles and Allen Dulles). In fact, they entered into an initial M$650 agreement with the then-Sha of Iran, Mohammad Reza, to develop Iranian oil in 1949.

Nevertheless, this did not transpire; in fact, it might have sparked the development of a hostile stance toward Iran. In 1951, Mohammad Mossadegh, a youthful activist educated in Europe, was elected prime minister of Iran. Motivated by his aversion to the Western nation's exploitative colonial attitudes and nationalistic ideology, Mossadegh emerged as a formidable adversary and was ultimately sworn in as prime minister. Oil production in Iran was nationalized at this time. This rendered him the sworn enemy of the Dulles brothers. Hostile intentions arose when destabilizing Iran and toppling the Iranian prime minister were proposed as courses of action. Additionally, this marked a pivotal moment in American politics and our diplomatic ties with Iran. Had America adopted Mossadegh's vision for his country, which closely resembles its own, the two countries might have been allies rather than adversaries. In the Middle East, Iran would have emerged as a stable nation-state. The grand qualifier of policy success or failure is "time." We especially see the resultant effects of years of American interference and "Coup d'État" in Latin America, where in many instances, we backed the "wrong horse," which appeared to be "a thing" for the United States' historical plan for advancement within the region (Panama, Argentina, Bolivia, Brazil, Chile, Cuba, Dominica Republic, Ecuador, Guatemala, Haiti, Nicaragua, Venezuela). Needless to say, the region is a disaster, ripe for the taking by another great

51

power competitor. As a lead-in, an additional pivotal moment of note in the economic history of the United States occurred with the establishment of the Federal Reserve in 1913.

The Federal Reserve: Although purportedly established to stabilize the financial system, it actually functioned as a manipulative center for questionable financial activities. Critics argue that the Federal Reserve and a small group of influential financial elites exerted significant control over the nation's monetary policy and manipulated economic outcomes to serve their interests. Curiously, that assertion continues to be made within certain groups today. The existence of a covert governing body, commonly referred to as the shadow government, is prevalent and deeply entrenched within the current political leadership of the United States. This is clearly apparent in the current Biden administration. An average prudent individual would concur that President Biden lacks the requisite mental acuity and cognitive capacity to make intricate decisions pertaining to the affairs of the state, let alone articulate a coherent statement to the public without engaging in incoherent rambling. The special prosecutor's report on storing classified documents also echoed questions concerning the President's acuity. The white house refuses to release the unclassified transcript to the public or Congress. The questions must be asked. Who, then, are the masterminds behind this manipulated puppet presidency? Who is running the government? Who are the unelected individuals that speak for us, the people?

The Military-Industrial Complex (MIC): During the post-World War II period, President Dwight D. Eisenhower warned Congress of the growing influence of the military-industrial complex[i]. This conglomeration of individuals working in the defense industry, members of the armed forces, and government officials held much sway over defense spending decisions and national security. The complex, which frequently carried out its activities in the background, evolved into a power that exerted substantial influence over internal and international policy choices. This industrial complex is even more formidable today, providing defensive and offensive systems to nations globally. It would be safe to assume that warfare is highly profitable to this complex so that lobbying would be skewed in this direction. Occasional usage of the phrase "Iron Triangle" refers to the Military Industrial Congressional Complex (MICC), which, in the context of the United States, includes the United States Congress. This tripartite association, the "MICC," encompasses political contributions, political endorsement of military expenditures, and lobbying efforts in support of bureaucratic entities to comprise the three primary components of this network. Additionally, the entirety of the contractual and financial transactional framework involving entities such as the Pentagon, Congress, the Executive branch, and private military contractors are embodied within this network. The Military-Industrial Congressional Complex (MICC) substantially impacts elite discourse. It influences the formulation of national security policies by endowing foreign policy think tanks with financial resources and access to supportive lobbyists.

Think tanks of this nature, in conjunction with their affiliated analysts, often emerge as the go-to sources for media coverage concerning subjects pertaining to peace and war. They form the narrative for the American public. War is an extraordinarily profitable endeavor, and ongoing conflict is also profitable. It is no stretch of the imagination to infer that the MIC has a vested economic interest in ensuring there is significant conflict in the global theater and that there exists in the world-defined adversarial alignments to sustain the viability of its very existence. This is also tied into the political and international economic posturing of the United States, the various propagation of hostilities, and the continuation of a Cold War doctrine in the global landscape. The deep state and shadow government entities have significantly influenced U.S. policy from the early 1900s until today. I am convinced that the locus of authority in our government does not reside in the Oval Office. If any President or group challenges the entrenched democratic and republican order, which includes the military-industrial complex and economic complex, all available resources will be mobilized to dismantle and undermine that President or group. Does this theory have any similarity to the current issues unfolding in American politics today, involving the vilification of a political opponent and former President, as well as his supporters, through coordinated attacks by the political, judicial, justice, and media establishments?

Secret Societies and Intelligence Agencies: The twentieth century witnessed the formation of intelligence agencies and covert organizations that were instrumental in determining the nation's course. Prominence was acquired by the Central Intelligence Agency (CIA) and groups such as the Council on Foreign Relations (CFR). These entities mainly functioned under the covert umbrella, giving rise to apprehensions regarding concealed motives and the manipulation of worldwide occurrences. These and other secret agencies have, from the past to the present, supported U.S. doctrine, regime change, and removal of key players that oppose U.S. philosophy for the furtherance of our foreign policy objectives. In government today, a key phrase that keeps emerging is "The Deep State," which has gained considerable traction. This seems one and the same, as it refers to the network of embedded bureaucrats and government officials, including the intelligence agencies that hold immense control over the governance of our nation. This seems evident today as we see the deep-state actions unfold. The democrat-influenced complex is systematically skewering the former President and main political rival in the upcoming election, and government institutions are weaponized to remove this candidate at all costs, regardless of the optics on display. Apart from all the current pressures in formulating strategically sound foreign and domestic policy, historical events and ideological factors can also influence and drive foreign policy initiatives. The lasting impact of many doctrines, such as the Monroe Doctrine, Truman Doctrine, and Wilsonian theory of promoting democracy, have significantly impacted the trajectory of United States foreign policy to date. Policy should and must not be created in a vacuum, shrouded in ignorance and lacking a comprehensive understanding of the region's geopolitics, as seems to be the case. The political parties seem to operate within their bubble of self-interest, self-preservation, party dominance, and personal economic gain, often to the detriment of the nation's long-term strategic positioning and ignoring, in many instances, the people's will.

Chapter 4
Global Issues And Policy

The 20th century saw major shifts in the realm of global politics, involving conflicts and diplomatic interactions that exerted a profound influence on the foreign policies undertaken by nations around the globe. Numerous key factors have impacted international relations during this volatile period. The policies that stemmed from these variables validate my theory that many of our policy formations were reactionary and are still today.

World Wars. The two World Wars brought significant changes in foreign policy. Following the First World War, the League of Nations was founded, state boundaries were changed, and defeated nations had to pay reparations. The emergence of totalitarian regimes and the ineffectiveness of the League of Nations created the conditions for the onset of World War II, thereby developing significant shifts in global power structures and culminating in the establishment of the United Nations, which in its inception, was a good framework, but unfortunately evolved into a liberal behemoth pushing a new world agenda.

The Cold War. This was characterized as an ideological and geopolitical conflict, which significantly influenced the formulation of foreign policies by both the United States and the Soviet Union. The Cold War precipitated the establishment of alliances such as NATO and the Warsaw Pact, proxy conflicts such as the Korean War and Vietnam War, and heightened competition in armament, from which the military-industrial complex benefited greatly. The foreign affairs of numerous nations were impacted by the concept of containment and the apprehension around mutually assured destruction. During this period, an economic component forced the USSR to spend more to stay abreast militarily, which limited their domestic growth.

Decolonization. This unfolded during the mid-20th century, marking the culmination of colonial empires when former colonies achieved their independence. The European countries' ability to sustain their colonial territories was significantly diminished due to the impact of World War II. The process of decolonization led to the formation of novel nation-states. It brought about significant changes in the worldwide distribution of power. The foreign policies of these newly independent states were significantly impacted as they endeavored to establish their autonomy and manage the complexities of international relations. When the colonial powers stepped back during this period, many nations hung in the balance between viability and failure, creating dictatorships where some vacuums were unfilled. I believe this period was a missed opportunity for American expansion.

Globalization. This refers to the phenomenon that emerged throughout the later part of the 20th century, which was characterized by heightened levels of economic interdependence, technological developments, and the exchange of cultural elements. Nations have strategically modified their foreign policies to participate actively in the global economy, forge international trade agreements, and effectively tackle cross-border issues such as climate change, pandemics, and terrorism. One of the main issues that arose in America was a significant push by nature activists and liberals to address the hyped climate change to limit our production of fossil fuels, therefore creating a national dependency. These harsh climate-associated policies have created growth setbacks and increased fuel costs dramatically. In 2019, under republican policies, the U.S. opened up drilling. It produced more energy than it had consumed since 1957, categorized as energy independence[ii].

To summarize, globalization facilitated unparalleled interconnectedness and interdependence utilizing economic integration. The interdependence between different aspects brought about economic expansion, cultural interchange, and technological progress in the United States. However, it also introduced numerous difficulties and alterations. The process of globalization has intensified competition and facilitated the global expansion of American companies. Globalization facilitated the dissemination of American culture internationally, resulting in increased diversity and multiculturalism within the United States. Technology enabled the globalization of information, goods, and services, thereby enhancing economic growth. Regrettably, it also resulted in heightened concerns and occurrences regarding cybersecurity breaches, cyber terrorism, and privacy issues. Escalated commerce resulted in worldwide ecological problems necessitating international collaboration, which affected the bottom line of many products because of restrictive regulations. Policymakers faced challenges in addressing the advantages and disadvantages of globalization and implementing regulations to manage its expansion and impact. International collaboration was required to tackle trade imbalances, safeguard intellectual property rights, and ensure environmental sustainability. The process of globalization has quickened, resulting in the United States becoming deeply interconnected with the international community. The nation's prosperity and advancement rely heavily on leading, influencing, collaborating, and adapting to geoeconomics, geopolitics, and global market forces.

Nuclear Proliferation. This phenomenon profoundly impacted international relations, as it entailed advancing and disseminating nuclear armaments throughout the mid-20th century. The acquisition of nuclear capabilities had emerged as a fundamental consideration in a nation's strategic deliberations, leading to the establishment of arms control treaties, the formulation of deterrence policies, and the implementation of non-proliferation initiatives. The overall premise of reducing nuclear weapons was sound, but the rapidly evolving geopolitical landscape was highly fluid. The Manhattan Project's clandestine progression and execution of atomic bombs underscored the incomparable destructive power and destructive potential of nuclear weapons. The Cold War, which followed, was characterized by a perilous arms race between the United States and the Soviet Union. This arms race culminated in the Nuclear Non-Proliferation Treaty

(NPT), a substantial effort to prevent the spread of nuclear weapons, being signed into force in 1968.

Additional challenges emerged when nations like Israel, South Africa, and India endeavored to obtain nuclear capabilities, thereby exemplifying the complex interplay of geopolitical influence. Questions were raised regarding the security of the Soviet Union's nuclear arsenal after it was disbanded, and the proliferation concerns in Iraq and Iran, along with North Korea's nuclear ambitions, added new intricacies to the global nuclear landscape. Major powers' modernization of nuclear arsenals and the emergence of cybersecurity and nuclear infrastructure threats demanded a renewed emphasis on sabotage and internal security. Proliferation aversion has been the focus of international endeavors, spearheaded by reputable organizations such as the United Nations (U.N.) and the International Atomic Energy Agency (IAEA), by implementing diplomatic initiatives and multilateral agreements. The historical trajectory of nuclear proliferation over the 20th century serves as a poignant reminder of the formidable obstacles that these weapons posed and the critical need for sustained international collaboration to ensure a secure and peaceful future.

FOREIGN POLICY EVOLUTION

The prevailing philosophy in U.S. international strategy during the twentieth century went through a few movements, mirroring the changing worldwide scene and the difficulties faced by the U.S. Here are the key philosophical patterns that affected U.S. international strategy during the 1900s and 2000s:

Isolationism (Pre-World War II). During the early 20th century, the United States adhered to a policy of relative isolationism, which was marked by a deliberate inclination to steer clear of involvement in hostilities occurring in Europe. This perspective was evident in the United States' hesitancy to become a member of the League of Nations subsequent to the conclusion of World War I[iii].

Interventionism (World War II and Post-War Era). The Pearl Harbor attack in 1941 signified a significant shift in the United States' foreign policy, prompting a departure from its previous isolationist position and a subsequent embrace of a more interventionist strategy. The period following World War II witnessed significant developments, including the formation of the United Nations, the implementation of the Marshall Plan to facilitate the reconstruction of Europe, and the introduction of the Truman Doctrine to curtail the expansion of communism[iv].

Containment (Cold War Era). The geopolitical and ideological conflict known as the Cold War exerted a significant influence on United States foreign policy for a substantial portion of the mid-20th century. The policy of containment[v], as formulated by George F. Kennan (Osgood, Robert E. "America, and the World." 2022.), aimed to impede the worldwide expansion of communism. This philosophy served as a guiding principle for the United States' engagement in conflicts such as the Korean War and the Vietnam War[vi].

Détente (Late Cold War). The 1970s saw a turning point in the détente era when the U.S. and the USSR adopted a new strategy to reduce tensions. The Strategic

Arms Limitation Talks (SALT I and II), the Anti-Ballistic Missile Treaty (ABM), and the Helsinki Accords were all landmark treaties and agreements that reduced and controlled nuclear weapons during this historical period. These treaties aimed to restrict the quantity and circulation of nuclear weapons and missiles while also fostering human rights and promoting security cooperation in Europe. As a result, the personal ties between U.S. and Soviet leaders, including Nixon and Brezhnev, as well as Ford and Carter, were strengthened. These leaders convened on multiple occasions and exchanged gifts and correspondence, fostering a congenial and respectful environment conducive to dialogue and negotiation. The measure diminished the likelihood of a direct armed conflict or a nuclear conflict between the United States and the Soviet Union, along with their respective allies. The U.S. was also able to devote more attention to other regions and concerns, including energy, human rights, and the Middle East, due to the détente[vii].

Post-Cold War Unipolarity[viii]. Following the conclusion of the Cold War during the latter part of the 1980s and early 1990s, the United States assumed the position of the singular global superpower. The prevailing worldview underwent a transformation, emphasizing the promotion of democracy, relaxed borders, free markets, and the establishment of a "New World Order" founded on principles of cooperation, modified socialism, and multilateralism. During these changes across the pond, American hegemony was being solidified globally. This would have been the perfect time, if any, to initiate aggressive foreign policy objectives of creating new alliances, projecting

economic power and establish a long-term geopolitical strategy for economic, market, and infrastructure investment backed by strong deployable home-based quick-reaction military forces.

Humanitarian Intervention. Humanitarian intervention refers to when a state (or states) employs or threatens to employ military force across international borders to end widespread and severe human rights violations in a state that has not authorized the use of force. Humanitarian interventions aim to end human rights violations against non-combatants of the state intervening, especially in the direst of situations. Efforts to establish political systems and institutions to attain favorable results in the medium to long term, including peacekeeping, peace-building, and development aid, are not encompassed within the scope of this definition of humanitarian intervention. Variations in definition pertain to the following aspects: whether humanitarian intervention is restricted to situations in which the host state has not consented, whether it is restricted to punitive actions, or whether it is limited to situations in which the United Nations Security Council has granted explicit authorization for action. Nonetheless, specific fundamental attributes will generally be agreed upon beforehand.

(a). Humanitarian intervention is predicated on the utilization and threat of military forces (b). Military intervention can be defined as the act of encroaching upon the internal affairs of a sovereign state through the deployment of military troops into its territory or airspace without the state having engaged in a specific act of aggression against another. (c). The intervention is undertaken in reaction to circumstances that may not directly imperil the strategic interests of the involved state; instead, it is driven by humanitarian goals. During the 1990s, there was a notable surge in the prioritization of humanitarian interventions, as evidenced by the active engagement of the United States in conflicts such as those in Bosnia and Kosovo. Regrettably, employing military force for humanitarian objectives had garnered support, overshadowing the humanistic approach to resolving crises and utilizing military power as a deterrent.

War on Terror (Early 2000s). The terrorist attacks that transpired on September 11, 2001, instigated a significant shift in the foreign policy of the United States. The George W. Bush administration launched a strategic initiative commonly referred to as the "War on Terror," which led to military interventions in Afghanistan in 2001 and Iraq in 2003. The main goals of these interventions were to mitigate acts of terrorism and eliminate the existence of weapons of mass destruction. Gaining a comprehensive understanding of Iran's engagement and underlying motivations is imperative for effectively devising long-term strategies to counter their actions. During the 1980s, Iran provided direct support to Muslim radicals in Malaysia and the Philippines while also serving as a source of inspiration for Shi'ite communities in North Yemen, Saudi Arabia, Turkey, and Pakistan. The writing by Bakhash, Vali Nasr's

"Reign of the Ayatollahs" (*New York: Basic Books, 1986*) is a significant academic work that delves into the subject matter of the Ayatollahs' rule. Iran had established networks of control and support through its Islamic Revolutionary Guard Corps (IRGC), collaborating with various Islamist organizations, including Hamas, the Palestine Islamic Jihad, the Turkish Islamic Action, Hezbollah, the Islamic Group in Egypt, al-Nahda in Tunisia, Houthi in Yemen, and the Islamic Salvation Front in Algeria. Additionally, Iran has formed alliances with radical secular groups such as the PFLP-GC and the Kurdish Workers Party, to name a few. Saying that Iran has a hand in most terrorist funding in the world in some manner is not a stretch of any imagination.

Neoconservatism. The initial ten-year period of the 21st century witnessed a significant prevalence of neoconservatism within the domain of United States foreign policy. This ideological perspective endorsed a proactive and assertive approach to advancing democratic principles and addressing perceived obstacles. The fundamentals of this specific ideology essentially determined the invasion of Iraq. This phenomenon may be classified as an offshoot of the conservative political ideology, distinguished by its fusion of traditional conservative principles, support for political individualism, and steadfast endorsement of free markets. Neoconservatives have taken on the role of vigilant monitors, particularly regarding perspectives that trend toward increased liberalization. Neoconservatives exhibit a pronounced proclivity towards cultural matters and mass media, encompassing various domains such as music, art, literature, theatre, film, television, and the Internet. This inclination arises from their conviction that the identity and values of a society are molded and conveyed through these mediums.

The prevailing consensus is that Western culture, particularly American society, has experienced a decline in moral standards, a lack of direction, and a deterioration in core principles. The moral decline of Western culture is exacerbated by the absence of accountability for individuals' actions, the consumption of violent and sexually explicit films, the proliferation of television programs that reinforce specific agendas, the glorification of death and lawlessness in video games, the manipulation of gender norms, and the widespread presence of popular music that is saturated with obscenities that no longer provoke surprise or disgust. Behaviors that were previously stigmatized and considered morally questionable are now regarded as socially acceptable in society. Neoconservatives argue that the widespread occurrence of such aberrant behavior signifies a broader and deeper cultural predicament that is impacting Western civilization. The intellectual movement, characterized by a liberalized approach and pushed in educational institutions, fosters a cultural environment that encourages the questioning of established authority, the critique of religious institutions, and the rejection of longstanding beliefs. Many neoconservatives argue that the perceived societal challenges can be attributed to the countercultural movement of the 1960s and the current push for socialism and liberalism in American culture. They contend that these ideologies undermine conventional values, as well as cultural and religious beliefs, by considering them outdated, insignificant, or backward. Regardless of its historical origins, neoconservatives contend that this decline presents a palpable and imminent peril to Western civilization.

Pragmatism – Multilateralism. The later years of the 20th century and the subsequent years of the 21st century witnessed a noticeable transition towards a more pragmatic and cooperative approach in the field of international relations, particularly during the period of the Obama administration, despite the absence of significant advancements in relations. Within the realm of domestic affairs, there witnessed an escalation in racial tensions instigated by progressive activists who advocated for narratives endorsing racial disparities, divisions, and instances of excessive force by law enforcement. Additionally, the President criticized police actions before guilt was established, which the police actions eventually proved aptly justified. This gave the fire of "racial targeting by police" all the fuel it needed to grow into the monster it is today, including the Black Lives Matter movement (BLM). The administration also stressed strengthening alliances, reducing climate change, and pursuing diplomatic solutions as their primary focus. The foreign policies enacted by President Obama can be categorized as "liberal-realist" due to their utilization of a combination of liberal and realist principles. However, it can be argued that foreign affairs have been an unambiguous disaster for the administration. The then-present geopolitical situation in various regions, including Russia, China, and the Middle East, seemed to be more uncertain when compared to the period prior to President Obama's inauguration. This is the inevitable consequence of an administration's tendency to ignore strategic military recommendations and refuse to place trust in military authorities. The administration also downplayed the repeated military and intelligence recommendations that called for the necessary military action to address the ongoing turmoil in the Middle East.

Nationalism and "America First" (Late 2010s). The Trump administration, which began in 2017, adopted a foreign policy approach that firmly focused on nationalism and transnationalism, placing American interests over international commitments while negotiating. The "America First" initiative comprehensively reassessed trade agreements and critically examined global institutions. The ideology that influenced policy and the National Security Strategy (2017 NSS) differed from the internationalist approach of the Obama administration, the transformative agenda pursued by the Bush administration, the Clinton administration's endorsement of globalization, and Biden's inclination towards liberalist Internationalism. Conversely, a steadfast commitment is shown in prioritizing supremacy and relieving the United States of its obligations in the realm of multilateralism. The "principled realism" ideology highlights significant divergences between the ideological underpinnings of Trump's nationalism and the predominant internationalist approach that has shaped U.S. foreign policy since 1945.

Critics, in trying to always downplay and make irrelevant the favorable policies of an opponent, push narratives emphasizing that although Trump's foreign policy approach brought average advancement, especially in Middle East peace, trade, and great power competition, it was often mishandled. The current scenario might be characterized as a clash between the forward-thinking viewpoints espoused by individuals within the Trump administration and the traditionalists (swamp, shadow government) that comprise the foreign policy establishment determined to maintain the status quo. This analysis effectively underscores the persistent conflict between Trumpism and traditionalism, leading to a notable schism within the realm of foreign policy decision-making in Washington and facing substantial criticism from proponents eager to restore the previous state of affairs. I have to note that even though Trump's LAC (Latin America and the Caribbean) policies helped curb illegal Immigration in the interim, the policies were disastrous for long-term strategic development in the region, as was the case with other administrations. Again, back to the old ideology, "long-term foreign policy doesn't translate to votes." In my opinion, this helped China to gain inroads much faster. A sad fact is that it is true of the Republicans and the Democrats that long-term foreign policies that don't yield immediate results at the voting booth take a back seat to band-aid quick return policies. Unfortunately, these band-aid policies do more harm than good. We are witnessing the effects of this ideology with the economic, immigration, and security issues impacting the U.S. in the Western hemisphere.

Appeasement[ix] (2021-2023). Mixed multilateralism[x]: "Foreign policy for the middle class." The current Biden administration promotes this as their primary guiding principle for foreign policy, in addition to Biden's seven (7) pillars aimed at preserving the "Liberal International Order." There are many apprehensions concerning President Biden's foreign affairs strategy or the absence thereof. The Australian and Japanese governments have concerns about Biden's stance towards China. The French are concerned about the Democrats potentially withdrawing from Europe as they aim to disengage from the Middle East and the fight against terrorism, specifically after the Afghanistan debacle. Biden's reception of the British continues to be lukewarm, making them feel uneasy in the light of Brexit. The administration's recognition of the urgent military threat posed by China has not yielded any significant revision in operational policy, defense budget, or the strategic positioning of U.S. forces outside of showboating. There seems to be an absence of any identifiable strategy regarding hostile probing actions or any change in U.S. forces' engagement protocol. Detractors in Washington contend that there is a significant degree of perplexity and a disconcerting lack of coherence between the administration's professed priorities and its tangible actions. China is getting ready to decouple on its terms and has strategically beat the West to the punch. Washington had hoped to use the threat of decoupling as a bargaining chip, but Beijing identified this vulnerability early on and has taken steps to correct it.

As a consequence of Washington's failure to garner allied support in the economic sphere, additional strain is placed on the armed forces and other U.S. facets to do the heavy lifting. The administration's understanding of the economic and foreign policy relationship has been complex and confusing, to say the least. A critical long-term component missing from Biden's national security strategy pertains to its economic outlook, which restricts the ability of the United States and other countries to reduce their dependence on Chinese goods and markets. The administration has ignored the pleas of East Asian allies to aid them in reducing their economic reliance on China. This strategy would have placed nations on a trajectory toward economic success that diminishes China's dominant influence over them, giving smaller nations maneuver room. Following this line of thinking, Australia, Japan, and South Korea have called on the United States to demonstrate a more resolute commitment to free trade in the Indo-Pacific region rather than being tunnel-visioned by merely seeking to isolate Beijing. Washington should develop a proactive strategic economic plan that persuades its allies to create independent markets and supply chains, eliminating dependence on China[xi].

Biden's[xii] helter-skelter economic strategy for his foreign policy seems to be centered mainly on the ups and downs of American domestic politics as well as social and gender issues, broadening the Democrat Party voter base and pressuring allies to bring their economies into line with American standards without any concessions. On the domestic front, President Biden conveniently disregards the actuality of his economic policies. Under the influence of "Bidenomics," American families' credit card debt has escalated to an unprecedented $1 trillion as individuals face difficulties in meeting their financial obligations and providing for their households due to the burden of inflation. As an example, the aspiration of owning a home has become unattainable for numerous Americans due to the rise in mortgage rates, which are nearing 8%, and the stricter lending criteria imposed by banks. Gas prices are experiencing a sudden increase across the entire country due to the energy policies implemented by the Biden administration, which are perceived as detrimental to American interests. Food prices have skyrocketed, placing many middle-to lower-income families in a food insecure status. Furthermore, American households have suffered an average loss of $33,000 in actual wealth this year alone. Unsurprisingly, nearly two-thirds of Americans view the President's economic initiatives negatively, and his approval rating is downward trending.

Now that we have an understanding of how our policies and the American vision have developed or changed over the course of the century, how the many political leaders have put their vision of leadership into effect, and a comprehension of our trajectory, it is time to address the current problems that are endangering America as we know it and understand what is at stake not only for our country but our current and future generations. America's survival is dependent on you, the electorate, having an informed understanding of our current trajectory, which party is morphing democracy into socialism, weaponizing government against the masses, eliminating political opposition, upholding Islamism, and allowing the changing of our societal construct towards immorality and the estrangement of society from Christianity. Some foresight and analytical thought are required for this task, and utilizing this save-all query has saved many in history from taking the incorrect path. "What if ?"

PART II

IDEOLOGICAL WARFARE

CHAPTER 5
THE DESTRUCTION OF DEMOCRACY, WESTERN VALUES, AND BELIEFS USING IDENTITY POLITICS

Understanding the Ideological War: Ideological and Political warfare has many crossover points, and the lines of distinction get blurry[2]. It is unnecessary to get bogged down in the exact labeling, but follow the arguments presented, draw from your relevant experiences, and the current state of anarchy we are experiencing in society. America is in the midst of an ideological civil war. Almost all of our domestic, foreign, and economic policies, values, and beliefs are being challenged at every turn. The "Zombie Electorate," whom I categorized earlier, shares a sentiment that, if it is on social media, it must be correct; that is how it should be, and without any constructive thinking whatsoever, they jump headfirst onto the ignorance bandwagon. Rational thought, critical thinking, and good old common sense are a thing of the past. This is so evident when observing the spread of false information through the Chinese Communist Party (CCP) propaganda platform, TikTok. Even though our President (Biden) is on various media outlets stating false economic information against his opponent, and even after it has been repeatedly debunked by both sides of the aisle, the lie still prevails. This follows the democrat machine premise that if

---

[2] Galantiere, Lewis. "Ideology and Political Warfare." *Confluence* 2 (1953): 43.

repeated frequently, it becomes truth, and the masses believe anything on social media without verification. The politically influential Democrat Nancy Pelosi publicly outlined in an interview the method employed to do this if you are so inclined to learn how to deceive the American public step by step.

Well, that irresponsible mindset contributes immensely to our societal decline, the dire consequences facing our nation, and the destruction of the fabric of our American political democracy, values, beliefs, and freedoms. We as a nation are now more polarized than ever before. Consider these points: identity politics has created more cultural and racial separation and animosity than probably ever witnessed in recent history[xiii]; rational and reasoning are a thing of the past; tolerance for opposing views is non-existent; meaningful dialogue and compromise are not tolerated; antisemitism is a condoned ideology pushed by educational institutions and social action groups; Islamist doctrine is increasingly popular propagated again by higher level education institutions and Islamist sponsored groups; and bipartisan political congruence on a policy that is citizen-centric is not attainable in our governing bodies.

Adding insult to injury, there is also a breakdown in effective governance of the nation, which is currently on display and evidenced by corruption within the Biden presidency, weaponization of institutions directed against citizens of opposing political beliefs, armed intrusion by federal agents into an ex-presidents and political opponent homes over document issues, collusion by party officials and state prosecutors to prevent the election of a political

77

figure and former president by the will of the people, and a double standard for judicial integrity and accountability. Another critical factor in this ideological civil war is the systematic effort to erase the democratic form of government that exists and replace it with a quasi-totalitarian-socialist form of government under a democratic party banner[xiv], with extreme left-wing socialist activists and, in some instances, Islamists posing as elected officials. This small group of politicians and their elitist backers aims to monopolize political power and control virtually every aspect of social life, including the economy, education system, science and arts, and private lives, by forcefully injecting their ideology to counter existing values and beliefs shared by the masses. No, this is not a foreign "banana republic" I am referring to, but the once aspiring to be great, ethically principled United States. Does any of this sound familiar, even in the least? The majority of people who advocate for socialism fail to acknowledge the fact that wealthy or powerful individuals (or both) will always find ways to insulate themselves from the insanity that they advocate for. "Socialism for thee, but not for me" has been the guiding principle for all Marxists and other socialists ever since it was first articulated. Stalin, Maduro, Lenin, Kim, Chavez, and Castro had all accumulated fortunes by taking what others had given them or confiscating and giving it back to themselves according to their "needs." The remaining members of the population, on the other hand, appear to either starve to death or devour garbage and creatures from zoos. In today's society, Soros and other democratic socialist liberal financiers contribute to most of the destabilizing events in American society.

Critics: To critics of my writing, please remember to be open-minded and analytical, look at the big picture, see what is transpiring in society, and not get trapped in listening to the pushed narratives and political talking points. Ask yourselves, is this the next evolution of American politicking? Think about what life will be like for your children and grandchildren on this political and social trajectory, and be honest with your assessment. My goal for you, the electorate, is assessing policy, foreign and domestic geopolitical awareness, and understanding the implications of changing our current societal construct, not changing your political ideology but holding all flawed politicians accountable for destroying the fabric of our nation. A call for action, be knowledgeable and make sound decisions at the ballot boxes. Reawaken your basic means of analysis and common sense, which is an elusively uncommon trait that is very much lacking in today's Gen Z society.

Weaponizing Ideology: The liberal democratic socialist machine aims to cultivate a devoted and robust voter base by strategically focusing on issues that evoke strong emotions and appeal to these specific demographics. The intentional deployment of identity politics by the Democratic party, liberal media outlets, liberal social activists, and socialist indoctrination is a clear indication of a calculated strategy to politicize matters concerning personal, social, and gender identity. This strategy aims to undermine the democratic process in America and suppress any opposing perspectives, especially those associated with the Republican party. While this strategy has successfully mobilized certain fringe factions, it has also led to substantial divisions along political, racial, and cultural lines, as well as a persistent assault on our Judeo-Christian values and ideology. With the growing polarization of the political landscape, the impact of identity politics on election outcomes is expected to remain a controversial topic of debate and analysis. A significant number of individuals will strongly object to this apparent decline in American freedoms and the relegation of faith-based values to a less important position. The responsibility lies with the well-informed and logical citizen to comprehend the current state of our society, including the degradation of our principles and convictions and the presence of corruption in our government. Only individuals have the ability to bring about change. Be an informed voter and American citizen.

Responsibility: This failure overlaps several political administrations, and the American political cycle is more often a hindrance to the continuity and synchronicity of policy. This writing is not meant to promote partisan politics or change political persuasions but to expose readers to differing viewpoints and create discussions to enable good decision-making as citizens. Let me be clear: both parties share enormous responsibility in most or all of the issues at hand, some more than others, so there is enough blame to allocate. Voters also have to share the accountability for our failures as a nation; we must identify and look beyond the party talking points, admonish the political and religious

80

slander prevalent in government today, and quash the infiltration of subverting influences using political office to push terroristic ideology and anti-Semitism on the masses. The electorate must recognize that our government representatives work for us and must perform for us, not in reverse. To gain a simple perspective of the state of our union, observe multiple (Important) news outlets about American domestic/global issues for one night (FOX, CNN, Sky News, India TV, DW, France 24, NHK World) and then compare this to what is happening in underdeveloped "banana republic" or war-torn nations, you would be surprised at the similarities with occurrences of government corruption, criminality in society, breakdown of judicial accountability, political strongarming, political and religious radicalization, and civil disruptions, in the United States. How does this make you feel about the place our elected leaders and our policies have brought America to? The major U.S. news networks have blocked many news stories that go against the narrative but are aired on foreign stations. That's when you realize that our networks are complicit in censoring information.

The Liberal Democratic Socialist Activist Complex: It is difficult to split a conversation about ideological differences and not reference political parties, as one party, in particular, is joined at the hip with liberal social activism. In the past, the democratic party was not a liberal socialist party but one of reason and sound policies. It was an outstanding balance to the conservative outlook for governance, and the parties kept each other in check down the middle for the betterment of the nation. The people had two great choices of governance based on the methodology used to achieve the overriding goal: the success of America and its people. Strong work ethic, God-fearing values, and beliefs were never in question. That is what democratic governance is all about: two strong parties with sound moral principles working toward the same end result but with differing approaches. None tried to sequester the other and silence their voice. This gives the people a choice to elect which governance methods they prefer. Still, regardless, both pathways are always people and nation-centric.

I have examined the pivotal historical events and prevailing social ideologies that have influenced our foreign policies and American society to this point. Considering this, let us look at the cultural animosity, racial aggression, Islamist doctrine, societal decay, liberalism, and immoral beliefs causing division and instability within our country. These divisions are primarily influenced by the political agenda of the left-leaning liberal-socialist faction during this decade. I relate to them collectively as the Liberal Democratic Socialist Activist Complex (L'DSAC), which includes the liberal international order (Biden coined), the democratic party, democratic socialists, socialist educators, prominent liberal media surrogates, social activist groups, legal activists, influential democrat-party donors, and foreign-financially-sponsored Islamist groups, all working in unison to destroy our democratic processes, subvert judicial jurisprudence, demonize conservative policies, racially divide and destabilize society, exacerbate lawlessness, attack Christianity and our Judeo-Christian principles, and silence opposing voices to bring about the "Fall of America." A political scholar made a comment about the American Democratic Party on a foreign national news outlet not too long ago, which made me pause. In their remarks, they made a reference to the concept of the American brand of selective democracy, which they defined as the protection and advocacy of freedoms for issues that their party supported while at the same time expressing disdain for similar issues that did not align with their belief structure (Trans rights vs. Gun rights). It was interesting that others viewed the U.S. brand of democracy in this manner.

Obama's Contribution to Racial Instability: I attribute some of the most deleterious acts a President could do to society and the propagation of a destructive ideology to former President Barack Obama. Most of the racial issues we face today and the empowerment of the democratic machine and social activist groups were set in motion by a few divisive acts. He took the successes of the African American experience, the civil rights accomplishments, and the advancement towards total integration in the fabric of America and unraveled it in one swoop. Obama emphasized that it wasn't just black against white anymore, but anyone who identifies as non-white forms a collective. From this point, the poison of division and diversity in society took center stage, and our national identity, "one nation under one flag," was in jeopardy. Everyone wanted to jump on the minority bandwagon to be identified as nonwhite, separated by ethnic grouping, and with no assimilation into American mainstream culture, thereby benefiting from the minority collective. As a result, our nation has become highly polarized and racially charged, and multiculturalism and a tribalism mentality have taken hold[xv].

Failure in Europe, Wisen up America: I guess Americans haven't witnessed the unfolding failures of liberal social experiments in Europe (multiculturalism, open borders, mass resettlement) thrust upon sovereign nations by the EU (European Union). European countries, including Great Britain, have been experiencing sharp racial and religious divisions in society, loss of national heritage and identity, overburdened social services, increased migrant unemployment, and increased migrant criminality, including drugs, gangs, and terrorism. The masses in Europe have spoken by saying enough is enough. Europe is experiencing a transformation and mass reversion to conservative governance, a rejection of Islamism, and the cessation of mass immigration resettlement policies, coupled with the forced removal of illegal immigrants and, in some cities, the activation of its military to curb criminal activity and return safety to the citizenry. Again, I might point out the news censorship experienced in the United States. Liberal media outlets in the U.S. have been blocked out for months now, reporting on the dramatic shift by many European nations from liberal governments, repudiation of harmful open border immigration policies, and the public rejection of the liberal brainchild experiment, multiculturalism. This is because it goes against the narrative and supported ideology of the left and the democratic party machine agenda. Treat the electorate in America like mushrooms, "keep them in the dark, and feed them excrement." America, get informed!

Reinforcing Racial Segregation: Throughout Obama's presidency, he consistently employed divisive tactics by subtly exploiting racial tensions, thus exacerbating racial animosity. Indeed, the expected outcome has been achieved since race relations in America have undeniably regressed significantly. I believe Martin Luther King would be disconcerted if he could witness the erosion of his ideal of harmony. Obama incited anger toward American law enforcement by making a false accusation against a white Cambridge police officer, claiming that the officer was "acting stupidly." He insinuated that the officer acted out of racial bias when he issued a justifiable and legal command to a black Harvard professor, who refused to comply. Another incident that sparked a separation in society and enforced the president's favoring black America was when Obama remarked, "If I had a son, he would resemble Trayvon Martin," when a self-proclaimed neighborhood watchman fatally shot and killed the black adolescent Martin in Florida. Another instance coming to mind is the statement referencing "middle America, flyover states" as loving to cling to their bible and guns in a demeaning manner. It actually meant nothing to the then-Obama administration, and didn't even solicit an apology when the jurors in the Trayvon case explicitly stated that race did not influence the incident; however, Obama, who eventually supported Black Lives Matter, once again promoted the inaccurate portrayal of anti-black "systemic racism."

He propagated these views with the help of the media machine, regardless of the facts and the many studies that demonstrate that police officers are more cautious and reluctant to use lethal force against black suspects compared to white suspects and the other corroborating FBI statistical data on black shootings. The argument of systemic racism was pushed and echoed by the media at his behest. Obama, in speeches, has acknowledged the enduring influence of historical events such as the Jim Crow laws and slavery and purported that widespread discrimination is still present across various societal institutions in American culture. He emphasized that these factors have impacted our society and continue to shape our collective identity. Obama also showed his hand again in extending invitations to Al Sharpton, a prominent figure known for his race-mongering, with more than 70 visits to the White House, and not condemning the sermons of his pastor spreading hate in declaring, "God Dam America," and many other racially divisive outbursts.

Eric Holder, the Attorney General under President Obama's administration, expressed his concern about the presence of deeply ingrained racism in America. He specifically cited the requirement of voter identification as an example. During Obama's second term, a black individual, influenced by the narrative presented by Obama regarding police discrimination against black people, killed two NYPD officers as they were seated in their patrol car. In Baton Rouge, a black man motivated by the same storyline deliberately attacked and killed three police officers. In Dallas, another African American individual, who was persuaded by this narrative, carried out a deliberate attack and killed five law enforcement officers. There is a direct correlation between Obama's language and the duration of the fatal and expensive 2020 Black

Lives Matter/George Floyd demonstrations. There was a total government and media disregard for the fact that the chief prosecutor, who is of African descent, did not assert that the cop-defendant acted out of racial bias, that the officer was not accused of committing a hate crime, and that George Floyd was an extremely dangerous criminal and repeat offender.

Adding a Splash of Socialism: With the seed of racial hatred, systemic racism, and police targeting African American males in some diabolic means to an end planted in their minds, plus the constant emphasis on these issues by the party spokespeople, media, and social activists, African Americans have been brainwashed into a state of mistrust, paranoia, and mental slavery. It is clear why America has since declined on several levels after our nation experienced these tumultuous years of reprogramming. We as a nation have become less influential on the international stage while experiencing unstable transformative changes in our domestic social framework and declivitous race relations. When Obama said he would change America, he meant every word of it. These ideologies continue to take root with the Joe Biden reign and the far-left democratic party enclave, as the former president still pulls the strings in a democratic party-led Washington. The ideology of socialism, often framed as "democratic socialism," as in the Bernie Sanders following, is becoming more popular in society and can be placed on a spectrum that spans between the economic systems of capitalism and communism. However, it clearly demonstrates a much stronger ideological alignment with Marxism and communism. These extreme views should not be mistaken for the conventional ideology of the Democratic Party but rather represent a radicalization and liberalization of the party towards the far left of the political spectrum. "The current democratic party is different from the democratic party of the past,"[xvi] as exemplified by the renowned democratic party President John F. Kennedy, in his inaugural address in 1961, when he stated, "Ask not what your country can do for you – ask what you can do for your country." With today's unengaged, irresponsible generation, patriotism and good work ethic are things of the past.

Deceptive Immigration Ideology to Secure Power: A newly uncovered revelation substantiates the argument regarding the deliberate manipulation of voting demographics in the United States to benefit the Democrat Party, irrespective of national security considerations or citizenry safety. Recently, through a Freedom of Information Request (FOIA) lawsuit, documents have been obtained that reveal the Biden administration's transportation of migrants on covert flights into the United States under the CHNV (Cuba, Haiti, Nicaragua, and Venezuela) parole program[xvii]. Lawyers representing the Democratic immigration agencies continue to be evasive, arguing that disclosing the locations could potentially pose national security 'vulnerabilities.' The Customs and Border Protection has declined to provide additional details regarding a covert program that has organized flights for more than 350,000 thousand illegal immigrants from international airports directly to cities within the United States, with the number continuing to rise. The government deceivingly claims that these individuals undergo a vetting process, which amounts to questions answered on a form by the applicant, with no follow-up, as most of the countries in question don't have any active criminal investigation departments complying with U.S. requests for information. Claiming "national security vulnerabilities" is absurd when the Democrats are recklessly transporting illegal immigrants without proper vetting and releasing them into U.S. cities without the knowledge of Americans and law enforcement. This act within itself poses a detrimental risk to citizens. This indicates that while there was a significant increase in the number of migrants entering the country through the southern border last year, the Biden administration was also secretly transporting them into the country without going through the border.[3]

Mark Morgan, the former Chief of Customs and Border Protection, joined Jan Jeffcoat from The National Desk to discuss the recently revealed information regarding the secret flights. *"It's unconscionable, but this is the shell game we've been talking about. This is what they've done, this administration. They've made a deal with migrants from all over the world,"* he said. *"They said, if you were framed from illegally entering along the southern border in between the ports of entry, what we'll do is we'll let you fill out a couple of lines of paperwork online, and we'll let you fly into 43 different airports in the United States who will process and release you. So it's absolutely to cover up bad political optics"* (Mark Morgan, 2023). According to the Center for Immigration Studies, in the period from January

---

[3] American Military News, 320,000 illegal immigrants flown into US by Biden admin: Report (03/2024).

2023 to December 2023, a minimum of 350K undocumented immigrants were permitted to enter the United States by air from their home countries. This was made possible through a contentious program implemented by the Biden administration, which was specifically designed to enable migrants to request parole entry into the United States without being processed through the border[4].

To add insult to what I deem as a treasonous act, all of them were granted employment permits without any means of being traced once released into our society. The Center for Immigration Studies discovered that Customs and Border Protection (CBP) authorized these covert flights from foreign nations under the Biden administration. These flights landed in at least 43 American airports between January and December of 2023. This reads like a spy novel in which covert forces are injected behind enemy lines to disrupt enemy operations and create dissent in society, which is my reasoning for labeling this as sabotage. This also aligns with the Democrat Party elite's vision of illegally manipulating the voter base to maintain power, articulated through California's efforts to expedite the voting process for undocumented immigrants, securing the vote for the political party that facilitated their access to the American dream ahead of both legal citizens and immigrants. The proposed Assembly Bill 1840, introduced by Democrat Assemblyman Joaquin Arambula, aims to provide interest-free state loans to illegal immigrants in California to purchase their first homes. I can guarantee

---

[4] The National Desk, Washington. 03/05/2024: https://thenationaldesk.com/

you that this was never offered to African Americans, economically disenfranchised Whites, Asians, or Veterans. Conversely, it will benefit and has garnered support from a large number of foreign military-age men and women who are illegally crossing the border from Mexico into the Golden State and illegals already residing in the country.

Even though late in realizing the impact, it has finally raised concerns as thousands of homeless Americans, African Americans, legal-resident Hispanics, and veterans in Democrat-run cities are realizing they have been discarded in favor of the illegals while living in challenging conditions and paying taxes that support their own demise. Democrats, including their model state, California, are promoting irresponsible pro-immigrant policies that prioritize the needs of immigrants over those of American citizens. They are advocating for nationwide changes such as free access to higher education, free access to healthcare and public benefits, protections for undocumented immigrant workers and work permits, prioritizing support for undocumented immigrant students over inner-city students within school districts, and providing economic opportunities and inclusion through access to driver's licenses and pro bono immigration services for undocumented individuals. California has also introduced the Comeback Plan, which includes significant investments to support individuals with illegal immigration status. This plan offers undocumented families an extra $1,000 in stimulus checks through the expanded Golden State Stimulus. Additionally, it includes the most extensive renter assistance program in the country, providing $5.2 billion to help low-income renters pay their overdue rent and cover future rent for several months. Furthermore, the plan allocates $2 billion to assist illegal immigrants and other Californians in paying their outstanding utility bills.

The California Comeback Plan includes a groundbreaking initiative to extend Medi-Cal coverage to illegal individuals in California who are 50 years of age or older. This will grant them access to essential healthcare services that legal residents cannot access. In addition to the billions of taxpayer dollars already spent in the past three years, America's tax dollars are being squandered in favor of political strategies to secure a power base of the largest growing minority demographic. Understand that every time you endorse a Democrat to elected positions across the political spectrum, you are supporting these destructive policies[5]. These Democrat party policies are an open invitation for everyone to flood our borders by whatever means necessary and violate our laws without consequence. How in God's name did we get here? Why have we, as Americans, sat back and allowed this to occur? This is positive proof that we as Americans need to be informed, take note of political policies' impact on our communities, and exercise our rights to either support or deny party agendas that run counter to our welfare and not allow them to slip destructive schemes by us.

Deceptive Identity Politics to Secure Power: The use of deceptive identity politics has significant implications for human rights, democratic principles, and the

---

[5] FitzGerald, David Scott, and John D. Skrentny, eds. *Immigrant California: understanding the past, present, and future of US policy.* Stanford University Press, 2021.

cohesiveness of society. Polarization and extremism are two outcomes that may occur as a consequence of a breach of trust and cooperation between different groups involved. In addition, it can potentially undermine the institutions and standards in place to protect minorities, the rule of law, and the separation of powers. As history has demonstrated, it also increases the probability of increased acts of violence and atrocities. This is the reasoning many share for the importance of advocating for critical thinking, media literacy, and unbiased civic education in schools. These practices are also essential to resist and counteract deceptive identity politics and critical race theory. Additionally, cultivating a sense of shared values and a common identity as Americans is paramount to transcending social group diversity. Furthermore, it is of the utmost importance to make sure that every group can express their opinions and have a stake in the political process, as well as to address the fundamental causes of identity politics, which include factors such as discrimination, inequality, and injustice as they present themselves.

Lies and deception are political arts that have been used and discussed throughout history, including in the present day. Without a shadow of a doubt, activists and political influencers consider deception to be an indispensable and logical component of the political sphere. Elitists, for example, argue that enlightened leaders in government must occasionally attempt to persuade the general public to believe something that is not true for the better good. In the realm of American politics, it would appear that Democrats continue to believe that political deception is essential to advancing democratic governance. This is especially true in extraordinary circumstances in which the will of the people does not align with their vision. By situating deceptive strategies within the context of organized political communication (OPC), which includes propaganda pushed by the media complex, one can acquire a more comprehensive understanding of how deceit and lying have come to be fundamental to the exercise of power, even in modern liberal democracies. This ideology, which is destroying the foundations of our democratic republic, has completely taken over the political landscape in the United States by storm.

Needless to say, with the level of deception and polarity being propagated in society, political, cultural, social, and racial discourse in the United States is at an all-time high. It has been profoundly shaped by the ideology of identity politics, which is centered on the disparity and marginalization of social groups according to characteristics such as sexual orientation, race, gender, and ethnic origin. The liberal democratic socialist machine has utilized identity politics as a strategy to appeal to these constituencies under the guise of fighting for infringed rights, using emotional overtones to disguise their true objective in plain sight. This approach involves shaping political discourse, attacking individual personalities, and promoting radical legislative goals in order to generate the fallacy that one is advocating for justice and equality. This strategy effectively activated distinct voter blocs, including African American women, racial minorities, and the LGBTQ+ communities. It indoctrinated them in the belief that mainstream America is against them, thus having to fight for their place in society and flaunt it publicly at every turn.

This ideological strategy, influenced by socialism, combines elements of liberalism and socialism to attract a dissatisfied demographic of young individuals unhappy with existing social hierarchies, patriotic service, preserving constitutional rights, loyalty to the nation, and support of pro-Islamist doctrine. Their grievances with society also include taxation, workplace regulations, accountability systems, complying with rules, law enforcement, institutional hierarchies, the pursuit of individual wealth and success, and any ideology that challenges their extreme laissez-faire, irresponsible way of life. This ideology gained popularity in the 1960s as socialism became less accepted in the United States. This led to the rise of a new perspective known as liberalism, which later evolved into democratic socialism. This phenomenon became popular in the United States and quickly spread among socially vulnerable individuals who oppose social norms. This has also contributed to the homeless crisis and drug epidemic we face.

Bureaucracy and Government Interference Inhibits State's Advancement: The Weberian ideal of bureaucracy is a pipe dream that describes a hierarchical structure that establishes distinct lines of command and domains of responsibility. This structure is characterized by a hierarchical structure. In accordance with the regulations that have been codified, decisions are supposed to be made fairly and impartially. It is expected that bureaucrats will be chosen through meritocratic procedures, receive specialized training, and advance within the organization based on objective criteria. The provision of public goods, the enhancement of the standard of living, and the promotion of economic growth within the nation depend on effective government operation in today's society. These functions are carried out by the government through a wide range of activities, which include, but are not limited to, education, professional licensing, foreign affairs, taxation, border integrity, and homeland security. The complexity of bureaucratic management and public administration has increased in tandem with the growth of society, which has led to an increase in the demand for different services provided by the government. Parts of public administration include both the academic field that trains individuals to work in government bureaucracies and the process of carrying out public policy. Both of these aspects are examples of public administration. Unfortunately, the big government bureaucracy creates specific barriers to competition among states and sometimes organizations. It encourages a level of protectionist rules that restrict the growth of professionals across state borders and eliminates competition between states.

For instance, the policy of "State Certification" and regulation of standards for professional occupations is essential to prevent practitioners of a given trade from falling below acceptable proficiency standards. It is a built-in protection so the citizenry can be exposed to an adequate and regulated level of professional services. However, the issue encountered is the bureaucracy that prevents many professionals certified under a state jurisdiction from plying their trade in another state[6]. To practice in another state jurisdiction, several criteria have to be met; for example, (a) an agreement of reciprocity has to exist, (b) approval granted to sit for that state's certification, (c) or some combination of training and certification before being allowed to practice, with sometimes steep application fees[7]. This actually restricts competition among States[8]. Suppose professional workers are allowed to seek employment in other locations; they then have the freedom to compete for salaries, quality of living, and location. This also makes States compete for workers by ensuring competitive pay, safe environments, good quality of life, and superior housing to be enticing to the worker. It is actually a positive-sum situation for the worker and the state. South Dakota has pioneered the way in erasing restrictions to work in that state with certification from other jurisdictions. The simple answer could be national certification standards with add-on competency home study for state-specific rules.

Drawing a Parallel: In order to emphasize a particular argument, I would like the reader to peruse this section containing factual information derived from historical data. Next, I will ask the reader to, without bias, contemplate the current reality of the Liberal Democratic Socialist

[6] UMEZ, CHIDI, and REBECCA PIRIUS. "Barriers to Work."

[7] Johnson, Janna E., and Morris M. Kleiner. "Is occupational licensing a barrier to interstate migration?." *American Economic Journal: Economic Policy* 12, no. 3 (2020): 347-373.

[8] Peterson, Brenton D., Sonal S. Pandya, and David Leblang. "Doctors with borders: occupational licensing as an implicit barrier to high skill migration." *Public Choice* 160 (2014): 45-63.

propaganda[9] and indoctrination campaigns, including the utilization of state agencies to subjugate the population, the prevalence of antisemitism, the indoctrination of liberal-socialist-Marxist ideologies in our schools and among our youth, the erosion of our social values and structure, the promotion of immoral behavior as normal, the endorsement of anti-Christian sentiment, the endorsement of anti-Jewish sentiment, the government's involvement in decades of social experimentation on African Americans[10], the incitement of racial hatred to divide and control, and the media industrial complex alignment with the narratives dictated by the Democratic Party's elitists. Subsequently, juxtapose it with the subsequent factual information regarding Hitler's indoctrination of Germany. Beginning in the 1920s, the Nazi Party specifically focused on German youth in schools as a targeted audience for its propaganda messages[11]. The messages highlighted the Party's social identity, characterized by its dynamism, resilience, forward-modern thinking, and optimism of a one-world order.

The Nazi ideology successfully indoctrinated millions of German youth through educational institutions and extracurricular programs. The purpose of education in the Third Reich was to instill students with the National Socialist ideology for subsequent generations[12]. Nazi

[9] Alexander, Gerard. "The myth of the racist Republicans." *Claremont Review of Books* 4, no. 2 (2004): 11-14.

[10] Bartlett, Bruce. *Wrong on race: The Democratic Party's buried past.* Palgrave Macmillan, 2008.

[11] Appleby, Kelsey Danielle. "Controlling information with propaganda: Indoctrinating the youth in Nazi Germany." *Dalhousie Journal of Interdisciplinary Management* 9, no. 1 (2013).

scholars and educators exalted Nordic and other "Aryan" races while denigrating Jews and other perceived inferior groups as parasitic "bastard races" lacking the ability to contribute to culture or civilization. Although certain books were taken out of the classroom by censors, German educators introduced new textbooks that instructed students in the admiration of Hitler, compliance with state authority, militarism, racism, and antisemitism. Following the Nazi electoral victories in July 1932, Adolf Hitler appointed Joseph Goebbels as the director of a newly established propaganda ministry once the Nazis assumed control of the national government. Goebbels quickly conceived of a dominion that would exert control over educational institutions, universities, film production, radio broadcasting, and the dissemination of propaganda. *"I will be responsible for the education of the German people,"* he stated. Editors and journalists were required to adhere to the mandates and instructions issued by the ministry[13]. They were obligated to be in line with the party directives. The objective of the Propaganda Ministry was to exert greater control over the news and editorial content by issuing directives during daily conferences in Berlin and disseminating them through the party's regional or local newspapers[14]. The guidelines provided explicit instructions

---

[12] Brickman, William W. "Ideological Indotrination Toward Immolation: The Inauguration of NationalSocialist Education in Germany in 1933." *Western European Education* 15, no. 1 (1983): iii-xxxii.

[13] Martin, Tracey. "Propaganda: How Germany convinced the masses." *History in the making* 13, no. 1 (2020): 8.

[14] Steinberg, James David. "Totalitarianism and the press: ideological justification used by Hitler, Peron, and Castro to control news media." (1974).

regarding the permissible and impermissible stories to be covered and the appropriate manner to report the news. Any noncompliance in society would face the wrath of the government's socialist agencies[15]. Are you able to see the similarities between what is transpiring today in the democrat's playbook and the evils of the past Nazi regime? It is a very true statement that those who fail to heed history and learn from its missteps are doomed to repeat the mistakes of the past. The Democrat Party elitists and liberal talking heads on the various media shows actually have the audacity to label conservative party members as Nazis. They can get away with this because the average voter is unfamiliar with historical information and is not interested in illuminating their minds, analyzing facts, and qualifying the accusations. The media shovels so many informational mistruths and biased opinions down America's throats and gets away with it that it is absolutely unbelievable. I wish the American Democrat Party and their surrogates would look in the mirror and realize how they are destroying democratic principles and the nation. The Democrat and Republican party leadership in America must get back to national and citizen-centric policies. Can we not see the destruction being perpetuated against the homeland? America is becoming like a "Banana Republic" where the political-criminal nexus becomes the natural order of operations. Wake up America.

[15] Woolley, Samuel C., and Philip N. Howard, eds. *Computational propaganda: Political parties, politicians, and political manipulation on social media.* Oxford University Press, 2018.

CHAPTER 6
THE EXPLOITATION OF BLACKS - SECURING POWER ON THE BACKS OF BLACK AMERICA

Our democracy in America is a representative democracy, contingent on an equal two-party system where party representatives vie for public support based on policy and other criteria, and then a winner is decided by a fair and open process of an election where the one citizen/one vote principle is applied. The preamble also lists six (6) principles that guide us. Consider the fact that the political left (liberals and Democratic Socialists) have strategically invested in the last sixty years by manipulating its most vulnerable citizens to preserve a controlled voting bloc for power retention (rigging power by ignoring the overall benefit to the nation and pandering to the needs of a few in exchange for votes). To create a power base, the systematic control of African Americans was the main show. Now, seventy-plus years later, as the African American culture starts to realize the misgivings of their political alignment, the Democrats turn to the Illegal Hispanic immigrants and the alternative lifestyle communities to create a power base. These two new groups are on the Democratic Party's radar and, in turn, the focus of the liberal media and socialist activist movements[xviii].

Social Experimentation/Indoctrination: If you read history and understand the roadmap of the Black enslavement and assimilation processes in America, you would look at this modern social experiment with disgust and anger[xix]. These social experiments encompass various actions, from the early days of forced rather than natural integration, eradicating the belief in meritocracy in our educational institutions through quotas, fostering a reliance on social entitlements that give rise to generational dependency on welfare, undermining black linguistic ability with Ebonics, minimizing family values and the male's role in fatherhood, advocating abortion as a control measure for population growth, advocating for segregation, evading accountability for one's actions and personal responsibility to advance by fabricating scapegoats, and attributing social conditions solely to "racism." By fostering a defeatist ideology within the African American segment of our society, their productivity is diminished and subjected to a state of dependency and victimhood, thereby facilitating their easy manipulation and control[16] by the government. This ideology, which has targeted the African-American culture since the early days of the democratic party, is ruthless and destructive[17]. The deliberate dismantling and sabotage of a culturally significant heritage to exert control and garner political support is a regrettable and deplorable act. African Americans should be very angry at the party and the wasted years of mental slavery endured under a

---

[16] Dickens, Billy R. "Book Review: Losing the Race: Self-Sabotage in Black America." (2001): 79-83.

[17] Forman Jr, James. *Locking up our own: Crime and punishment in Black America*. Farrar, Straus and Giroux, 2017.

mentally and socially engineered experiment in maintaining a "political power base." I wish more would study the writings of Thomas Sowell, Robert Woodson Sr. (1776 project), Jason L. Riley, Jason D. Hill, and many more African American authors. There is an abundance of literature that exposes the mental slavery that the Democrat Party and Liberal Elitists inflicted on African Americans and how they shaped a culture of victimhood and self-defeating ideology over several decades with the help of the complicit media in crafting narratives evoking racism, and stoking anger.

It is disheartening that most African-American leaders have not vociferously denounced this injustice, and the culture is screaming for positive leadership. Unfortunately, the prominent figures with the bully pulpit are opportunists and leach on their own communities. They possess the ability to provoke Black society emotionally and divert their attention away from critical inquiries regarding their subjugation. In order to infuriate and divert the attention of Black youth and the voter base from the truth, the media complex, social activists, and Democrats persistently promote key phrases such as "racism," "institutional racism," "John Crow," "Uncle Tom," "back in chains," "slavery," "voter suppression," "White privilege," "discrimination," and "police killing blacks" to achieve their desired objective (BLM riots). As one navigates history, recognizes the deception, and hears the perspectives of numerous African Americans, the indoctrination of African American society becomes glaringly evident and saddening. The poison of indoctrination transcends all levels of the African American community and functions against the best interests of Black America. An additional concern that troubles and angers me is the Democrats and their agents' conceitful belief that Black Americans are not the smartest and are incapable of making independent political decisions; therefore, they will forever be obligated to support the Democrat Party. Furthermore, this attitude implies that the party elitists know best and must speak for the Black American culture. What puzzles me is why has the African American community tolerated this heinous act against their culture, dignity, and intellect for so long. Why?

I propose an argument that there is a genuine rationale for "racism" and "disenfranchisement" against Black Americans in our nation. However, not in the way we are led to perceive it. It is actually perpetrated by the Democrat Party, Democrat Elitists, and their propaganda arm, the Legacy Media outlets, to mislead, mentally enslave, and create a victimhood societal norm among Black Americans. As a result of these indoctrinations, the arguments, beliefs, and traits floated repeatedly in the African American community reflect (a) low self-esteem and a feeling of being a second-class citizen, (b) lack of opportunities because of color, (c) needing affirmative action programs to get ahead or get an education, (d) existing in a sphere of victimhood, (e) dubiety for other races, (f) deep resentment and distrust for all whites,(g) tolerance of whites but underlying distrust (h) a belief in welfare dependency[xx], (i) a failure to see the merits of a meritocratic society as it would exclude blacks, (j) a profound sense of "not belonging," and a dire need to "belong," (k) a notable disconnect with their African heritage, religious practices, cultural practices, social practices, and traditions, (l) a congenital distrust of institutions, authority, and enforcement organizations, and (m) capitalizing on a highly volatile sensitivity reinforced by over a century of subjugation to slavery, colonialism, racism, cultural inequality in economic advancement, inadequate societal advancement, and standing, and the subversion of their culture. Yes, it is a mouthful. Unfortunately, as previously discussed, this last attribute (m) is often exploited by the Democratic Complex to distract and enrage the culture into aggression and prevent the focus on relevant issues[18]. This is very clear when examining causation, agitators, activists, democratic party condonation, and media involvement during the unrest between 2020-2023.

In summary, it is a culture that was ripped from its motherland, irrelevant to the politics of the time, and stripped of everything that culturally identifies them as a people except for memories and phenotype. Then, they are assimilated into a culture at a level of servitude and reinforced with subservient indoctrination. As history progressed relating to the forced integration of blacks into society, political or societal support for advancing the culture was subdued[19]. They were subjected to incomprehensible exposure to racism, inequality, indignity, cruelty, ignorance, and the overall premise espousing the superiority of Whites. Regardless of the adversity faced,

---

[18] Hinton, Elizabeth, and DeAnza Cook. "The mass criminalization of Black Americans: A historical overview." *Annual Review of Criminology* 4 (2021): 261-286.

[19] Best, Wallace. ""The Right Achieved and the Wrong Way Conquered": JH Jackson, Martin Luther King, Jr., and the Conflict over Civil Rights." *Religion and American Culture* 16, no. 2 (2006): 195-226.

many African Americans have prevailed and taken their rightful place professionally, economically, and socially in American society. It is time to continue that trend en masse and erase any disparity in success and opportunity between cultures. A cultural change and awakening needs to occur in the Black mindset. Educational opportunity and education must be pushed at all levels, as it is the great equalizer in society.

The Democratic party's segregation of African Americans from mainstream American society was also apparent in the 1970s when the NAACP criticized Biden's proposition of *"an anti-black amendment."* At that time, the sole African-American member of the Senate, Ed Brooke, referred to it as *"the greatest symbolic defeat for civil rights since 1964"* (https://nymag.com/intelligencer/2019/03/joe-biden-record-on-busing-incarceration-racial-justice).
Irrespective of the long-term harm to African Americans, Biden assisted his fellow liberals in accepting the fact that they were supporting the incorrect side of history by portraying integrationists as actual racists. *"The new integration plans being offered are really just quota systems to assure a certain number of blacks, Chicanos, or whatever in each school. That, to me, is the most racist concept you can come up with,"* Biden said in a 1975 interview regarding the issue, *"What it says is, 'In order for your child with curly black hair, brown eyes, and dark skin to be able to learn anything, he needs to sit next to my blond-haired, blue-eyed son.' That's racist."*(https://realnews45.com/abrams-adviser-rips-exploitative-bidens-entitlement-he-wants-her-to-save-his-ass/) It is crucial to acknowledge the historical context that

predominantly black schools lacked resources, funding, and opportunities for students to compete equally with their white counterparts. (nymag.com/intelligencer, Biden 1975).

Integration provided black students with access to opportunities and resources that were previously unavailable to them. This action would ultimately achieve educational equality for Black students, but liberal democrats opposed racial integration. In the same year, Biden reiterated this sentiment during his remarks to the NPR news outlet, saying, *"I think the concept of busing that we are going to integrate people so that they all have the same access and they learn to grow up with one another and all the rest is a rejection of the whole movement of black pride ... a rejection of the entire black awareness concept, where black is beautiful, black culture should be studied; and the cultural awareness of the importance of their own identity, their own individuality[20]."* The tactics employed by the Democratic Party elitists, who exploited social identity and pitted it against African Americans in order to hinder their long-term progress, are truly astonishing[21]. It is utterly disgraceful. Do African American leaders lack awareness of the actions carried out by the Liberal Democratic machine, or are they simply exhausted by the long-standing oppression they have endured? How many negative experiences must your culture endure

---

[20]Joe Biden's Problematic Record On Racial Justice Explained.
https://nymag.com/intelligencer/2019/03/joe-biden-record-on-busing-incarceration-racial-justice-democratic-primary-2020-explained.html

[21] Masket, Seth. *Learning from loss: The democrats, 2016–2020.* Cambridge University Press, 2020.

before recognizing the political party that is more likely to promote your collective prosperity as Americans?

The liberal democratic socialist complex consistently diverts the attention of African Americans by presenting them with unfounded allegations and speculations about injustices and racism perpetrated against them by Caucasians, republicans, and individuals from other ethnicities. This serves as the catalyst to enrage the racial group and foster division and hatred in society while diverting their attention from the real issues in question. The media complex also derives its messaging from the democratic party machine and, in so, instructs the demonizing and suppressing of dissenting voices that reveal the genuine goals of the Liberal Democratic Socialist Machine. I am going to be very blunt here and strongly suggest that the "African American culture wakes up, gets informed with truth, and takes stock."[22] You are a vital part of our collective American culture, and no one can ever change that, so take your place by uplifting each other, denouncing destructive ideologies forced upon you, and being a part of the most significant social experiment ever undertaken: true democracy and the freedom to be great.

Finally, Realization: I fervently desire that African American communities in America become aware of the harsh truths of their betrayal[23], as seen by the recent expression of discontent by vocal residents and community

---

[22] Sowell, Thomas. "Three black histories." *Wilson Quarterly* (1979): 6-106.

[23] Sterba, James P. "Completing Thomas Sowell's Study of Affirmative Action and Then Drawing Different Conclusions." (2004): 657-693.

leaders in numerous town hall meetings. African American grassroots spokespersons are actually calling for the republican party and Trump to step in and help them on public platforms. Of course, these public outcries are censored from CNN, MSNBC, CBS, ABC, and other liberal democratic outlets, so if one doesn't watch other outlets, they would never be aware of these turn of events. African Americans in Chicago, New York, California, and other states designated as "sanctuary states" are now recognizing that they have been used as mere instruments to achieve specific party goals. The policies that were supposed to assist Black Americans have merely deprived them of their rights and privileges, and this knowledge is gradually being internalized. As residents in these communities witness the deterioration of infrastructure, lack of social, educational, and healthcare programs, inadequate facilities, limited crime prevention efforts, and limited opportunities, they are now publicly observing the actions taken by the governing political party to secure power by pandering to another group. These actions include opening the borders and appealing to the Hispanic voting bloc by providing more community opportunities, free resources, healthcare, access to social programs, housing, food, education programs, and significant other funding. This starkly contrasts the African American communities, who have been requesting similar support for years without success. How is that for a slap in the face of hard-working, tax-paying African Americans?

Take a moment to contemplate this evaluation: If the millions of dollars used to manipulate the immigration system and pander to the illegal immigrant population for political gain had been initially invested in improving the African American communities, enhancing their opportunities, developing their community infrastructures, and promoting their socio-economic progress in America, their culture would not be in its current state of distress[24]. Instead, it would have achieved levels of cultural advancement similar to those of other ethnic groups in America. This assessment is regrettable and concerning, particularly for the African American community, which has consistently shown loyalty to the political party that has consistently let them down over many years. Another concerning situation created by the open borders is the increase in criminality. This has created a trickle-down effect, causing increased crime within the cities, as criminals and gang operatives come across undetected in the open system and vie for power within these already crime-infested cities, thereby causing mayhem and social instability.

The rise in black-on-black crime and gang violence is reprehensible in these and other cities. It is inconceivable that in a developed nation like America, African American and socially depressed residents of all nationalities have to live in macabre fear as their kids and loved ones are slaughtered senselessly in the streets, and human security is threatened on a mass scale. The American government, regardless of party, sends troops or funding overseas to stop atrocities similar to this from happening, so how is it even possible to overlook what is transpiring in our own

---

[24] Doleac, Jennifer L. "A Review of Thomas Sowell's Discrimination and Disparities." *Journal of Economic Literature* 59, no. 2 (2021): 574-589.

cities? This, to me, is absolutely unequivocally unacceptable governance by both parties, and the question has to be asked: what ideology is driving this train? Assuming for a moment, that the leaders of this society are unable to eliminate the long-standing deception, transcend political party divisions and indoctrination methods, and objectively perceive the truths of their American existence and the present policies that affect them, then under those circumstances, African Americans are destined to become a marginalized culture within American civilization[25].

Replacing Blacks, History Repeating: On a historical note, A federal court rendered a decision on June 30, 2020, in opposition to the third-country transit bar prohibition that had been enforced during the Trump administration. As per the initial bar, individuals who have entered the United States after passing through a non-origin country en route must lodge an asylum application in one of those non-origin countries. Failure to comply would result in ineligibility for asylum benefits within the United States. The bar issue affected every individual who entered the U.S. on or after 16 July 2019. This was done to prevent those individuals from using the asylum crutch to enter the U.S. versus actually seeking safety for themselves or their family at the first port of entry that verified their threat and vetted their application. This also took the pressure off the southern border, allowing for the more timely processing of legitimate applications. Conversely, recent occurrences and a liberal democrat party push have prompted a court to

---

[25] Horne, Gerald. "Race Backward, Race Forward: Thomas Sowell, William Julius Wilson & Derrick Bell Considered." *Black Renaissance* 1, no. 2 (1997): 76.

declare the third country transit bar null and void. This suggests that immigrants may seek asylum in the United States even if they entered the country subsequent to departing from their country of origin and passing through other nations en route. The sentiment was that preventing someone from seeking refuge in their country of choice was against the new world order and, of course, the underlying objective of changing the voting demographics of America to a democratic socialist monocracy. Imagine with over 10 million illegal migrants and counting; this group will be the largest sympathetic voting block for the party. It doesn't take a genius to figure out this strategy. This is also a countermeasure for the loss of African American support as they become aware of the true nature of the democratic party complex. The social experiment of keeping this growing segment of society dependent on big government and social programs to erode personal responsibility and work ethic and achieve excellence through meritocracy is being repeated. This was the same approach that was and is still being used to destroy and restrict economic growth, family expansion, and the social advancement of many in the African American culture. It would be a crying shame if history was ignored and the democratic elites were allowed to perpetrate this injustice on yet another unsuspecting culture for the sole purpose of maintaining "Party Power." Wake up, Black America. Wake up and educate yourselves about what is happening around you, and do not hop on the disinformation train.

Cultural Separation, Loss of Cultural Legacy, and Isolation of African Americans: Neglecting to highlight the primary obstacle impeding cultural pride that afflicts the

African American culture would be an oversight of immense proportions. The social, educational, and religious leaders of this proud old culture, as well as the well-endowed members of society and politics, are the ones I believe are responsible for this cultural failure[26]. The fact that opportunists like the Jessie Jacksons and Sharptons, who have the podium, are unwilling to acknowledge these misgivings or simply do not care because it is not a lucrative venture is contemptible. For any culture that has moved away from its original homeland and cultural heritage, it is crucial to maintain contact and connection with its heritage and/or religion to safeguard its cultural identity, pride, and sense of belonging. I have personally observed this occurrence of maintaining cultural ties among the Indian diaspora in the Caribbean, the US, the UK, and other regions beyond India; the African diaspora in Europe and the Caribbean; and the Chinese diaspora in the Caribbean and the United States also share this phenomenon. From language to food, customs, religion, family values, traditions, and beliefs are passed down and maintained while still assimilating to the host nation's core values. It is a fact that the two can coexist if the cultural or religious belief structures are somewhat aligned. As an example, Indians, other Asians, Africans, Latin Americans, and the Caribbean diaspora have no issues assimilating to the American culture at varying levels while maintaining their individual heritage. I can attest to this.

---

[26] Delgado, Richard. "Explaining the rise and fall of African American fortunes-interest convergence and civil rights gains." (2002): 369.

Note* It seems that only the individuals from these regions affiliated with a jihadist or Islamist doctrine will not assimilate because of the stark difference in ideology and unwillingness to coexist with other cultures.

Questions to ponder: Establishing Pride.

(a). What does the average African American know about their cultural heritage, Ideology, the tribal legacy of their originating region, ancestral religious practices, or basic African history dating back to biblical times or the pre-slavery era?

(b). What constitutes your heritage, how do you establish your identity within your culture, and what is the significance of your ancestral roots in relation to your heritage? Are African Americans capable of responding to this inquiry?

(c). In navigating cultural identity and belonging, young African American adolescents cannot reference ancestral and cultural pride. Are levels three, four, and five of Maslow's Hierarchy of psychological requirements met by these young adults?

(d). Are the African American culture and heritage, which are uniquely shaped by their ancestral regions and history in Africa, thoroughly examined in schools as part of a civics curriculum? Additionally, is it compared to other immigrant cultures in America, highlighting the struggles and contributions of each culture in shaping the new world of America?

Assessment: From my perspective, the forced cultural decapitation and purposeful denial of a socially identifiable heritage experienced by African Americans in the United States are elements that contributed to their cultural paucity, a tendency toward overexpression, identity crisis, diminished self-esteem, compliant progress, and undefinable customs and beliefs. This, unfortunately, results in the culture constantly existing in a state of flux, trying to define itself and establish a foundation for its family values, beliefs, and traditions. This state of fluidity also allows the culture to be easily manipulated by rancorous liberal socialist actors and identity politics indoctrination to reinforce that everyone is against them and that African Americans are inferior, which in turn encourages racial hatred and separation in society.

I echoed these sentiments in an interview with a colleague and educator last year, and it still holds true. - *"The African American culture is akin to a young child of about eight years old, not like in the Caribbean where you and I grew up and loved. This Black American child is imbued with a disdain for whites, a sense of mediocrity, a lack of self-worth, contempt for all Republicans, a segregated mentality masked as Black pride, and no structured social and cultural framework to guide them for, say, the next 20 years; so what end result do you expect to get. Well, you achieve the desired result that is prevalent in the culture today, a culture brought to the brink of hysteria and instability and sabotaged into a state of cultural regression, where the mere mention of race or discrimination can cause national disruptions of an unimaginable scale, and bloodshed and rioting in the cities against a manufactured injustice. All this to distract and anger the masses, and mask the true injustice that has been perpetrated against this culture for generations by their own democrat "masta's" and the liberal social activists and liberal media, the modern-day "house slaves" that do the "masta's" bidding – one of the most despicable social experiments of the last 30 years in my opinion. In America, these Blacks are not taught from early on anything about their proud cultural existence, no pride in belonging, no ties to their ancestral heritage pre-slavery, and nothing ingrained about striving for the mountain top, a cultural temperament drawn together from so many years of vicissitudes, a denouement of sorts..." (Transcript #4, SurajPersad, Jam.23).* African Americans, your own cultural leaders, have deceived you for generations, and those who spoke against this deception and advocated early on for integration and equitability were either assassinated or socially silenced (Medgar Evers, Harriette Moore, Harry Moore, Martin Luther King, and Malcolm X). Research President Biden's speeches and voting record, and you will find that then-Senator Biden and the party elitists did not advocate for many unification policies, and their words echo the sentiment of the party even from then.

Framework, No One Left Behind: For the overall benefit of the homeland and for the uplifting of this integral part of our American experience, the Republican party must, at all costs, take the reigns in redefining this prominent and stalwart culture by promoting programs to rebuild a cultural connection between African Americans and their proud heritage, educating all individuals through civic education in schools regarding the significant contributions African Americans have made to the American landscape, and elucidating the reasons why they must remain an integral part of our future-defined American culture. This would fulfill the requirement for cultural identity, a sense of belonging, knowledge, and mutual respect, and the foundation for further exploration of heritage and identity as individuals advance in society. It would also erase the notion of racial inequality in our society as we become more integrated at all levels of the socioeconomic spectrum in a meritocratic society. It is incumbent upon our nation as a whole to alter the course of this culture's marginalization. Irrelevant of your racial, economic, or political construct, it is an undeniable fact that this cultural segment of our society has been the subject of the most botched Democrat Party "social experiment" in American history, and it is incumbent upon those who govern the nation to correct the mistakes of the past governments.

Underlying Objective: Drawing inspiration from the severe economic challenges of the Great Depression, the Roosevelt administration recognized the imperative for more extensive reforms to avert a repetition of the situation in which the economy failed to furnish unemployed workers and their families with essential public assistance and employment opportunities. On June 8, 1934, in a message to Congress, President Roosevelt delineated his perception of the imperative measures that were in order during that period: "*of the men, women, and children of the Nation first. This security for the individual and for the family concerns itself particular period. Among our objectives I place the security primarily with three factors.*

People want decent homes to live in; they want to locate them where they can engage in productive work, and they want some safeguard against misfortunes which cannot be wholly eliminated in this man-made world of ours...[27]" This concept created the underlying motives of the Social Security Act of 1935, which comprised eleven distinct "titles" and established three different types of programs to provide economic protections to various populations in palpable ways, as is outlined herein. (1) A framework comprising state-administered Unemployment Insurance programs, which aim to furnish able-bodied workers who are unjustly laid off with temporary financial aid; (2) The Old Age and Survivors Insurance Program, which is a contributory and universal social insurance program for eligible wage-earners who have deceased or retired, leaving behind a spouse or family; and (3) A network of public assistance programs operated by the states and federal government, catering to the needs of elderly, blind, and dependent children[28].

Weaponization: These programs seemed to operate efficiently as a "means-tested" initiative until they were repurposed in 1973. The program comprised several noteworthy components, and the original intentions were justified. Nonetheless, these programs were weaponized

---

[27] Social Welfare History Project Origins of the State and Federal Public Welfare Programs (1932 – 1935).
https://socialwelfare.library.vcu.edu/public-welfare/origins-of-the-state-federal-public-welfare-programs/

[28] Davies, Gareth, and Martha Derthick. "Race and social welfare policy: The Social Security Act of 1935." *political science Quarterly* 112, no. 2 (1997): 217-235.

for political gain at some point in history by Democratic Party elitists intent on establishing a monocratic government with a minimal opposition party to still create the facade of a Democratic two-party nation. The achievements of a disproportionate number of individuals in the African American culture—or perhaps it is time to say "American African" culture—provide irrefutable evidence that a national reeducation initiative would yield widespread extraordinary results for the American African nation and the homeland. American leaders need to step away from the shackling liberal democratic-socialist framework of developing a dependency on government and social welfare programs, handouts, and social pacifiers within society by building a power base of loyal recipients[29]. Establishing a dynamic society that values individual accomplishments is hindered by this illogical experiment, which originated in the Democratic Party. Rather than coddling our populace, we should encourage them to strive for greatness and assume their rightful position in a meritocratic society. Individual or collective empowerment promotes advancement and personal development, a positive outlook on society, participation, and a feeling of belonging. We are most formidable when united under the Red-White and Blue but weakest when we are divided as a nation. To the best of my knowledge, this is the only country in which social activists advocate for two distinct "National Anthems": one for "Whites and others" and one for "Blacks." To the displeasure of most, it has been allowed to be sung at ball games and other national

---

[29] Hansan, J.E. (2011). Origins of the state and federal public welfare programs (1932-1935).

sporting events. Should this not incite alarm or ignite the hair of Americans, then the public either does not comprehend or is indifferent to the explicit goals of our adversary; at worst, a civil war in its infancy and the division of our nation along the lines of North and South, Conservative and Liberal, or Black and White plus Others may ensue. A recurring question in my mind is, who would this weakening of America benefit, perhaps China, Russia, Iran, and others that share the Islamist ideology?

Equality or Hinderance for Minorities: Another investment in destroying the competitive nature and subduing the pride of achievement was the institution of affirmative action (A.A.) quotas in the workforce, primarily targeting the African-American culture, where advancement and opportunity were afforded based on ethnicity. This program nonetheless had a hook and was framed as "democrats advocating for African Americans." It actually has fostered enormous prejudice and bias in society, and If the objective was to eradicate discrimination from society, then implementing a program that fosters discrimination was not a viable approach to achieving this goal. Advancement should not occur to the detriment of others, and with affirmative action, that is almost always the case. Granting preferential treatment to an individual based on their minority status rather than their qualifications is an erroneous viewpoint, particularly in systems that rely on quotas. It perpetuates cultural stereotypes, which are very pronounced in our current society.

Whenever a program is available that enables individuals to secure a position in an educational institution, a professional setting, or the military, it has the potential to establish a basis for stereotypes based on minority groups or, in some cases, genders. Despite the qualifications of all individuals, Affirmative Action (AA) creates the premise that African Americans, women, or other minorities are somehow "inferior" to white men, thereby fostering a sense of superiority among the majority group and placing minorities and women in a diminished capacity. This belief has permeated society, and one catalyst is AA. When a program such as Affirmative Action is in place, its focus often shifts toward fulfilling requirements or regulations rather than actively seeking out individuals with exceptional qualifications. An indisputable fact is that universities have been using AA as a means to discriminate against Asian and White students in admissions rather than a system of meritocracy until the Supreme Court ruled against the practice in 2023.

Equality entails providing each individual with an equitable opportunity at the commencement of a venture, and it diminishes the accomplishments that minority groups or individuals achieve. If an individual obtains a position through a program such as affirmative action, their accomplishments are perceived as being attributed to the policy itself rather than their own individual abilities and professional aptitude. This societal perception hurts the merits of cultural achievement and acceptance of the beneficiaries of AA within the workforce. Consequently, individuals belonging to minority groups often face the challenge of exerting more effort to attain an equal degree of esteem compared to individuals in majority groups, as they must counteract the prevailing policy perceptions. This is a stigma that women in the military face, especially female officers. They inevitably work three times harder than their male counterparts to ward off the veil of accomplishment through "entitlement" versus "exceptionalism." When affirmative action programs are in place, it is routine that the news cycles will always be filled with stories that revolve around racism, classism, cultural divide, and political polarization. African Americans and other minorities are smart enough to hold their own. Given the laws in place, discrimination would mean career and institutional suicide to any offender and possibly early retirement for the discriminated.

Education for all: Leveling the playing field, no preferential treatment based on race, finances, or gender. Fixing the system is not complicated by any means if the desire is there. For starters, the educational playing field must be level, elementary through high school. This can be achieved by a national standard curriculum, comprehensive testing to advance by grade, equal access to remedial training regardless of location, mandatory technology requirements, funding and access by every school, standardized compulsory training for teachers by subject matter, final prep classes for all students and acceptance to college where cumulative and final grades are weighted heavily for admission. Teachers are also graded for pay increases based on students' success/passing rate. This will develop a climate of meritocracy in our educational system. Additional funding must also be available by need to support financially disadvantaged students requiring food, transport, or after-school monitoring. Consequences must also be in place for absences and belligerence. Many more checks and balances can be worked into the system, such as funding incentives and protections against dropouts. We have intelligent individuals who can improve the system if it is prioritized. As I alluded to, education is the great equalizer; our youth and our nation's health depend on it, so it is a worthwhile investment. Fix this, and we will change the race, income, and equality disparity in America. An area of particular concern that has the propensity to alter America's trajectory is our institutions of higher learning. A refocusing on America's tertiary institutions must also be undertaken to emphasize the purpose of these institutions. These institutions are supposed to foster learning, debate, and dialogue, encourage appreciation of diverse approaches, and develop critical thinking, ethics, the emancipation of ideas, leadership, and the accumulation of knowledge. On the contrary, students are not there to practice Marxist ideology and be involved in social activism, rioting, and public displays of aggression endorsing Anti-Semitism, Islamism, and anti-Americanism. That is not the role of educational institutions of higher learning in America. These institutions that are infiltrated and economically supported by social activist groups, Islamists, democrat left-wing donors, and other disruptive forces must not be allowed to indoctrinate our youth and alter the social construct of American society and the future generations of Americans.

CHAPTER 7

DEMOCRATS ARE AT IT AGAIN

IRREGULAR MIGRATION – ILLEGAL IMMIGRATION

Targeting Hispanics, Using Irregular Migration for Benefit: Let me preface this section by saying, in my opinion, this liberal no-border ideology is a treasonous action by the fringe elements of the democratic party machine, and the orchestrated compromise of our borders amounts to nothing less than "Sabotage of American National Security and Citizen Welfare." For fear of sounding like a conspiracy theorist, I have to wonder how much of these destructive anti-American policies are driven by foreign actors or states. The facts are there for your scrutiny; use your own intelligence and research to fully understand the situation and repercussions on our society.

Irregular Migration: Millions of individuals across the globe reside in and traverse perilous and unconventional routes in an effort to escape violence, corrupt governments, and weak and failed states; they are compelled to migrate irregularly and without proper documentation in pursuit of employment, education, healthcare, food, safety, and other essential services. The presence of irregular migration can be attributed to the insufficiency of domestic opportunities for security and prosperity, coupled with the scarcity of conventional methods to address this dearth of prospects. In light of the critical, understudied, and frequently misunderstood characteristics of this worldwide phenomenon, it is indisputable that large numbers of individuals will strive for security and improved economic conditions.

Illegal immigrant: Refers to an individual who enters or attempts to enter a country unlawfully in violation of a deportation order or immigration laws. This term also encompasses individuals who have already entered the country in such a manner. (The Immigration Act of 1971). Aliens can be classified as unlawfully present for three distinct reasons: unauthorized entry or inspection, surpassing the permitted duration after lawful entry, or violating the terms of legal entry. Section 1325 in Title 8 of the United States Code, referred to as "Improper entry of alien," states that any individual who is not a citizen and enters the United States without proper documentation and authorization may face a fine, imprisonment, or both penalty. Section 1325 delineates three illegal activities related to (1) the unpermitted entry of a non-citizen into the United States, (2) entering into a marriage to bypass immigration regulations, and (3) establishing a business to avoid immigration laws. The legislation made it a crime for specific individuals to cross the border. Section 1325 stipulates that entering a country without authorization is classified as a federal misdemeanor for the initial offense and as a felony for subsequent offenses. Both charges have the possibility of resulting in financial penalties or imprisonment. The Illegal Immigration Reform and Immigrant Responsibility Act (IIRIRA) amended 8 U.S.C. § 1325 to incorporate a provision stipulating that if an individual of foreign nationality is apprehended while attempting to enter or actually entering the United States at a location or time that immigration officers do not sanction, they will be subject to a civil penalty.

As eluded to before, one of the demographics focused on in this governing party cycle is the Hispanic voting bloc, whereby democrats strategically disregard any actions or policies to secure the southern border so as to increase that demographic's numbers and then pander to their needs by providing free education, healthcare, housing assistance, and sustenance policies to ensure the votes for the party that provides for them. By catering to this demographic, the extreme left of the democratic party aims to secure the exploding Hispanic vote in elections. The democratic party machine also creates a disconnect between the enforcement of immigration policy and local law enforcement, especially in the creation of "Sanctuary Cities." According to the U.S. Bureau of Labor Statistics report, October 6, 2023, "in the third quarter of 2023, the nation's 47.7 million Hispanics accounted for 17.8 percent of the U.S. civilian noninstitutional population ages 16 and older. Mexicans accounted for 10.7 percent of the U.S. population and nearly 60 percent of the Hispanic population." The open border and acceptance of everyone without proper intake, vetting, and tracking sends the wrong message to the millions waiting in the wings. These actions are overtly practiced by the liberal democratic socialist complex and are highly destructive to our nation's security. More than 1.7 million known elopements at the Southwest frontier have been confirmed by U.S. Customs and Frontier Protection (CBP) sources during the administrations of President Biden and Department of

Homeland Security (DHS) Secretary Alejandro Mayorkas. An even more alarming development occurred during a field hearing in March 2023, where then-U.S. Border Patrol Chief Raul Ortiz stated that the actual number of escaped individuals may have exceeded the publicly disclosed figures by as much as 20 percent.

Statistics from the Border Security Subcommittee: Here are some current statistics extracted from the subcommittee's Border Security and Enforcement report, October 26, 2023, Washington DC, published for Congress and public consumption.[xxi] The House Committee on Homeland Security released its latest "Startling Stats" factsheet outlining U.S. Customs and Border Protection's (CBP) September and Fiscal Year (F.Y.) 2023 border encounter data. The quotes from this document are in the section below. *(Homeland Security Committee, 10/26/2023.)*

• *Encounters at the Southwest border (SWB) in FY2023 increased over 40% since FY2021, 4% compared to FY2022, and more than 100% compared to FY2019, making last fiscal year the worst on record under the Biden administration.*

• *Last month, U.S. Customs and Border Protection (CBP) reported a 40% increase compared to September 2021 and 18% compared to September 2022. This monthly number also represents an 86% increase from June 2023, when the Biden administration celebrated a short-lived drop in illegal crossings following the end of Title 42.*

‧ In FY2023, 169 individuals whose names appear on the terrorist watchlist were stopped trying to cross the U.S.-Mexico border between ports of entry. Eighteen were apprehended in September alone.

• FY2023 represents a 72% increase from FY2022 for apprehensions of individuals on the terrorist watchlist and is the most on record. Of these encounters, 218,763 individuals were apprehended attempting to cross illegally between ports of entry. This is a 20% increase since the previous month.

• Encounters by the Office of Field Operations (OFO) in September increased by 155% compared to September 2022.

• Around 43,000 inadmissible aliens were processed by OFO with CBP One app appointments in September. Almost all of these inadmissible aliens will ultimately be released into the interior, regardless of whether they are granted parole or claim asylum.

• In response to a subpoena threat, the Committee on Homeland Security has received startling information and documents regarding the expanded use of the CBP One app by DHS Secretary Alejandro Mayorkas.

• In FY2023, 240,000 Cubans, Haitians, Nicaraguans, and Venezuelans have been granted parole under the administration's CHNV parole process at ports of entry nationwide.

• Since President Biden took office, there have been 7.5 million encounters nationwide and 6.2 million

encounters at the Southwest border, in addition to 1.7 million known gotaways who evaded U.S. Border Patrol.

• At the S.W. border in September 2023, CBP encountered 132,017 single adults, 123,815 family unit individuals, and 13,771 unaccompanied children along the Southwest border.

• Encounters at the Northern border in September 2023 increased by 409% compared to September 2021 and 41% compared to September 2022.

• In FY2023, encounters along the busiest sector of the Northern border, the Swanton Sector, increased by 1,797% compared to FY2021 and 550% in FY2022.

• So far in FY2023, CBP has arrested 35,433 aliens with criminal convictions or outstanding warrants nationwide, including 598 known gang members, 178 of those being MS-13 members.

• In FY2023, CBP, including Air and Marine Operations, has seized 27,293 pounds of fentanyl, coming across the Southwest border—enough to kill around 6 billion people.

• Total CBP fentanyl seizures in FY2023 increased 88% compared to FY2022. Notably, Federal officials estimate they are only able to seize 5-10% of all illegal drugs smuggled across the Southwest border.

•Reported by the New York Post on September 2, Venezuelan immigrant Daniel Hernandez Martinez, who crossed the Southwest border illegally in July, has been

arrested six times on 14 different charges since arriving in New York.

• An illegal immigrant from Peru was charged with murder in Eagle Pass, Texas, on September 19. He had initially crossed illegally into Eagle Pass in May and was released into the U.S. with a 2025 court date.

•On September 6, Border Patrol agents patrolling near Fronton, Texas, discovered backpacks with ammo and a homemade explosive in the same area where cartel gunmen have been repeatedly seen on cameras crossing illegally into the U.S.

•On September 13 and September 15, mass street releases of aliens were conducted due to CBP facilities being overcapacity. CBP released 13,000 aliens in San Diego over the last month alone. On September 14, CBP in Cochise County, Arizona, announced their facilities were overcapacity, and they were forced to begin releasing aliens into the community.

•On September 19, the city of Eagle Pass issued an Emergency Declaration after around 4,000 aliens crossed into the city in the span of just four days.

•On September 27, Eagle Pass Border Patrol released an <u>internal memo stating no</u> agents were in the field

---

[30] **FACTSHEET:https://homeland.house.gov/2023/08/23/factsheet-illegal-encounters-at-southwest-border-jump-from-june-as-border-crisis-continues/ End of Document: (Homeland Security Committee, 10/26/2023.) *News Update: In December 2023, over 302,000 people have crossed the border for the month, according to border control officials. (Fox Breaking News, MSNBC Nightly News).*

between ports of entry because many had been diverted to help process aliens into the interior.

To put this report[30] in perspective, these numbers are still staggering if the supporting documentation and even half of everything reported is accurate. They also represent severe National Security implications, which will be realized down the pike. America cannot under any circumstance sustain this irregular migration crisis, and it will need to enact harsh measures to reverse the damage to our society and economy. Nefarious foreign agents and proxy actors are coming across our border undetected. It only takes one group and the correct explosive components to strike a blow to our infrastructure and or soft population targets like a school with hundreds of children to strike a crippling emotional (hearts and minds) blow to our society. What happened in Israel shows the barbarism and an insight into the enemy's psyche. Don't be fooled and fall into a state of complacency; these ideologies and policies harm our national security. The blood will be on your hands.

Voting Security and Voter Identification: Voting is an honored privilege and the right of a legally naturalized or American-born citizen(person). This responsibility must never be taken lightly. Another ploy to secure votes through illegitimate processes is the ongoing fight to eliminate accountability by advocating for no identification requirements to vote. This would mean a totally insecure "banana republic" voting system in the United States, coupled with a porous border and an unstemmed flow of illegal immigrants. This would increase the already present "deceased voting bloc" and the "illegal undocumented bloc numbers" to overwhelmingly win the elections. According to federal law, voting as an illegal alien in federal elections is considered a criminal offense that can result in a substantial fine, imprisonment, deportation, or inadmissibility (depending on the circumstances). Nevertheless, not all individuals who contravene these statutes are apprehended or prosecuted; many loopholes and acceptance of inadequate or fraudulent identification contribute to this dilemma. Proponents of undocumented and noncitizen groups under the liberal democratic banner of social justice argue that the number is undeterminable as to the precise incidences of unlawful aliens who have cast ballots in the United States; however, many academic estimates, along with Hispanic investigative news place that number at a level sufficient to "alter meaningful election outcomes" in a Democratic-leaning direction.

Many democratic governed states have passed legislation to allow non-citizen immigrants to vote in city and state elections and even a push to allow illegal residents to secure sensitive city jobs such as upholding the law in the capacity of a police officer. I couldn't make this up even if I tried. It has been eluded to and demonstrated through politicking by several key members of the Biden administration that the ultimate goal is to have illegals vote in the very near future, which would guarantee singular political power and a majority sway in their liberal-socialist anti-American ideology. If this is allowed to occur, I am fearful that the only way to secure our American way of life and the integrity of our constitutional freedoms is an actual American civil war and republican state separation from the federal government. With another four possibilities, at least twenty-five of these powerhouse states could seek separation from the Democratic-Socialist-Liberal Government. These manufacturing, agricultural, dairy, and oil-rich states will be financially viable and self-supporting. Many of these states also share international borders and access to shipping ports to facilitate imports and exports.

Currently, the District of Columbia and twelve states permit noncitizens to obtain driver's licenses. On numerous occasions, when these unauthorized individuals renew their driver's licenses, their voter records are supplemented without any endeavor on the part of the government to authenticate their citizenship in the United States. Therefore, this systemic vulnerability constitutes a component of the issue. The issuing of state identification and the push for no identification requirement to vote also exasperates the situation. I would think that reasonable, prudent individuals, regardless of political affiliation, would agree to secure the one vote, one citizen concept to prevent foreign actors and non-citizens with allegiance to another country from influencing domestic policies and elections. The argument the democratic machine frequently espouses is these immigrants pay taxes and work in America, so they should have a say. Many legal immigrants do not want American citizenship; they still have a vested stake in their own countries, and many send their excess funds to a bank at home for retirement. Others who are illegal do not pay taxes, send most of their money home to family ($millions in remittance), and really don't care two hoots about American policy except what they can obtain for free. Those who care about America's policies and welfare gain citizenship when they are eligible, and those individuals have the right to vote and are sometimes more engaged than the average citizen.

Multiculturalism is a Failed Social Experiment in Europe: Europe is now faced with hard decisions. The welfare, security, and integrity of their nation's culture and values are threatened by extinction. Several world leaders and prominent left-leaning scholars such as Nicolas Sarkozy of France, Angela Merkel of Germany, David Cameron of the UK, Gaad Saad Ph.D., and Paul Cliteur, to name a few, have declared that Europe's experiment with multiculturalism has shown to be a complete failure, damaging the social construct of their collective societies. The confusion arises when individuals mistakenly equate multiculturalism as a political normative theory with its colloquial usage, representing cultural, religious, and ethnic diversity (pluralism). The latter interpretation is a highly commendable goal to strive for; as such, diversity contributes to a more intricate and vibrant social fabric.

Conversely, Multiculturalism's primary definition extends beyond being a mere unsuccessful political ideology. It is a primary factor contributing to the gradual decline of Western civilization. This also brings to the table the acceptance and practice of Sharia law in the U.S. as the governing law for Islamic followers and disregarding stated country laws. In Western Europe, particularly in the Netherlands, Denmark, the United Kingdom, Norway, Sweden, Poland, Austria, and Germany, hatred is growing for the concept and implementation of multiculturalism. The rationale underlying this opposition to diversity is that it generates social discord and disrupts the social construct of the nation[xxii].

The liberal international order, or new world order, and the democratic machine push a fundamentally flawed ideology distinguishing multiculturalism as its core: the conviction that every culture possesses equal worth merits admiration, and deserves celebration rather than assimilation. This stems from a combination of liberal postmodernism *("There are no objective truths")* and the rejection of moral/cultural relativism *("Who are we to judge the moral and/or cultural precepts of another people?"),* which are mainly to blame for this mixture. This multiculturalist perspective proposes that host nations and cultures should not expect newly arrived immigrants to assimilate the defining ethos of the host nation. Instead, it is presumed that every cultural group would retain its unique identity, regardless of whether its fundamental cultural values oppose those of the host nation.

Multiculturalism posits that failure to integrate and assimilate does not inherently equate to negative consequences; instead, it perceives isolationism as a material manifestation of cultural pride. Disregarding the ideas and beliefs of the host nation is unimportant, and it is advisable to maintain a distinct cultural group identity separate from the larger society. This social experimentation with multiculturalism in our society, which prioritizes the interests of specific groups over the collective national interests, will lead to the erosion of the collective interests in favor of minority interests and create racial hatred and divisions in our society, as is experienced in mass today. Time proves all theories, and the adverse effects in Europe are staggering.

The attainment of national unity may be rendered unattainable if individuals perceive themselves primarily as constituents of ethnic or racial factions rather than citizens of a shared nation. This phenomenon leads to societal divisions, as it is advocated by the left in the context of American identity politics. The second point is that multiculturalism erodes the concept of equal individual rights, thereby diminishing the political significance of equal treatment, which can potentially lead to racism. This concept has failed in Europe, but when will the liberal democratic socialist machine learn, or is that their intention for America all along? This concept of multiculturalism is flawed on so many levels; it amazes me that sane-minded people would even consider giving this theory serious consideration, to the detriment of their own national heritage. Why would a nation even allow immigration under that premise?

I would ask the reader to entertain this question: Who benefits from this ideology? The immigrant, obviously, if the nation they are attaching themselves to is not worthy enough for them to adopt its core values, then their loyalty lies not with that adopted nation, so they cannot have the nation's well-being or its citizens at heart. Now, I can see this as a great way to create an immigrant base within a nation for the purpose of causing division, upsetting societal norms, and trying to introduce an alien set of norms into an established system to create havoc.

Destabilization tactics at its best. Now ask, what can the motivations of the sponsoring group advocating multiculturalism really be, and who is the guiding force behind the push?

Multiculturalism Weaponized against the West: Multiculturalism is increasingly being utilized as a significant means to erode national identities. At the same time, the term "populism" is employed to suppress a reasoned response to the profound anxieties that have plagued Western societies for many years. These anxieties include the "right of center" apprehension of dealing with large-scale, uncontrolled Immigration, the concern that Western culture will disintegrate into a state of relativism and fragmented communities, and the fear of nations lacking both external borders and internal moral authority. This apprehension regarding cultural disintegration has been subtly reinforced by the likelihood of the gradual disappearance of the sociological majority and, ultimately, the Judeo-Christian fabric of society. Indeed, the events are unfolding precisely as anticipated, to the benefit of the Islamists who have a holy mission to spread their warped version of Islam in the West.

This liberal-inspired social experiment has failed, and it has left nations and their citizens bearing the effects of this failure. For Europeans, the stakes are high. Over centuries, national identities have been formed with commonality in heritage, language, religion, customs, moral values, and history. Illegal Immigration and irregular migration together threaten to destabilize or destroy those commonalities, as immigrants from many of these Islamic nations will not acculturate or assimilate to a level of successful integration. With one coalition already toppled in the Netherlands, experts say leaders in Germany, Italy, and perhaps France and Spain face similar issues. A Pew Research report found that majorities or pluralities in most E.U. nations want less Immigration into their countries. Many that Pew polled believe that immigrants remain distinct from the broader culture, and they further worry that Immigration increases terrorism risks because of their hatred of Western or Christian philosophy[xxiii].

Recent official statistics from Britain indicate that the number of foreign-born individuals in England and Wales has reached 10 million, which accounts for one-sixth of the population. This represents a significant increase of 2.5 million since 2011, despite the government's stated efforts to restrict Immigration. However, England's prime Minister has recently approved the mass removal of illegal immigrants after pressures from the constituents and the deplorable conditions present. Currently, Immigration accounts for 90% of the population growth in Britain. Regrettably, Europe is running out of time to stop and make a definitive choice regarding its commitment to the liberal principles of open borders, multiculturalism, and globalism. If Europe remains passive, it risks the rapid extinction of its hard-earned Judeo-Christian values, freedoms, and identity. Europe is experiencing a rapid erosion of its cultural identity, and a similar phenomenon is occurring in America[xxiv]. Europe, from late 2021 through 2024, has been feeling the disastrous effects of its liberal policies and a dramatic increase in the crime-terror nexus.

Within this framework of renewed nationalism and preserving their national heritage, the five Nordic nations (Finland, Denmark, Norway, Iceland, and Sweden) have agreed to enhance cooperation in expulsing undocumented migrants and curbing the influx of migrants into their territories. As of January 2024, more European countries are coming on board, driven by the realization of the spread of Islamism in their nations. Poland is one of the latest to say, "Enough is enough; we need to preserve the integrity of our nation and traditions." Behind the scenes, each Nordic country has been progressively adopting stricter immigration policies, following the example set by Denmark. However, Sweden's increase in crime is not an isolated occurrence in Europe. Homicide rates have been on the rise over the past decade throughout the European Union, including countries such as Hungary, Germany, Denmark, and Finland. An examination of crime data from the E.U. and United Nations conducted by "RealClearInvestigations" reveals a significant correlation between Immigration and the overall increase in criminal activities, similar to the situation observed in Sweden. In the span of only ten years, the Nordic Nation has experienced a significant shift from having one of the lowest rates of deadly firearm incidents in Europe to one of the highest.

Established criminal syndicates, predominantly led by second-generation immigrants, are no longer solely targeting rival groups but are increasingly causing harm to their families and innocent individuals. A significant number of the culprits are Islamic adolescent individuals, some as young as fourteen (14) years old, who are brainwashed by criminal organizations to execute targeted acts of violence. During a televised address in late September, Ulf Kristersson, the Prime Minister of Sweden, provided his analysis of the unprecedented violence, explicitly attributing it to *"reckless immigration policy and unsuccessful integration."* Additionally, it demonstrates that these liberal policies have ruined formerly prosperous, secure nations and engulfed them in a culture of drugs, crime, gangs, and war, just as in the homeland of the immigrants themselves. Wisen up, America[xxv]. We are rapidly en route to joining our European colleagues in one of the possibly most significant failures of our time. Suppose I were to tease out one positive from the shameful public antisemitic display in the United States. In that case, it is the realization of how extensive Islamist doctrine has permeated our society and tangible proof of the failure of multiculturalism in American society. I am afraid that this is only the beginning for America.

In a surprisingly shocking revelation, for me, at least, a recent (December 2023) poll of Gen Z (18-29) constituents revealed one in every five polled supported Osama Bin Laden and viewed the 9/11 attacks as America's fault and deserving *(Washington Times, News Media Outlets, MSNBC, FOX)*. America, it is time to wake up, get off the proverbial fence, and observe the permeation of Islamist doctrine in our society. Mainly the indoctrination of our future generations through institutions of higher learning and democratic social activists, funded by foreign actors with the intention of making America irrelevant in the world. There are many ways to fight a war, head-on or covertly, in an underhanded manner by infiltrating and imploding the targeted society. Don't kid yourselves; we are at war, and the Biden administration is handing America over to the enemy by allowing our societal infrastructure to be compromised by adverse ideological infiltration, weakening our national unity by engaging in identity politics, practicing appeasement foreign relations posturing, and abandoning support for allies in favor of domestic support for Islamism.

Normalizing Alternative Lifestyle Ideology and Indoctrination of our Children: Another identity group that has been identified for special attention and pandered to by the Biden administration within the past few years for securing the voting bloc of the liberal democratic socialist machine in power is the 2SLGBTQIA+ group (Evolving). This group keeps evolving in definition and classification and has been given special rights and afforded privileges that others may find hard to acquire, not to mention a high level of social protection based on the fabricated notion that they are being discriminated against. These groups are allowed to flaunt vulgarism and their warped value systems that attack the very fabric of our Judeo-Christian society, including the indoctrination of our youth.

Imagine laws have to be placed on the books in some states to protect some public spaces from being bombarded with lewd and vociferous sexual displays (drag shows, twerking, stripping, and other explicit displays) by the 2SLGBTQIA+ practitioners, where children might be exposed with their parents, to include schools. It is coming to a point where immorality and vulgarity are becoming the norm in the American landscape. If these groups are challenged, we, the majority, face dire consequences for bringing the challenge. The liberal democratic machine ignores the most basic of realities in that while spouting freedom for these groups, they are effectively dividing society and compromising the freedom of conservative values, democracy, speech, and a morally infused way of life. President Biden has assured the transgender community in a public speech that he supports them; well, this is from a President who documented media reports stating that he had showers with a grown daughter, sniffs young women, and likes to expose himself to Secret Service female agents under the guise of taking a swim in the buff; no surprises there. The current administration is not expected to impose any limitations on the teaching of transgender topics to our children in schools and will allow cross-dressing displays and sexually explicit materials and ideology that are morally offensive and against the principles of all four major religious bases (Christian-Hindu-Islamic-Jewish) in the United States, in schools.

At several educational institutions, drag queens are invited to read books during storytime, sometimes displaying inappropriate conduct. Some sexually explicit books that have been allowed by school administrators and exposed by Congress are often read for storytime. The content would make a prostitute blush, much less children. Even our military institutions have been infiltrated with DEI and gender-blurring ideology. The recruiting command has solicited cross-dressers to aid in recruiting, and the Department of Defense-sponsored drag shows on base until being called out in Congress. Basic training has been redesigned to eliminate the shock and awe approach and to create a calmer learning environment. I can almost guarantee that with the new training emphasis in the military, our psychological and physical casualty rate in a conflict will be enormous. The new breed of military just won't be equipped to absorb the shock and reality of combat. I directly blame the upper military echelons for caving into this woke nonsense. In all my years serving as both an enlisted soldier and an officer, my peers and I had one shared "Army" identity and one "Green" color. That seemed pretty inclusive to me, and to boot, I was really a minority representation, and it never crossed my mind.

The liberal Democrats have taken things to another level of insanity in proposing the Equality Act, which aims to expand the scope of Title IV of the 1964 Civil Rights Act to include sexual orientation and gender identity (SOGI) as protected categories. This may result in modifications to the educational content in public schools, mandating the inclusion of texts that endorse and advocate unconventional perspectives on gender and sexuality. Parents in the United States and globally have effectively resisted these modifications to the curriculum, expressing their entitlement to nurture and instruct their children in accordance with their own principles and preferences, to no avail. In addition, several parents express apprehensions regarding the propagation of gender ideology, which may result in an increase in the number of young individuals suffering from gender dysphoria and pursuing "transgender medical treatment" that can have harmful health consequences. Regrettably, the liberal democratic machine disregards the significance of parental rights and, with the help of the ruling party, is shoving it down our throats, disregarding the constitutional freedoms afforded to us as Americans. I wonder why many of us feel as if we live under an autocratic system.

Regarding the contentious subject of alternative sexual lifestyles, new "gender blurring" identification, sexual indoctrination and mutilation of minors (Under 21), and transgender anomalies, it is crucial to maintain a clear understanding of their true nature. These are, by and large, deliberate personal lifestyle choices driven by various motivations such as the desire for exclusivity, rebellion against societal norms and traditions, deviant behaviors, conformity to popular trends, or simply personal preference, often shrouded in a belief that nature made a mistake in their physiological design. I would even entertain the line of thinking that some of these conditions fall under mental illness, which would require compassion and treatment. Under the support and encouragement of activists, these organizations have veiled themselves within the realm of identity politics and gender identity in order to obtain special assignments and preferential treatment. This phenomenon, which is supported by a large number of professionals, requires psychological treatment and is, in my opinion, a plea for assistance and attention. If an individual is in psychological conflict with their own anatomy and identity, then they are unstable and should not be placed in positions of authority or potentially injurious fields requiring mental stability and rational reasoning capabilities.

This social trend has created confusion among the rational in society and the impressionable children who lack a solid family foundation and are vulnerable in society with no direction or aspirations to excel. This bursting desire for self-expressionism is evidenced by the vast examples of sexual showboating and vulgar attempts to be recognized as a relevant societal entity. In today's unstable, indecisive, social media-driven, self-imposed sensitive environment, numerous decisions are influenced by social trends and the desire to distinguish oneself from others and stand out rather than be afflicted by true psychological dysfunction. Sexual preference and intimate choices should not be a topic of public discourse, as many professional individuals with whom I have conversed who practice their freedom to choose a same-sex partner find the association with vulgarity and transgenderism disconcerting and intrudes negatively in their private spheres; thus, placing their private lives in an unhealthy spotlight. What is the final objective of the liberal social activists rallying behind the creation of numerous genders and this nonsensical categorization of human identity? What could possibly be the endgame for America and our children? How did this perversion ever become normalized behavior? I also have to point out that, in my opinion, those in the mental health profession who coddle and support these ridiculous notions of not belonging to the sex or body assigned at birth being a normal process are hurting those misguided, infatuated individuals and not addressing the actual root causes, for the rebellion against normal behaviors. A cry for help comes in many forms.

Regardless of the reasoning we may ascribe to this phenomenon, unconventional personal lifestyle choices and behaviors should not be forcibly assimilated into mainstream society, disregarding our religious, cultural, and conservative belief systems that are based on Judeo-Christian values, which have played a significant role in our development as a moral and devout society. Regrettably, the liberal democratic socialist complex has been manipulating and empowering these marginalized groups for their own political gain, using any means necessary to secure a voting bloc. The demonization of Christianity and its doctrine is a heavily pushed agenda, especially when juxtaposed against alternative sexual lifestyles and gender confusion doctrine. This manipulation has led to an emphasis on narratives of discrimination, marginalization, and exclusion, creating the illusion of fighting for human rights and advocating for social justice.

Rational thinking should be dominant in a country that upholds liberty; these chosen ways of life should exist in the realm of personal and private decisions made by individuals regarding how to lead their own lives. Individuals have the freedom to pursue alternative lifestyles within the confines of their own private sphere, similar to how other members of society exercise their personal rights with respect for others. Here is an interview conducted with administrators after a board meeting on another unrelated topic that illustrates many educators' predominant way of thinking.

Interview: As one senior administrator and Ph.D. educator at a prominent school told me in a private fact-finding interview regarding education: *"Sir, I have been a Democrat, an educator and administrator for 31 years, and I have never been more disgusted with the pressures educators are under, and how many have turned a blind eye to the children's welfare; if a child wants to be called a cat or other identifiable thing, they will do so and laugh under their breath at their stupidity, and that of their parents, so they can keep their jobs. Most of her teachers turn a blind eye. If parents want to invite these mentally unstable individuals to mentor their children, we cannot stop them; only cringe in disgust. It is sad and unfortunate for these minors; the odds of them becoming productive and contributing members of society are slim to none. It's all about keeping your job today and retiring. If you speak up, the unions will decimate you, and they will make it known. We cannot go against the system, or we will be destroyed. After looking at everything happening, I cannot in good conscience support the party anymore. There are no more values...."*

This particular educator, now retired, has kept her three children in private catholic school through high school, and now all three are pursuing professional degrees in college. Over several months, I have concluded that this is a common consensus among many responsible and concerned educators who are disappointed in the education system, regardless of political affiliation. It is truly a shame how many parents are disenfranchising their children and contributing to their delinquency with support from so-called professional pundits and the government's help. For comparison, I have never encountered any documentation of heterosexual individuals going to schools and displaying vulgarity or twerking and trying to lobby for pornographic material to be accepted as part of the curriculum. I think that would qualify them as pedophiles, immediate removal from premises and arrest. Neither have I seen heterosexual individuals in public spaces trying to ply their trade of stripping, public exposure, or playing dress up like a retarded (not challenged) imbecile. I think they have laws against that sort of behavior; indecent exposure may come to mind. Enforcing alternative beliefs on others is likewise a transgression of our entitlements and a violation of our freedoms. If someone invades your private space, sufficient legal provisions are in place to safeguard an individual's rights, thus obviating the necessity of publicly promoting one's chosen lifestyle for acceptance in mainstream society. Welcome to our new government, the democratic socialist "autocratic party." Never have I witnessed so much hypocrisy in society. Do you think, for one instance, reasonable and intelligent democrats would willingly allow their children to descend into this brand of societal madness that they publicly support? Of course not, just like I alluded to earlier, a "lifestyle for you, but not us." Those with the money will always find a means to insulate themselves and significant others from the poison they spew in society.

Although late to the "Awakening Party," I am relieved to see so many young African Americans seeking information and clarity and finally coming to the realization of which political party has been instrumental to their cultural disenfranchisement. As more of this younger African American electorate become informed self-thinkers, I believe we have a unique opportunity in society to get all

Americans on an equal footing, right the wrongs of the past, and strive for American unity, success, and greatness. This would be in direct opposition to the destructive divisions and racial hatred the democratic party and the liberal media machine have been inciting within our American society. While observing the state of affairs in our nation, occasionally, one has to step back in bewilderment and ask, why?

PART III

CHAPTER 8
POLITICAL WARFARE

The Democratic Party Complex is effectively engaging in political warfare to undermine the American democratic process and change the nation's governance from within. The strategic and skillfully executed manipulation of society, along with the governmental endorsement of immoral behaviors while vilifying Christian perspectives, is concerning and indicates a shift in our societal framework. The evolution of American government, society, institutions, and political doctrine is remarkably well coordinated. The dissemination of ideas, narratives, and ideology from the top down is highly effective in its messaging, targeting, and persuasiveness due to the support and coordination involved. The Party effectively controls the narrative and distribution of information through mainstream media outlets, suppressing opposing views and influencing the audience. Opposing opinions to the Party's official story are suppressed through organized institutional, governmental, media, or societal coercion to achieve a powerful impact. Powerful nations like China, Russia, Iran, North Korea, and the Arab League of Nations have mastered the art of controlling the flow of information and messaging within their own countries. This allows them to shape national views, influence national trajectories, impose their will on society, and implement ideological shifts that reflect less tolerance of Christianity, personal freedom, wealth accumulation, societal control, military occupation of sovereign nations, and similar beliefs. The facts are clearly visible and presented for everyone to observe. The reader does not need to be persuaded of the imminent threat we face in losing our nation. All information is readily accessible for society to scrutinize and decide how to respond and what to believe. To prevent such an operation from succeeding, there is a strategy consisting of three parts: (1). Millions of Americans believe that our traditional values, earned freedoms, and Judeo-Christian beliefs should be strongly and equally advocated for in society. (2). The public should insist on accurate reporting and compel media organizations to be impartial in presenting information for the public to evaluate independently rather than being influenced on what to believe. (3). In order to achieve these outcomes, the electorate must get involved, seek information, evaluate the facts, observe the course and effects of harmful policies in our country, and make wise decisions through our democratic processes in the areas of economics, quality of life, and personal freedom. Without question, instead of power being manipulated and corrupted by the government, power must be returned to the people for democracy to survive.

As previously stated, distinguishing between an ideological conflict and a political war becomes challenging in the context of the Democratic Party's present administration. This is primarily due to the fact that the Democratic Political Party orchestrates and integrates the ideological warfare currently engulfing the United States, which is directed at conservative practitioners, the religious establishment, the Republican Party, and all right-of-center organizations. The mainstream media and news outlets are employing a deceptive strategy of disinformation by echoing the Democratic Party's talking points and spinning conservative doctrines, withholding pertinent and accurate information, and provoking racial discontent. Additionally, foreign actors have infiltrated our institutions of higher education and imposed their worldviews on the present and future generations of statesmen and stateswomen as part of the indoctrination process. All of this is a component of the Democratic Party's demographic reengineering, which they are doing to have a captive audience from which to spread their ideology since the majority of patriotic Americans would reject such destructive views. In the United States, the Democratic Party and its affiliated organizations have been saturated with Marxist doctrine (BLM), liberalism, progressivism, antisemitism, as well as socialism at every level. The confluence of these ideologies represents the most deleterious influence that America and American society have ever before been confronted with. Under the guise of oppression and systemic racism, destructive narratives have been introduced into social activism by these ideological groups, which receive support from the Democratic Party. The goal is to incite riots, looting, racial unrest, and racial ostracization among immigrants. These endeavors pursued by the left wing of our political spectrum are calculated to sow discord in society and alter the composition of the country's population.

These destructive ideological movements have evolved in America and redefined themselves for better

153

penetration and acceptance by the younger, liberated, socially irresponsible electorate. Even among these younger Democratic socialists, a conflict of ideologies emerges; they challenge the legitimacy of categorizing communism as a legitimate form of socialism. They argue that command economies are managed efficiently by a limited bureaucracy that owns private interests in the means of production. Democratic socialists disagree with social democrats regarding using capitalism to finance a comprehensive welfare state. They argue that maintaining private enterprise ownership in mixed economies, which blend aspects of socialism and capitalism, is an undemocratic practice. The implementation of self-management or democratic control should be the prevailing norm for all employees in the workplace. Those who advocate democratic socialism argue that markets can be included in a socialist economy if the businesses operating in those markets are owned by collectives like the public or cooperatives. Democratic socialists, akin to their social democratic counterparts, advocate for enforcing government regulations and implementing extensive welfare programs, which actually form a dependency relationship and loyalty to the government. Some political leaders perceive these measures as a means to gradually reform the system and as temporary remedies to mitigate capitalism's "so-called" adverse effects.

The terms "social democrat" and "democratic socialist" have historically been used interchangeably, which could cause readers who follow 20th-century socialist ideologies to become confused, especially when advocating for some Marxist ideologies. In every instance, the goal was to establish a fully socialist economy. On the other hand, individuals who aligned with the social democratic party may have supported either revolution or reform. In contrast, democratic socialists generally preferred gradual and incremental changes. Consolidating diverse New Left factions in Europe and then in America broadened democratic socialist interests beyond their previous scope. Currently, these issues consist of environmental activism, anti-colonialism, anti-immigration, LGBTQ+ rights, and opposition to Israel and Zionism. Following this, democratic socialist groups, such as the Democratic Socialists Organizing Committee (DSOC) and the New American Movement (NAM), embraced the inclination towards supporting various causes, which came to be recognized as intersectional or multi-tendency, both within the United States and globally. In the United States, Democratic Socialist Bernie Sanders received more than twenty-five percent of the total votes cast in the 2020 Democratic Primary Elections and over forty percent in the 2016 Democratic Primary Elections. Membership in the Democratic Socialists of America (DSA) skyrocketed, going from 6,500 in 2014 to more than 100,000 by 2020. Democratic socialists have strategically employed these recent statistics to achieve electoral victories and, as a result, secure nominations for federal and state offices from the Democratic party. There is some strange allure to the socialist ideology in America by the younger college-educated individuals that I haven't been able to decipher.

IDEOLOGY DRIVING POLITICAL WARFARE

To understand the objectives of the democratic party, one must first understand the root drivers acting on the party and the prevailing destructive ideology that has overtaken the party doctrine.

Root Drivers: In short, the erosion of our democratic system of government and institutional processes, followed by the destabilization of our society and the restructuring of our social construct, ultimately led to our relinquishment of hegemonic status on the international stage. These individuals espouse radical liberalist ideas that incorporate a jumbled assortment of socialist and Marxist principles in an attempt to placate a more moderate audience. With its inception in Europe, this movement has evolved through a series of strategic maneuvers, manipulations, and transformations to assume its present form with the intention of sowing discord in conservative societies of the West. Additionally, it is worth noting that hostile foreign actors have identified an opportunity to piggyback on these movements, provide financial backing and institutional support to entities that propagate destabilizing ideologies, and exert pressure on democratic governing bodies in the United States. Iran, China, Russia, North Korea, and their proxies have all been engaged in some form of destabilizing action towards the U.S. and financially supporting homegrown insurrectionists. Indoctrinating our liberal educators and institutions of higher learning gives these hostile actors access to undermining and controlling current and future generations of leaders in American society without firing a single shot. All of these supported ideologies are in direct contravention of American ideals, conservatism, and our Judeo-Christian value system head-

156

on. It is imperative to remain cognizant of the present political climate, as all indicators suggest an increased assault on conservative doctrine, the economy, education, religious freedoms, freedoms for "all speech," our social composition, law enforcement, judicial jurisprudence, and the conservative demographic voter blocs by the democratic party. America is, in essence, under attack. The liberal democratic left has been responsible for promoting and popularizing fallacious conspiracy theories, which use fear-mongering "buzz words" such as "Non-Inclusive, Anti-Gay, Anti-Islam, Systemic Racism, Institutional Racism, Gender Discrimination," and the African American culture as a scapegoat to incite an uprising that would further divide America. A divided nation is weak at its core. Recent memory recalls the glorification of "Black Lives Matter" and the incitement of looting and rioting by vulnerable adolescents. Sometimes, I contemplate how most Americans could be so naïve to what is happening around them. Ignorance of current events, attacks on our values and beliefs, destructive ideologies, and being unengaged will eventually lead to our downfall.

Ideologies/Effect: Within the book, I frequently allude to these ideologies, specifically democratic socialism, liberalism, and Marxism, renowned for their deleterious characteristics. According to my research, no country or nation has successfully implemented these ideologies and achieved the idealistic vision promised by their doctrine[31].

---

[31] Kuziemko, Ilyana, Nicolas Longuet Marx, and Suresh Naidu. *"Compensate the Losers?" Economic Policy and Partisan Realignment in the US*. No. w31794. National Bureau of Economic Research, 2023.

Presented here is an examination of how this ideology is depicted and practiced within society. Open societies guarantee and protect rational discussion, while monocratic or closed societies force individuals to submit to authority, whether it be religious, political, or economic[32]. Europe adopted a policy of open-border liberalism in its governance, which resulted in adverse outcomes. The issues encompassed irregular migration, tribalism, crime, terrorism, civil unrest, religious intolerance, and economic burdens. Those countries (Denmark, Sweden, Italy, Germany, France, Spain, United Kingdom, Poland, and Norway) are presently exerting immediate efforts to seal their borders and reverse the detrimental trajectory that their nations are undergoing. The aim of a liberal world-order vision is to establish a global community that transcends sovereign states and national boundaries. In this perceived world, individuals acknowledge their shared interest in freedom, equality, and economic growth without engaging in conflicting power dynamics.

The crucial factor that appears to have been overlooked in this idealistic vision is the inherent characteristics of "human nature," particularly the inclination toward "greed." Realizing a global, all-encompassing society devoid of territorial limitations is unfeasible and a utopian ambition. They propose that their rigid ideology is the only method to ensure humanity's victory over the urgent challenges of climate change, food scarcity, conflicts, geopolitical rivalries, and nuclear

---

[32] Kanna, Ahmed. "Enlisted in struggle: Being Marxist in a time of protracted crisis." *Focaal* 2023, no. 95 (2023): 61-73.

proliferation. This ideology has gained support from many influential liberals in America, who embrace it as an ideal of a perfect society. Nevertheless, this ideology is viewed by many nefarious actors representing diverse factions as a strategic advantage to undermine and deconstruct American society, thus hindering the internal power and influence of the United States. A nation's preoccupation with addressing internal disruptions and restoring social stability results in a diminished focus on external affairs and geopolitical positioning. This diversion of attention provides an opportunity for adversaries to take advantage of the situation.

Political Correctness: This is a meticulously planned component of a broader strategy aimed at controlling the thoughts and behaviors of society. In order to undermine a society internally, it is necessary to systematically undermine or challenge the fundamental principles of rationality, prevailing norms and values, and the sense of national unity. It is essential to take advantage of ethnic and racial conflicts and to create divisions within social classes by presenting them as disparate and unequal treatment and discriminatory in nature. Gender equality and women's rights would also be highlighted to expose the supposed marginalization in society caused by targeted misinformation and manipulation of the truth. The unwavering embrace of fascism by liberals, demonizing opposing perspectives on university campuses or within society at large, creates the desired effect of shutting down opposing views on several levels.

Young individuals and college students who are privileged and receive financial support from social disruptors (such as Soros, Sixteen Thirty Fund, Tides Foundation, liberal activist groups, and the Democratic Party hardliners) forcefully suppress conservative speech and perspectives backed by their socialist liberal indoctrinated educational institutions. They do so under the mistaken belief that they are championing the oppressed and acting as social warriors for the disadvantaged. Merely discussing border security often leads to widespread condemnation and the advocacy of anti-immigration beliefs, nationalistic ideologies, white supremacist rhetoric, and criticism that undermines credibility. To align with their liberal democratic socialist Marxist vision, it is deemed optimal to alter the demographics of society by advocating for open borders and unregulated irregular migration, allowing unrestricted access and eroding national identity.

Under the democratic party leadership and followers' definition of freedoms, only speech and actions authorized by the liberal democratic socialist machine are deemed eligible for protection. It appears that the entire nation is engaged with a group or an individual who experiences borderline personality disorder, or BPD, with a confusing psychotic twist. Living in today's society is akin to having awoken in a dreamscape or entered an alternate reality with a complete reversal of all norms as we know them[33]. When dialogue is eliminated, and dissenting viewpoints are rejected, society collapses, leading to a halt in progress,

---

[33] Stivers, Richard. *The culture of cynicism: American morality in decline.* Wipf and Stock Publishers, 2023.

increased conflict and divisions, and ultimately, paralysis, and there lies another strategy for destroying Western societies.

Victimhood and Dependency: Only in the United States do individuals display such intense enthusiasm for the concept of victimhood that they would fabricate hate crimes against themselves to achieve that social status and receive preferential treatment. In the United States, the liberal democratic socialist movement, along with social activists and the liberal elite, has intentionally and strategically undermined the African American culture,[34]as detailed in another section. Their aim is to influence and persuade the vulnerable members of this community to perceive themselves as victims of unequal treatment and systemic prejudice, specifically by corporate America, Republicans, and White individuals. The lower educational rates, lack of home ownership, increased crime rates, plus the state of depressed inner cities are all interconnected with this misinformation campaign. The recent closures of numerous store branches and pharmacies in democratic cities, which are located in crime-ridden neighborhoods plagued by frequent rioting, theft, and armed robberies, are being attributed to corporate greed and discrimination. The liberal democratic machine promotes these narratives in order to foster divisions. This convenient messaging disregards the genuine underlying factors and fails to hold responsible the unlawful actions of the so-called susceptible young individuals and criminals who are

[34] Fraser, Nancy, and Linda Gordon. "A genealogy of dependency: Tracing a keyword of the US welfare state." *Signs: Journal of women in culture and society* 19, no. 2 (1994): 309-336.

emboldened in society due to social activism. The liberal establishment in power promotes criminal actions without any law enforcement or legal repercussions.

As a part of the playbook, the liberal apparatus also pushes DEI to stoke racial animosity towards Caucasians and other immigrant communities, all the while advocating for social initiatives aimed at fostering a state of reliance within the society. Implementing specific quota programs undermines the notion of success achieved through diligence and meritocracy. Instead, it promotes a perception that minority success and selection are not merit-based but preference-based on race and gender. This concept or handout is not only objectionable to many within the culture but also alters societal perceptions and undermines the accomplishments of African American individuals, other minorities, and females who have achieved success in society based on merit, thereby forcing them to justify their own success[35]. In America, it is necessary to acknowledge the existence of manufactured concepts like white privilege and institutional racism, even though actual instances of racism may not be widespread enough to fully validate the experiences of marginalized minorities who hold liberal beliefs. In a previous era in the United States, people aimed to have strength, competence, and self-reliance rather than adopting a victim

---

[35] Schiele, Jerome H. "Black Political Ideologies: Conceptions of African-American Subjugation and Social Welfare Policy Intervention." *Journal of Policy practice* 8, no. 3 (2009).

mentality. Conservatives are individuals in modern society who still exhibit these traits.

Black neoconservative[36] criticisms revolve around the notion that African Americans embrace a victim-centric identity, which in turn magnifies the gravity of racism in order to instill remorse in white people and thus contributes to the emergence of the "white privilege" movement. Their argument is that welfare and affirmative action are both ineffectual policies that impede racial progress and perpetuate a sense of dependency and victimhood among African Americans. Black neoconservatives contest the prevailing notion that racism and white supremacy have diminished in overt manifestation yet continue to wield significant influence. They assert that liberal programs, civil rights legislation, and government intervention have all contributed to the development of pathological dependence among African Americans. Black neoconservatives contend that the profound obstacles encountered by the Black underclass and the restricted progress of African Americans are primarily attributable to their reliance on external assistance. The analysis centers on the ideology of archconservative George S. Schuyler, who is regarded as a prototypical forerunner of Black neoconservatives, notwithstanding their assertion that their own ideology finds its origins in Booker T. Washington's philosophy[37]. For context, a comprehensive analysis was conducted on the

---

[36] Gooding-Williams, Robert. "Black Neo-Conservatism: A Critical Introduction." *Praxis International* 7, no. 2 (1987): 133-142.

[37] Bracey, Christopher Alan. "The Black Neoconservative Intellectuals." *The Journal of Blacks in Higher Education* 58 (2007): 64.

works of Shelby Steele, Thomas Sowell, John McWhorter, Star Parker, Stephen Carter, Ward Connerly, and Glenn Loury.

The Politicization Phenomenon: Virtually every action you take in contemporary society carries a hidden motive aligned with the liberal movement. Engaging in seemingly harmless actions and expressing oneself verbally can lead to social exclusion, being mocked, financial loss, and even having one's reputation severely damaged. Engaging in racial endogamy or exclusively hosting individuals from your own racial group for meals could potentially be interpreted as manifestations of racism. It is essential to exercise caution when expressing opinions: say if your young daughter is sharing a bathroom with an adult male who identifies as female, you had better not try and mitigate the risk to your daughter for fear of legal consequences or social ostracization, with accusations of homophobia being leveled against you. If you do not support or accept "gender confusion" in society, some may perceive you as oppressive, homophobic, and potentially aligned with Republican white supremacist ideologies. One's race is inconsequential, regardless of whether or not they are of Caucasian descent. Well, we as a rational nation need to stand our ground and delegitimize these ridiculous attempts at resocialization.

A prominent MSNBC host (Joy Reid) recently remarked on the Iowa caucuses, where former President Trump was a landslide winner, that "Evangelical Christians" were "White Nationalists" and they want black people to bow down to them. It doesn't get any more absurd, divisive, and hateful than that, and her employers have not admonished her because this is the predetermined narrative. Because of the hatred and separation forming in society, there is a growing trend of individuals refraining from engaging in various forms of public interaction that foster national unity, such as organized sports and other types of entertainment, due to the apprehension of being stigmatized for not conforming to these ridiculous ideologies. When society emphasizes tribalism and individualism instead of unity based on national identity and the preservation of the nation's fundamental principles, then diversity, discrimination, hatred, and conflict will inevitably arise. The age-old ideology of one nation under God is now a distant memory; this is definitely not the country I fought for. The very foundation of American society is being methodically disassembled.

Tribalism/Separatism: Using a concerted and blanketing misinformation campaign coupled with a tribalism mentality propagated by the Liberal Democratic Socialist Complex facilitates the polarization of the electorate, creating separation of our population, driving racial hatred and institutional mistrust, creating more dependency on government, and spreading the concept of victimhood in society. Liberals strive ceaselessly to fragment the American populace into factions that are increasingly engaged in violent conflict. They will exploit any circumstance that may occur. Promoting and endorsing immoral, sexually explicit, and deceitful conduct in order to undermine the Judeo-Christian values and belief system of the United States is an additional strategy for sowing discord in society[38]. In light of the gravity of the situation, vigorous public discourse is presently taking place concerning transsexual individuals, whose proportion varies from 0.25% to 0.75% of the total population, contingent upon the precise definition. A discernible paradigm shift has occurred, wherein the objectionable notion that an individual's ability to understand is limited by their race, color, or gender has given way to a heightened sense of animosity between individuals on the basis of immutable distinctions.

This presents a substantial peril to the trajectory of our country, given that preserving cohesion within any collective, including a nation, becomes unfeasible when members no longer share a common comprehension and consent regarding their common objectives and guiding principles. The European endeavor to implement multiculturalism ultimately demonstrated a profound lack of success, as it unintentionally contributed to the spread of Islamism throughout Western civilizations. Consequentially, cohesive communities were disrupted, national pride and traditions trampled, and their once peaceful cities transformed into war zones. America is on track to follow along; as a matter of fact, some may argue that we are already there. Our nation's current condition renders obsolete our motto, "E pluribus unum" (Out of many, one). A correction in society and how Americans perceive their country is vital for a change from this destructive trajectory. What consequences can be expected if liberals continue to assert their multicultural

---

[38] Fanning, Bryan. "The Future of Public Morality." In *Public Morality and the Culture Wars: The Triple Divide,* pp. 183-206. Emerald Publishing Limited, 2023.

ideology concerning immigration that the parts of the group are incapable of coming together? To answer this, view the European news stations and Europe's reversal of liberal immigration policies and cessation of accepting refugees in mass.

Nonjudgmental Attitudes: It has become ingrained in popular culture that being nonjudgmental is vital, as liberals have repeatedly emphasized its importance (on the fence society). This instantly removed accountability of action, qualifying right from wrong in society, and broke our moral compass. When faced with a decision between prioritizing the welfare of society or safeguarding the interests of an individual who has committed a wrongdoing, we consistently prioritize the protection of the individual, as it was society or some other force that caused the individual's action, negating them of responsibility. From an early age, and further emphasized during my military career, I learned that a larger group's collective needs and security take precedence over an individual's needs. Here are some thoughts to ponder on the loss of values because of indecisiveness: Given the diminished social disapproval surrounding divorce, non-marital childbirth, and abortion all the way till birth, are we experiencing a net improvement or decline? Do children who are aborted or raised by a single parent instead of a family experience better outcomes? Is it considered as safeguarding a child's mental health when they are allowed to indulge in sex change therapy and operations that mentally scar them for life? Are individuals who identify as a different gender and play a grown-up version of "dress up" psychologically unbalanced and need treatment? Is it ok for same-sex marriages to be accepted as wholesome unions and upheld as model family units? The inherent reluctance to establish clear boundaries and unequivocally distinguish between what is morally correct and incorrect has resulted in the decline and corruption of our society[39]. We currently reside in a society that hesitates to assert its beliefs or values and take a firm position. This hesitancy stems from a fear of facing criticism from liberal groups and individuals who may aim to undermine and dismantle those who hold opposing ideas. Perhaps an increase in individuals who experience remorse for actions that "fall short of their mothers' expectations" would result in a significant rise in the number of morally upright individuals[40]. It's perplexing to witness the behavior of the liberals in action. For some unknown, unfounded, and unproven reason, the liberals act as if they possess the moral high ground, are intellectually superior, are all trained psychologists, and have all the correct answers on life and how we should live. It must be the Kool-Aid or an advanced affliction of "ethical egoism."

Liberal Feminism: Given the widespread acceptance of its fundamental principle that "Women should have equal rights as men," feminism is now regarded as obsolete. Women occupy positions of authority and wield significant influence across all aspects of American society. The absence of women poses a substantial threat to the

[39] Fanning, Bryan. "Sex Differences and Gender Identities." In *Public Morality and the Culture Wars: The Triple Divide*, pp. 147-181. Emerald Publishing Limited, 2023.

[40] Ayoub, Phillip, and Kristina Stoeckl. "The Global Resistance to LGBTIQ Rights." *Journal of Democracy* 35, no. 1 (2024): 59-73.

survival of the nuclear family. The male and female counterparts contribute to the natural equilibrium, creating an ideal union where they fulfill the roles of nurturing and providing for the family unit according to their specific circumstances. Liberal feminists reimagined feminism by merging victimization and man-hatred. Foresee the prevalence of rape culture and patriarchy! It is absolutely unacceptable to hold the door for me. Please refrain from providing excessive explanations or engaging in what is commonly referred to as "mansplaining"! Remove the expression "Not all men!" As you reflect on your role in oppressing women, you remain still and silent. Many men are concerned about the reaction they will receive from women when they exhibit masculine behavior, as liberal feminism falsely convinces women that they can attain success and satisfaction without any obstacles. Reject the outdated belief that men should conform to traditional masculine roles and women should conform to traditional feminine roles. Liberal feminism promotes the idea that women should take on the same roles as men while simultaneously devaluing men. Sorry, it doesn't work both ways. Both are equally important and have unique skill sets.

Weaponization, How Better to Destroy America: An individual who remains apathetic towards the present condition of our government is hindering progress toward a resolution. The Democratic party machine made a substantial error when it attempted to manipulate the democratic process in the United States by circumventing the will of the people. This has backfired, resulting in overwhelming support for former president Trump. The people have recognized the earmarks of a political hatchet job to eliminate the people's choice, so much for democracy. They accomplished this by employing the Justice Department (lawfare) to impede the election of the former president and candidate of the opposition party. The indictments filed were grasping at straws, failing the requirements for prosecution scrutiny, and were, at the very least, absurd in character. This sentiment was echoed by many judicial and scholarly experts from both sides of the political aisle. The most egregious aspect is that the government makes no effort to conceal the obvious, a flagrant disregard for legal statutes and the preservation of our democratic procedures. Regardless of the analysis employed, the outcome remains unchanged. This unequivocally demonstrates that the American Democratic Party, along with its left-leaning liberal socialist Marxist entities, including the state Democratic media complex, is actively involved in a campaign to dismantle democracy in America and establish a Socialist or monocratic regime.

The Democratic party has utilized the Department of Homeland Security and Immigration Customs Enforcement as a means to achieve their political goals. They have implemented policies that hinder these agencies from carrying out their responsibilities and have also relaxed border controls, granting unrestricted entry to millions of illegal immigrants. These individuals, who do not share the fundamental principles of the United States, have no intention of supporting or defending the nation, nor do they seek to integrate into society. Instead, they aim to exploit entitlements and health and welfare benefits intended for legal residents, thereby draining resources from our country. In addition, they also introduce their illicit activities, and numerous terrorist organizations have deployed bad actors undetected by any authorized surveillance[xxvi]. This in itself is a dire threat to our national security and the safety of our citizens. They can literally disappear from society and prepare to strike. The multitude of shocks our nation faces cannot be absorbed, as our system was not designed to handle such large volumes, financial burdens, or mismanagement of protocol. States are facing significant challenges due to the increasing number of illegal immigrants, with no foreseeable resolution from the Biden administration.

As a result, our system is under immense pressure, leading to the displacement and marginalization of our citizens in order to accommodate individuals without legal status. Illegal immigrants are eligible for free medical care, food, housing, debit cards, winter clothing, and housing. Still, so many legal citizens working two or three jobs to make ends meet cannot afford adequate medical care, and many Americans lack the basic necessities such as food, clothing, and housing. African American communities, especially those living in urban regions, heavily depend on police protection, crime prevention initiatives, after-school services, community programs, and essential aid; however, these services are provided to illegal immigrants even though our citizens begged for more support and were denied.

There is no version of this transgression to our needy citizens and veterans that can be explained away by the Biden Democrats. Preferential funding allocations must be made for the preservation of infrastructure and programs within these communities immediately, as opposed to allocating resources towards the accommodation and support of illegal immigrants. These communities continually witness their own government allotting millions of dollars to undocumented immigrants, the funding they themselves were denied countless times before, and that has created a political migration from the Democrat party. It's incredible how funding can materialize when the government wants to support a program that translates to votes. What does that say about inner city programs, better housing, infrastructure development, crime prevention, better-funded schools, and employment training and growth opportunities? Sorry, it's not important enough, as we already have your votes.

These inner cities and many economically marginal communities nationwide have repeatedly requested and sought funding to enhance their lives, only to be rejected due to funding streams being redirected to illegal migrant upkeep and resettlement. Unless the government's objective is to depress these communities, it is implausible for any rational government to intentionally cause such damage to their own country and disregard their own citizens. To all African American communities, sanctuary cities, democratically run enclaves, and other economically marginalized communities—regardless of color or culture—that have been sidelined, used for political gain, and then abandoned, I have a direct message for you. "You were cautioned; you consumed the Kool-aid; you neglected to broaden your perspectives and permitted yourselves to be deceived." Regrettably, the veracity of the matter is arduous to acknowledge. Given our current understanding of the situation, it is imperative that we collectively put an end to the chaos and disloyalty toward America. Let us unite as one nation with a solid resolve to support and protect the land we refer to as America and the legal occupants referred to as Americans. Utilize your cognitive faculties and employ logical reasoning to articulate the phrase "Never Again," "Never Again."

The Justice system exacerbates criminality in our nation through the withdrawal of financial support for police forces, lack of assistance in policing operations, endorsement of riots and looting by eliminating accountability through legal prosecution, implementation of a revolving door system for grave offenses, and prosecution of individuals in society who protect their rights and property. The party in power remained silent as our nation's historic national monuments and statues were demolished, and directing the media surrogates to push the "peaceful demonstration" messaging, even when they were reporting in front of burning buildings and looting mobs on live television. The organization known as Black Lives Matter, which espouses Marxist ideology and has been accused of promoting racist rhetoric, received backing from the President (Biden), Vice President (Harris), and numerous Democrat party political figures. The extent of the damage these individuals have caused to communities is inconceivable, yet no form of responsibility has been assigned. Criminals of various degrees have become more confident, and it will be challenging to control their activities. The magnitude of crime, disorder, and devastation in our country is unparalleled. If these actions do not constitute treasonous acts against our nation, and if the officials of the ruling party are not held responsible to the people, then America as we know it will be gone and relegated into history. If no accountability of action is forthcoming, then what measures can prevent future maniacal party leaders from implementing similar destructive actions or a party under the influence of a foreign power from seizing control? We are drawing closer and closer to "Destroying the Homeland."

CHAPTER 9
ELIMINATING CONSTITUTIONAL PROTECTIONS

The Democratic Complex, which reemerged prominently during the Hillary Clinton administration and the Democratic Party elites in 2014, had long since sought to diminish the Constitution's importance. This was most notably demonstrated through their explicit efforts to regulate and impede free speech. An amendment to the United States Constitution that would revoke the First Amendment's protection of political speech consumed considerable Senate time. Dick Durbin, the Democratic Whip at the time, accurately predicted that the vote would be entirely partisan prior to the debate's start. According to Section 1 of the proposed amendment (S. J. Res. 19), the jurisdiction to regulate and impose reasonable limitations on the acquisition and use of funds by candidates and other individuals seeking to exert influence over elections resides with Congress and the States. The key phrases in this context are "and others," which pertains to any group that Congress elects to regulate, and "to influence elections," which encompasses any form of communication that politicians believe could affect an election, including political speech concerning significant public policy issues relating to incumbents and explicit advocacy urging voters to support or oppose a candidate[41]. Considerable

---

[41] Edelson, Chris. "How to Keep the Republic (Before It's Too Late): Why a New Constitution Is Necessary to Strengthen Liberal Democracy in the United

segments of essential political dialogue, encompassing material completely divorced from electoral procedures, would be susceptible to restrictions. Politicians would advocate for controversial policies with the knowledge that dissenting opinions could be arbitrarily disallowed. This would significantly curtail the right to free speech and undermine the integrity of the democratic process.

Democracy or Autocracy: Democrats in California have proposed a state bill that aimed to make it a crime to express doubt or skepticism about the widely accepted understanding of climate change. During that time, Attorney General Loretta Lynch informed the Senate Judiciary Committee that she had deliberated with her colleagues about the potential of initiating civil proceedings against individuals who deny the existence of climate change. What implications does this have for suppressing dialogue or dissenting opinions in society? Please correct me if I am mistaken, but these policy views do not align with democratic principles. Democrats have consistently shown dissatisfaction, and sometimes even open disdain, for the Constitution whenever it obstructs their capacity to implement new government initiatives[42]. President Obama has frequently expressed dissatisfaction with the complex procedures established by the Constitution's co-equal branches. Consequently, he has claimed to assume the role of disregarding the limitations imposed by the

---

States." *Presidential Leadership and the Trump Presidency: Executive Power and Democratic Government* (2020): 121-149.

[42] Perry Jr, H. W., and Lucas A. Powe Jr. "The Political Battle for the Constitution." *Const. Comment.* 21 (2004): 641.

Constitution on the president's powers to accomplish tasks. I have observed that this mindset is quite common among Democratic elitists. The evidence is widely dispersed throughout the records of political journals and media reports, available for anyone to examine. In my many exhaustive hours of research, I have found that Google Scholar and other research sites on the web are clearly democratic, leaning toward providing access to or restricting search results concerning documentation and views that oppose the liberal democratic socialist party's complex messaging[43]. No surprises there; democratic socialism is alive and growing among the naïve and uninformed youth.

AMERICAN SHADOW GOVERNMENT WIELDS POWER

The shadow government, or "swamp," is alive and well and continues to wield power and dictate policy for America. As stated earlier, the terms "swamp," "deep state," or "shadow government" refer to an organization or group of unelected officials, past presidents, bureaucrats, lobbyists, military officers, intelligence agents, and corporate elites who wield influence and power inconspicuously, irrespective of the will of the people or elected representatives. Another name that references elements of these power brokers is the Military Industrial Congressional Complex (MICC), which wields enormous government leverage. The national security apparatus of the federal government is confronted by an ever-growing

---

[43] Dawood, Yasmin. "The Fragility of Constitutional Democracy." *Md. L. Rev.* 77 (2017): 192.

and impactful network of organizations and individuals willing to subvert the Constitution, the rule of law, and our national security interests in pursuit of their own ideological and financial goals. These individuals collectively are also powerful enough to dictate the trajectory of our foreign policy for their benefit[44]. Collectively, as the power behind the Oval Office, the trust in the electorate to choose leaders and our democratic process has an entirely different interpretation. The deep state influences presidential selection, maintains the Beltway status quo, dictates foreign and domestic policy trajectories, and works with intelligence, military, and regulatory agencies to ensure the MIC is dialed into a global conflict.

This network has gained publicity and unwanted exposure since the first Trump presidency. Their matrix comprises coalitions of organizations and individuals bound together by a unifying ideology and monetary gain irrespective of party affiliation. From this standpoint, those united by the overarching ideological objective of expanding the administrative state should hold power. It is pretty evident with the opposition hatchet jobs that the power brokers in America, the ruling class of elitists that form the shadow government, will not relinquish power and will do whatever is necessary to protect their positions, as seen with the opposition to President Trump during his presidency, and his reelection[45]. This enclave considers

---

[44] Lofgren, Mike. *The deep state: The fall of the constitution and the rise of a shadow government*. Penguin, 2016.

[45] Michaels, Jon D. "Trump and the deep state: The government strikes back." *Foreign Aff.* 96 (2017): 52.

itself to be the guardian of the United States. The basis of this agenda is predicated on the tendency of progressives to entrust authority to unaccountable experts operating outside the jurisdiction of democratic institutions. In other words, the credibility of experts surpasses that of democratically elected officials, such as the Constitution, the President, and Congress. During times of conflict and war, the United States, the shadow government (including the manufacturing sector and the Military Industrial Complex), the economic complex (including the energy, banking, and financial sectors), and the media complex all gain financially. For the arms race to continue and be profitable, it is also in their best interest to push a foreign policy that maintains a global landscape of opposing forces, conflict, or a dominant foe. In other words, the mindset is we must always "have a bogeyman and an enemy for America to battle." Peaceful existence is counterproductive to the shadow government's financial empire.

In accordance with the proponents of the shadow government, the duly elected government ought to be subordinate to its shadow, which holds or ought to hold authentic executive authority. Advocates of the shadow government are personnel employed in administrative bureaucracies. They maintain that until one of their elected representatives assumes the presidency, elites who wish to conceal their desire to manipulate policy should secretly control the government, or at least particular government levers. However, relatively recent developments concerning Biden's cognitive decline and the overt weaponization of the DOJ have caused apprehension even among certain Democrats, as it has become clear that some group or person has been directing the Biden puppet presidency from the beginning. One organization that seems to pop up frequently on their radars is the Organizing for America (OFA) group[46], which has operational ties to President Obama. It has been at the forefront of leading the opposition to the Trump administration, a democratic power broker in Washington advising Biden, and changing the construct of the Democratic Party. OFA serves as a manifestation of the views held by a considerable number of Obama supporters who lack confidence in the state party's structure and instead advocate for forming independent organizations staffed by insiders whose official stances on a range of matters are not necessarily disclosed. If this doesn't meet the standard of subversion of our democratic processes and an attack on our governance, then I don't know how else to categorize it.

Furthermore, revelations have emerged regarding covert alliances between Obama supporters, external actors, and administrative state personnel, some of whom are affiliated with the Deep State bureaucracy situated within the intelligence community of the United States. According to Bryan Dean Wright (the Wright Report), a former CIA agent and current Democrat, *"certain American spies demonstrate a greater degree of hostility towards a partisan agenda as opposed to the Constitution in order to further their resistance against President Trump.*

---

[46] Stone, Erica M. "Content Strategy or Strategic Content? Suggestions for Developing Sustainable Content Strategy in Advocacy Organizations." *Journal of Technical Writing and Communication* 53, no. 4 (2023): 382-397.

Consequently, it is indisputable that those who have betrayed the organization in pursuit of personal ambitions and objectives are willing to divulge classified information. The multitude of instances of wrongdoing in the legal system, coupled with the efforts by the Democratic Party establishment to undermine our constitution, is profoundly disconcerting. Fortunately, the proceedings are transparent, enabling citizens to make informed voting choices with the hope that the process remains secure." (The Wright Report on Apple Podcasts. 2023).

Republican lawmakers strongly condemned President Biden for employing the federal government as a means of political vengeance after it was revealed that the Justice Department had pressed charges against the former President, Donald Trump, for his alleged mishandling of classified documents. Several State district attorneys who have been in contact with the White House have also initiated indictments in order to prevent the opposition frontrunner from being on the ballot. This is how low and corrupt our justice system has gotten in stooping to "lawfare." Providing context, this coincides with the previous president's significant popularity increase and emergence as a strong political rival in the upcoming elections. The Florida Governor, Mr. DeSantis, who was widely regarded as a strong potential challenger to Trump in the 2024 GOP presidential primaries, strongly condemned the unprecedented indictment. Another candidate, Vivek Ramaswamy, a constitutional lawyer, wealthy entrepreneur, and former presidential candidate, has expressed dissatisfaction with the unethical and immoral use of the justice department's power. Prior to this, no former president has ever been indicted on federal criminal charges in the annals of American history. "The utilization of federal law enforcement for political purposes poses a grave danger to a society that values freedom," DeSantis expressed on Twitter. "This matter requires immediate attention." We have noticed a conspicuous discrepancy in the application of legal onslaughts depending on an individual's political affiliation for a considerable duration of time. Looking ahead, DeSantis, Vivek, and Haley could soon be joining Trump's campaign if they are politically ambitious and willing to speak out about the weaponization of the system. The governor of Florida, a lawyer with judicial experience, and a naval officer inquired about the President's intense commitment to investigating Trump while showing little interest in Hillary or Hunter Biden. These judicial witchhunts continue today as the republican primary is upon us. Surprisingly, the masses are cognizant of the monumental breakdown in democracy, and the support for former President Trump has skyrocketed to astronomical numbers and continues to do so throughout the trials.

Kevin McCarthy, the former Speaker of the House, conveyed his apprehension regarding the recent events, characterizing it as a "bleak day" for the nation. He emphasized that former President Trump is being charged in connection with the uncovering of classified material at his Mar-a-Lago estate while under Secret Service purview. McCarthy highlighted various factual aspects concerning the resemblance and aggravated conditions related to President Biden's handling and protection of classified materials before assuming the presidency. Additionally, it was noted that President Biden is presently being investigated for his involvement with classified documents discovered at his Delaware residence in an unprotected garage drawer and an unprotected office in Chinatown. However, chatter and disposition from the Justice Department have gone dark. "It is morally indefensible for a President to accuse the main candidate who is opposing him," McCarthy asserted. Before his presidency, it was discovered that Biden maintained classified documents unsecured for a prolonged duration. After the Justice Department investigation was concluded, the special prosecutor made a judgment not to prosecute Biden because he was too old and forgetful to stand trial. In not so many words, he had cognitive issues. With this revelation, how can this individual be fit to execute the office of president? This is currently a comedy show that could turn into a horror show if V.P. Harris were to take the reigns. I couldn't make up this story even if I tried. Later on, former President Trump made a public announcement on social media stating that a federal grand jury had officially charged him with mishandling classified White House documents that were seized from his property in Florida. The legitimacy of our criminal justice system will face additional scrutiny in the preceding period until the next elections. In the absence of intervention, the ruling party will exploit the Judicial system as a tool to target and harm both regular citizens and Political Officials opposed to its views. There is even talk of bringing charges against the former President in Atlanta and New York on "trumped up" charges. Navigating this route is extremely dangerous for all involved. We have officially descended to the ranks of a corrupt third-world dictatorship[47]. I can guarantee that the public will see through the charade and political persecution.

The actions of the democratic party have gradually undermined constitutional safeguards and attacked the Bill of Rights over time. It is very evident for all to witness, especially with the current developments, where numerous protections that are explicitly guaranteed by the Constitution are in jeopardy, which is profoundly disconcerting, to say the least. An escalating, countrywide threat to the principles of fair legal proceedings and the First, Second, and Fifth Amendments of the U.S. Constitution is unfolding in America. Frequently, we come across news articles that emphasize the flaws of our legal system and the blatant miscarriage of justice. With the probability that I may be coining a new phrase, it seems that "Judicial Immorality" is running rampant in today's political landscape of lawfare and constitutional violations, that it has probably never been so crucial for the average electorate to be informed for the next election.

CONTROLLING THE NARRATIVE, MEDIA, AND SPEECH

The increasing division in public discussions and the rising lack of tolerance among citizens towards differing political perspectives (W. Bennett & S. Iyengar, 2008) jeopardize the effective operation of democratic procedures. Journalism is a fundamental indicator of the

---

[47] Dershowitz, Alan. *Get Trump: The Threat to Civil Liberties, Due Process, and Our Constitutional Rule of Law.* Simon and Schuster, 2023.

vitality of a democracy. The relationship between democracy and the media is commonly conceptualized as a social contract (Strömbäck, 2005). Due to the gravity of this mutually beneficial relationship, ensuring that media maintains impartiality and adheres to its core principles is paramount to the democratic process. Given that the majority relies on media as their primary information source, any bias present can distort the democratic dialogue, as evidenced today (Strömbäck, Jesper & Dimitrova, Daniela. (2006). The dissonance between the media, conservatives, and the public is perturbing and can result in irreversible harm to our republic. This arises from recognizing the significant bias exhibited by major news outlets and the Associated Press, which is both flagrantly skewed and opinionated. Anyone who denies this is either intentionally oblivious or so deeply radicalized in their hatred towards the Republican party that they endorse this manner of media coverage on Trump and conservatives, which is highly disturbing for the journalistic field, to say the least. Media are the watchdogs and information gatherers of our democratic society and not the enforcers and messaging outlets for political parties.

Indeed, they sincerely believe that it is beneficial for the nation when the AP and other prime-time media organizations exclusively emphasize the drawbacks of Trump's proposals, refrain from broadcasting primary election results and speeches, deemphasize the current president's state of cognitive decline, or disseminate false information about the former president and his staff. This was evident when they asserted that the former president had caused hardships for minority groups and that white supremacists were proliferating in society. At the same time, it was pushed that black men were being targeted and shot by law enforcement officers to create fear and panic in the African American communities. They conveniently forgot to remark that it was President Biden who targeted Black men with his legislation while in the Senate (Crime Bill, 1994)[48] and made racial statements consistently in public. Such coverage and assertions go far beyond mere bias in reporting and, in my book, are borderline treasonous acts. Patriotic Americans can send a message to these news outlets through the audience support they don't receive.

Controlling Information: Another arm of the shadow government is the Liberal Democratic Socialist media complex, which has a very deliberate mission statement to further the changing of the American social, political, and governance landscape[xxvii]. They collectively focus on controlling ideas and forming perceptions in the public forum without the masses having access to accurate and unbiased information. Any opposing voices that contradict the overall narrative and democratic socialist party doctrine must be railroaded, silenced, or demonized by whatever means necessary. American democracy is enhanced by the constitutional right of free speech, especially in the media. We, the people, depend on news organizations to investigate and inform us without coercing our thoughts and perceptions concerning the facts. In socialist and communist doctrine, this is a known and practiced state

---

[48] Biale, Noam, Elizabeth Hinton, and Elizabeth Ross. "The Discriminatory Purpose of the 1994 Crime Bill." *Harv. L. & Pol'y Rev.* 16 (2021): 115.

tool, "control the messaging and information; you control the people." It is very evident from actions unfolding in the Western world that the majority of the large media outlets serve the state as opposed to the people. Take, for instance, the news giants of CNN, MSNBC, CNBC, ABC, NBC, AP, BBC, and all their social media and print affiliates; when a particular event is of concern, or the democrat party controllers push a supported narrative, all the outlets parrot the message without question and disseminate the compromised information for public consumption. Seeing how every agency falls in step with the State-sponsored narrative without any scrutiny is disconcerting and very transpicuous as to the motives[xxviii]. The common theme among the "State Sponsored Media Complex" is always the same: we know best, we are the judges of truth, we decide what you should hear, we report only what we think is relevant, we decide on the messaging you receive, we are the architects of democracy, we are the freedom fighters of the underserved, we reserve the right to shut down all opposing speech as racist, or white supremacist propaganda, and damaging to democracy[49] as we see fit. Incidentally, this controlling of information is how socialist and communist states have historically reinforced party ideology and formed public perceptions in society.

The Democratic Party has a most effective circle of influencers and operators working towards America's destruction of democratic principles. They are the: (a).

---

[49] Cooper, Horace. *Put Y'all Back in Chains: How Joe Biden's Policies Hurt Black Americans*. Simon and Schuster, 2023.

Deep State, (b). Planted State Prosecutors, (c). Weaponized Justice Department, (d). Internal Revenue System, (e). Elected State and City Officials, (f). School boards, (g). Higher learning Institutions, (h). The Media Complex, and last but not least, (i). Liberal, Marxist, and Socialist sponsored Social Activists create physical and societal disruptions. If you were to regroup and analyze the past three years of political and societal turmoil, the architects of these disruptions would be clear. To name just a few, (a). The mass rioting and public property destruction in mainly democratic-run cities were induced by a coordinated media push of State narratives and false flag information campaigns, pushing claims of racial injustice and white police supremacy in society. (b). The shutting down of conservative and opposing arguments on almost all media outlets. (c). The censoring of all reporting and views on mass and social media sites, plus the demonization and government attacks on political opponents, including our former republican President, (d). The continued attempt to silence more than half of our nation (Labeled as the Deplorables) in the democratic process of voting in the next election by removing the people's choice for President through a weaponized judicial and justice system and (e). The continued silencing of conservative reporters, republican political pundits, and anyone who enlightens the public to opposing views or challenges the narrative[xxix] of the Liberal Democratic Socialist Complex will receive the wrath of the party's State actors and surrogates.

Now more than ever, we must demand and uphold the principles, protection, and preservation of the rights of individuals confronted with the full authority of the government, or our constitutionally formed Democratic Republic will cease to exist. Instituting this perversion of autocratic democracy is the underlying mission of the Democratic Party Machine, which includes the liberalist, Globalist, Socialist, Islamist, Social Activists, Climate Activists, and Marxist factions operating in concert with the Party to undermine our democracy, destroy our conservative values, and drastically change the construct of American Social Structure and Society.

FAILURE TO PROTECT AMERICAN STATES: A CONSTITUTIONAL PROTECTION

The playbook to change the voting demographics of America is well underway. On the contrary, the open border debacle is not by chance poor leadership but a deliberate ploy to absorb as many immigrants as possible while in power. The developments of the past few months are incredibly problematic, to say the least. Our present political party in power (the Democratic Party) has purposely negated its responsibility to follow one of the articles in the constitution regarding the protection of states. This section concentrates on **Article IV, Section 4** of the Constitution, protecting states[xxx]. Under Article Four, the federal government of the United States guarantees every state a democratic form of government and will protect each state against foreign invasion. States' rights pertain to the exclusive powers and privileges that state governments retain under the U.S. Constitution, in contrast to the federal government. State sovereignty has been a prominent issue in the United States for over two centuries, starting from the Constitutional Convention of 1787 and continuing through the Civil War of 1861, the civil rights movement of the 1960s, and the current marijuana legalization movement.

The principle of states' rights asserts that the 10th Amendment to the United States Constitution grants certain rights exclusively to individual states, which are not subject to the federal government's authority. Article IV, Section 4 of the U.S. Constitution establishes the specific arrangements governing the interactions among states and between individual states and the federal government. It delineates the duties and liabilities of the states, as well as the federal government's obligations towards the states. As mandated in Article IV, the federal government of the United States guarantees that every state upholds a democratic system of governance and is protected from external aggression and invasion. In Federalist No. 43, James Madison asserted that every society is responsible for safeguarding its constituent parts from invasion. The expression in question seems to provide protection for each state, not only against hostile foreign forces but also against the vengeful or ambitious actions of its more powerful neighboring states. The historical evidence from both ancient and modern confederacies clearly shows that the weaker members of the Union should not ignore the principles described in this article.

The Argument of Invasion: The comprehensive and equitable definition of the broad term *"invasion"* in Section 4 of Article IV encompasses any unauthorized and unlawful entry that causes or poses a threat to harm the interests of the invaded state or states and its citizens. In the absence of any explicit indication to the contrary, Section 4 does not impose any restrictions on the blanket term *"invasion"* (U.S. Const. art. IV, § 4). *"Without some indication to the contrary, general words (like all words, general or not) that are contained in any legal instrument are to be accorded their full and fair scope. They are not to be arbitrarily limited."* (Scalia & Garner, at 101.).

Article 1, Section 10. Texas is also justified in its actions to secure its established borders and state sovereignty under Article 1, Section 10 of the Constitution. "No State shall, without the Consent of Congress, lay any duty of Tonnage, keep Troops, or Ships of War in time of Peace, enter into any Agreement or Compact with another State, or with a foreign Power, or engage in War, unless actually invaded, or in such imminent Danger as will not admit of delay." (U.S. Const. art. I, § 10).[xxxi]

In December alone, an unprecedented number of over 300,000 undocumented immigrants crossed the southern border. Between October 2022 and September 2023, there were 3.1 million crossings along the U.S. southern border. Of that, an estimated 600,000 migrants were able to cross the border undetected, according to the Department of Homeland Security, and a majority of these immigrants are *"prime war fighting age."* According to DHS (Department of Homeland Security) reports, approximately 300,000 (+) migrants were granted humanitarian parole at the border and released into society[50]. They were given temporary

---

[50] Ingber, Matthew, Conner Muth, and Nathanael Hall. "The Migrant Crisis at the US Southern Border." (2022).

residency in the United States and issued work permits. This status is commonly extended to migrants originating from a restricted set of countries, such as Venezuela and Nicaragua.

The consequences of these detrimental liberal democratic social policies regarding unrestricted immigration have resulted in strong adverse reactions within society, with our urban communities experiencing the full impact of this influx. African American and Hispanic communities in liberal cities are experiencing disenfranchisement, with resources and funds being redirected towards programs that support illegal immigrants. This has an immediate detrimental effect on the Hispanic, Homeless veterans, and African American communities in terms of opportunities for entry-level and temporary employment, accessible community services, food, education, healthcare, and housing, to name a few. This issue cannot be concealed or obscured by the deceitful democrat media complex, as the residents are expressing their opinions openly, and numerous members of the democratic party have initiated legal action and are publicly critical of the city leaders.

The disturbing situation in our society is demonstrated by the displacement of American citizens and legal residents in numerous vulnerable communities with regard to social services (such as healthcare, dental care, housing, food, and clothing), policing efforts, infrastructure projects, and community resources (such as after-school programs, utilization of schools, government buildings, and recreation centers), which should be given priority to our residents. Ironically, Democratic politicians in sanctuary cities are expressing dissatisfaction and declaring emergencies due to the burden of supporting a population of 80-100,000+ undocumented residents. However, they refuse to recognize the economic and societal crisis and imminent danger that millions of illegals have caused to border states since the start of the Biden Presidency. They only cry foul when it is their city in the migrant crosshairs.

Biden Starts Border Crisis: It is well-documented that Biden, upon assuming office, promptly and publicly reversed the majority of President Trump's immigration policies, which were sound. Biden expressed his belief that the executive orders issued by the previous president were detrimental to our national security and our identity as a nation, especially in the realm of immigration. In addition to that, Biden has also issued 25 additional executive orders since assuming office on January 20th[51]. These orders encompass a range of actions, such as suspending the construction of the US-Mexico border wall initiated by Trump, as well as reaffirming the Deferred Action for Childhood Arrivals program, which provides work permits and deportation protection to individuals who were brought to the US illegally as children. After the reversal of former president Trump's republican policies on immigration, it sent a ripple effect throughout the world, announcing "open borders, come to America." The massive immigration debacle we are experiencing currently and the National

---

[51] Castaneda, Ernesto, Reilly Phelan, and Joseph Fournier. "The Backlash to the Backlash: The Moral and Electoral Failure of Anti-Immigrant Political Campaigns in the US 2018-2023." *Castañeda, Ernesto, Phelan, Reilly, Fournier, Joseph* (2024): 2018-2023.

Security threat to our nation is the direct result of those nonsensical Biden reversals. No smoke screen, political gotchas, or talking points are present here. The issues and resultant social impact are public for all to see and are deliberate by design. It fits into the larger picture of altering the voting base of power in future elections. Supporting this theory and adding more insult to injury, the attorneys for the immigration agencies of President Joe Biden acknowledged that the recently exposed "covert flights" did occur, but disclosure of secret migrant flight locations could potentially expose vulnerabilities for the 43 cities they were released into. Information regarding a program that secretly chartered flights for thousands of illegal immigrants from foreign airports to U.S. cities last year is withheld by Customs and Border Protection. According to the most recent evidence regarding the clandestine migration schemes of his administration, 320,000 (+) otherwise inadmissible migrants were granted entry to the country via air last year; however, their final destination remains unknown to even local law enforcement. This is a blatant act of irresponsible governance with unfathomable national security consequences[52].

The financial burden on the State of Texas's infrastructure and medical resources has been under siege, not to mention the increased cost associated with battling crime and drugs as a spinoff of the border issue. Texas took a stand, as it was declared by the State

---

[52] Pavlich, Katie. "Biden's Bad Faith on Border Opens Gap for Crime To Thrive." *The Hill* 30, no. 58 (2023): 20-21.

leadership that this was an "Invasion," which was causing egregious harm to their infrastructure and creating an imminent danger to its citizens. In the ensuing weeks, the Biden Administration engaged in a legal, media propaganda, and verbal war with Texas. On Thursday, a collective statement was issued by twenty-five (25) Republican governors expressing their support for Governor Abbott's efforts to safeguard American citizens from unprecedented numbers of undocumented immigrants, lethal substances such as fentanyl, and potential bad actors infiltrating our nation[53]. Regardless of the threat to America, the Justice Department and the Biden Administration contended that the fencing impedes the efforts of Border Patrol agents by presenting a risk to both migrants and law enforcement personnel.

Several illegal immigrants have sustained injuries from the barbed wire, they claim. Imagine the insensitivity and disregard for our citizens in this statement as the illegals overrun our border. It is only a matter of time before I fear these migrants will actually rush our border in mass and injure any State military or Texas law enforcement personnel. This act would set a bad precedent for border control going forward. At this specific location, the federal agents have been using it as a processing station; the border agents have refrained from deterring access but actively assisted in migrants illegal entry into the country, processing them and then subsequently released to proceed with their journey within the United States as

---

[53] Dwinell, Erin, and Hannah Davis. "The Costs of Biden's Border Crisis: The First Two Years."

ordered to by the Administration. Numerous civilian organizations have thoroughly documented this recurring trend, which involves the tracking of migrants to specific locations within the State for the purpose of recruitment by members of criminal cartels. It is essential to note Border Patrol local leadership and officers have stated on the record that there is no intention to remove these barriers, and the methods employed are effectively stemming the flow of illegal border crossings. An appropriate question to ask would be, what is the specific objective of the administration regarding the ongoing influx of undocumented immigrants?

The Texas initiative has successfully halted the influx at that specific site, which is a straightforward achievement. However, the Biden Administration is actively working to oppose and undermine this desired result. The administration has disregarded the National Security risks posed by this open border practice. Large numbers of men of military age from various countries, including those with hostile relations with the United States, are arriving in significant numbers on our territory. They do not arrive via maritime or aerial means as much but traverse the border on foot. This border has gained significant publicity in the "illegal migrant sphere" and also from publications distributed by American and UN-backed "NGOs" supporting open borders. Human caravans consisting primarily of military-aged adults, with a smaller number of young women and children, are able to freely travel through Latin America and reach our border due to the perceived lack of defense, the catch-and-release in America policy implemented by the Biden administration, and the ease of access. While no foreign invasion of American soil has occurred in recent history, a scenario similar to one is unfolding at the moment, with significant representation from China, Pakistan, Africa, Iran, Sudan, and other Arab nations.

State officials who corresponded with the Biden Administration in a letter of concern affirmed this fact in detail without any answer from the Administration. The participating members, all respected National Security experts, Timothy Healy, the ex-director of the Terrorist Screening Center, Kevin Brock, Chris Swecker, two ex-assistant directors of the FBI, and Mark Morgan, the former acting commissioner of US Customs and Border Protection and a former FBI superintendent, were part of the officials' group that made the statement out of concern. *"This letter from senior federal law enforcement officers is crystal clear that under Joe Biden's failed leadership, the United States is facing a dangerous invasion threatening our national security and our sovereignty,"* said State Rep. Elise Stefanik and other republican lawmakers.

CHAPTER 10
DIVISION OF THE HOMELAND

America is being targeted and divided into three categories: geographical, class, and ideological. This is a tactic being used by the Liberal Democratic Socialist complex to propagate retribalization and rebranding in American society as part of changing the social construct and separating from the unifying central ideology of our collective union. This invasive doctrine acting on our society is directed by the democratic party and proponents of the liberal new world order. It directly contributes to our nation's weakness and disintegration of unity as we pull away from our central traditions and ideology. Polarization, particularly in the realms of politics and race, has evolved into a self-perpetuating phenomenon, growing more potent as it engenders animosity and finds support from both the liberal and conservative factions of the political spectrum.

The American political system has been recently affected by a series of societal disruptions, which clearly demonstrate the harmful impact of polarization[54]. The United States stands out among nations due to its polarization, fueled by an electorate that displays a laissez-faire attitude, ignorance, and a revolutionary, unpatriotic stance toward American beliefs, traditions, and values.

[54] Shepperd, Taryn. "The United States' identity crisis: Emotions, image, and US foreign policy under Trump and Biden." In *Soft power and the future of US foreign policy*, pp. 59-77. Manchester University Press, 2023.

Prominent academics are raising questions that Americans have not been required to ponder since the era of the American Civil War in light of the emergence of a more communal and instinctive political style. Does the nation stand on the precipice of a political upheaval that could potentially lead to explicit discord, division, or a resurgence of authoritarian governance? Simply put, could we be witnessing the end of democracy as it is currently understood in the United States?

The traditional understanding of American politics, which reduces it to a partisan struggle between the left and right, Democrats and Republicans, overlooks the current historical milieu in light of the magnitude of these profound inquiries. A new facet of politics has surfaced recently, exposing a deep schism transcending traditional party lines and policy preferences. One perspective posits that an increasing number of Americans are becoming further divided along partisan lines due to the steadfast commitment of specific party influences, forcing ideologies counter to traditional belief systems, democratic processes, and moral behavior. This division potentially will lead to a political crisis, as the nation's democratic institutions and values are at risk. On the other hand, there are those who are committed to actively changing the social construct of America, regardless of the instability and destruction to the republic, and believe that America is an "imperfect union" to begin with. One of these contentious political division points in our political landscape is the liberal democratic socialist complex push for open borders, even though that social experiment has failed miserably in Europe, causing economic and social catastrophes. Many of these EU nations are abandoning this liberal ideology and globalist doctrine for nationalist-conservative policies. This border issue between a federal government that pushes open borders to change the national voting demographics regardless of the societal harm caused and States that are fighting to safeguard their constituents and economy might just be the straw that breaks the camel's back and forces more serious action regarding a modified form of civil war and separation of at least twenty-five States from the union.

Governor Greg Abbott of Texas and the Department of Justice (DOJ) have been involved in a multitude of legal conflicts concerning his tactics designed to deter migrants. The majority of Republican governors in the United States have endorsed a statement supporting Texas Governor Greg Abbott in his contentious dispute with the federal government regarding border control. The Republican Governors Association issued a statement on Thursday criticizing the Biden administration. It explicitly asserted that Texas has a constitutional right to defend itself. The letter, signed by twenty-five (25) Republican governors, stated, *"We stand in solidarity with our fellow Governor, Greg Abbott, and the State of Texas as we employ every tool and strategy at our disposal to secure the border, including razor wire fences."* The organization also stated, *"The Biden Administration has neglected its constitutional compact obligations to the states; as a result, Texas possesses every legal basis to safeguard the sovereignty of our states and the nation."* To bring this issue into focus, the Biden administration is utilizing the courts and creating divisions in the nation to advocate for illegals to invade and destroy our country and support the spread of transnational criminal enterprises[55]. The states, on the other hand, are trying to prevent this and support the safety and welfare of their citizens. There is no other way to interpret the current policy.

The Liberal Domestic Socialist Complex has mounted a massive disinformation campaign against Texas. Governor Abbott has implemented various measures to deter migrants in response to the escalating number of unauthorized border crossings, the increases in transnational criminal enterprises, and the overwhelming flow of deadly narcotics entering our nation. These measures include the deployment of the Texas National Guard assets, other Republican states' National Guards, and Law enforcement personnel, the installation of razor wire along specific segments of the southern border, and the utilization of a floating barrier in the Rio Grande River that is equipped with a circular saw-like contraption. The implementation of these successful strategies has led to a substantial reduction in border crossings across the majority of regions. It should be noted, however, that in areas where federal agencies manage easily accessible border crossings, the volume of traffic remains high. It is essential to mention, as factually reported in publicized statistics, that the level of illegal crossings and drug proliferation across the border has never been higher in the past few decades than in the previous three (3) Biden years to date. It would be offensive and a great disservice

---

[55] Kirkwood, R. Cort. "IMPEACH BIDEN ON HIS IMMIGRATION POLICIES." *The New American* 39, no. 17 (2023): 19-22.

not to recognize the selfless service of the many militia citizen civilian groups, including American Veterans, that have been voluntarily assisting in patrolling the US/Texas and other state border territories and continuing to serve in the capacity of our sworn oath in part: *"to support and defend the constitution of the United States against all enemies, foreign and domestic" (Soldiers handbook).* It is so bewildering to me how so many Americans are willing to sell out our nation to liberal, socialist, and even Islamist ideology without any conscious thought as to the ramifications of such action. It is an action against the United States of America and should not be tolerated. It is treason. If America falls, where do we go?

Democrat Border Deceit: The administration, in its media propaganda campaign, has stated that the "perilous" and "inhumane" measures employed by the Texas administration to secure its border are being directed at the migrants attempting to traverse the two countries. Unless I am grossly mistaken, isn't that the mission statement? It is a known and documented fact that the Biden administration can effectively stop the flow of illegal immigration into our country with the stroke of a pen. Doesn't he remember the same executive orders he rescinded with his pen? Probably can't remember a thing. This narrative that the "Republicans are stalling" is outrageous and a downright mistruth. The media complex is repeating the White House's message that blames Congress for the border crisis. It is essential to analyze the facts thoroughly before making assumptions. The Biden administration has the power to address the border situation through executive action. Still, Democrats will choose to delay this to advance their strategic political goals[56]. President Joe Biden signed executive orders shortly after taking the reigns to begin dismantling former President Donald Trump's stringent immigration policies, with a focus on stopping the wall from being completed and removing border restrictions for illegal entry. "I'm not making new law. I'm eliminating bad policy," Biden stated as he revoked the former administration's policies with the stroke of a pen.

Immediate reinstatement of the authority utilized by former President Trump to secure the border, which was rescinded by President Biden upon assuming office, is possible. In regards to the Democratic Party's "Bill Showboating" misinformation campaign, which is echoed verbatim by the party's media machine, it is illogical to support the legislation due to the inclusion of so much extraneous material (funding Ukraine) that it becomes impractical to approve. Consider a border bill that does not include astronomical funding for Ukraine. What does our border have to do with Ukraine? Even their politicians have stated on air that we need this signed to fund Ukraine. No, we need to be talking about our border and amend the exorbitant numbers on entry to, say, 200 refugees per month(estimate), not 5500 per day, which is preposterous. That amounts to over 2.2M refugees per year plus our legal entries[57]. That is unsustainable.

---

[56] Anderson, Jeffrey H. "Impeachable?; Joe Biden's refusal, as president, to enforce immigration law and secure the nation's border deserves as much scrutiny as his behavior as vice president." *City Journal* (2023).

[57] Marsai, Viktor. "Gatekeeper Countries—Key to Stopping Illegal Immigration."

We have a viable and fair legal immigration system that must be returned to for stability to be realized. The determination of immigration quotas should not be arbitrary; instead, they should be supported by the level of economic and social strain each state can or is willing to endure without compromising citizen benefits. To add insult to injury, the United States allocates taxpayer funds to support organizations that enable unauthorized migration across our borders. The UN agencies participating in the operation, namely the Office of the UN High Commissioner for Refugees (UNHCR), the International Organization for Migration (IOM), and the UN Children's Fund (UNICEF), are carrying out registrations in person. The UN Secretary-General expressed his approval of the new Biden administration's actions regarding migrants and refugees during a photo opportunity. Additionally, the head of the UN Refugee Agency (UNHCR) congratulated the President and Vice President on assuming office and promised to collaborate with them to enhance international assistance for refugees and their admission into the United States, which President Trump had curbed.

We are accommodating a significant number of illegal migrants, as well as refugees, at the cost of our own citizens. What is the situation regarding our "refugees" residing in urban areas, our homeless population, our disabled and homeless veterans, and Americans living below the poverty threshold? With our destructive Democratic Socialist policies, we are continuing to disenfranchise the African American, Hispanic, Asian, Veteran, and Caucasian segments of our society that operate in the economically vulnerable range. Without proper opportunities, education incentives, jobs, food, medical care, and housing assistance, we will lose these citizens to the ranks of the homeless and destitute in America. Instead of addressing these critical areas, the administration provides financial support to non-governmental organizations (NGOs) operating in the southern region to assist and encourage individuals from other countries to violate our immigration laws and flood an already saturated environment. How is this even considered acceptable in the United States? Do African Americans and Hispanics, in particular, living in urban centers that are already stretched thin for resources, understand the gravity of how they are being railroaded? Have there been any concerns raised? Are we that naive, America? How can the United Nations, an external organization, exert influence over American immigration policies and aid in the mass overrun at our territorial boundary? I contend that the United States should either disengage from the United Nations and NATO or prioritize selective programs that provide advantages for the country and its citizens. Priority must be given to our citizens, no question. Why should we give our votes to a government that neglects its responsibility to protect and uphold the welfare of its citizens and our Constitution? Unfortunately, the fact remains that our nation must take precedence in the international arena, given that every other country is preoccupied with its own interests. This mindset does not imply isolationism but rather an America-first presumption. America can and must be engaged globally but with shrewdness, placing national interests paramount in policy making.

The government's primary obligations are to its citizens and residents; there should be no room for debate on the contrary. Currently, illegal immigrants are disenfranchising our citizens, which cannot be tolerated. It is beyond comprehension that the Democratic Party would attempt to act as if nothing has transpired while displaying such a flagrant disregard for American citizens. In March 2024, there is a discernible shift of African Americans and Hispanics from the Democrat Party to the Republican Party, particularly due to their support for Donald Trump and his "America First" policies. This is the outcome of decades of negligent policies by the Democratic party, with political candidates attempting to appeal to voters by using stereotypical symbols such as hot sauce and fried chicken and making promises to provide undocumented immigrants with access to our taxpayer-funded benefits. Additionally, the party has made a significant error in underestimating the intelligence of these influential demographics. The Democratic establishment was confident that African American and Hispanic voters would continue to support the party unquestioningly, particularly due to the relentless dissemination of misleading narratives by their media representatives. The nauseating realization for Black Americans is that the party has been using them without consideration for their cultural progress for decades, leading to a sense of deceit and pain. Democrat politicians and elitists routinely misjudge the intellectual capacity of the "Black culture," assuming that Blacks can be easily manipulated through insincere pledges and gratuitous offerings, as has been the pattern throughout history. Undoubtedly, the Democrats would have orchestrated an extensive disinformation campaign in collaboration with the Democratic media complex to manipulate their voting base.

Recognizing the change in political support within their major voting blocs, democratic elitists resorted to opening borders and constructing an additional powerful voting base in an effort to alter the long-term voting demographics of America. As a consequence of these ill-conceived policies, the occurrence of "Migrant Crime" has escalated. It has spread from border states to Georgia and states in the Mid-East U.S. via government resettlement programs that disregard background and character checks. The FBI, by its own admission, is alarmed by the expansion of the Venezuelan gang "Tren de Aragua" into American cities; they have issued warnings regarding a possible merger with MS13. There is also an increase in the cartel infrastructure expansion in small-town America and a crime-terrorism nexus that is emerging and quite troubling. These policies serve as evidence of the Democratic Party's intentions to create an autocratic style of government shrouded under the democratic banner. Securing a permanent and overwhelming voter base will ensure continued long-term power, even under the democratic facade of being a democratically elected government under fair elections. It is time to demonstrate to the African American, Hispanic, and all other voting blocs that Republicans are committed to gaining their support and allegiance for the greater good of the nation, not through manipulation but by implementing policies that treat their culture and all cultures equally[xxxii]. We as a nation have to get the various internal threats to our national security under check or suffer the consequences of mass terror and the destabilization of America and a relatively safe environment in which to raise our families. Republicans must get back to basics, educate the electorate, and start correcting the shortfalls in society rapidly.

HATE NARRATIVE AND DIVISION PROPAGATED BY THE DEMOCRAT AND MEDIA COMPLEX

Civil War Talk: Numerous individuals are expressing their opinions on this subject in the media[58]. The narrative has already been formulated and is being promoted by the usual Democrat-controlled talk show pundits as a form of "Trump and Republican White American Christian Uprising." By closely observing articles, political pundits, and news outlets, it becomes evident how the narrative is being shaped, and the talking points are continuously being evaluated for their resonance and impact on the public. This is done to determine the most persuasive messaging that can distract, instill fear, and create instability during the election cycle. We as a nation have already been exposed to the so-called democrat party version of "peaceful protest."

While perusing different media platforms, such as YouTube, podcasts, and radio talk shows, I have come across articles and absurd remarks regarding white Christians, American patriots, the deplorable, and so much racially inspired rhetoric. Additionally, there is the claim that the number of guns in predominantly white states

---

[58] Marche, Stephen. *The next civil war: Dispatches from the American future.* Simon and Schuster, 2023.

surpasses those in minority states, and whites are ready to use them in some "insurrection." It is also suggested that Republicans possess a greater quantity of firearms compared to Democrats and have the necessary skills to utilize them. Furthermore, there is the insinuation that genuine American patriots might need to employ violence as a means to safeguard our nation. This list of observations continues indefinitely. The media is exacerbating racial tensions and fostering animosity between different ethnic groups, instilling fear, particularly among minorities, notably African Americans, and inciting them against the perceived "White Oppressor." Several articles cite statistics indicating that white supremacists are preparing for a confrontation, possessing over 40 million firearms in predominantly white Christian southern states. In my view, the liberal democratic socialist apparatus has already manipulated the media and public opinion in its favor. I wonder, is this the same racist America that voted in power a Black President for two consecutive terms, and a country that has had Black Secretaries of State representing America overseas, or Black congressional, senatorial, and ambassadors representing our government, and last but not least, high ranked African American military leaders in our armed forces and the joint chiefs of staff?

Step Back and Observe the Hate and Poisonous Ideology of the Liberal Democratic Socialist Movement: This section may anger those who operate in the bubble of deniability, but it contains important points to analyze and absorb regarding the forced racial animus, deceptive political smokescreen and what the agitation and division of America could manifest into. America could potentially be eventuating the reality of a quasi-civil war based on race, ideology, citizenry safety, and the preservation of our American Judeo-Christian social construct. Apart from witnessing the liberal activism, Islamist indoctrination of our youth, democrat-orchestrated Soros-funded destruction of our cities, the invasion of marauding rioters in our communities, and the vandalization of our national monuments and buildings, other more subtle plays were being deployed[59] to destabilize the nation. The liberal socialist democrat media complex was employed to continuously push narratives by the democrat echo chamber saturating the information space with labeling "White Christian Males" as the evil segment of society who are deemed as a significant threat to the democracy of America and the evil, deplorable "White people" and "Republicans" who spread racism and hate crimes throughout America. Surprisingly, this was not the demographic makeup of the rioters, lawbreakers, and aggressors during the year of destruction. Any Republicans, reporters, or public figures that stood up and denounced the actions of the left were lumped into the evil portfolio along with the flyover states of whites, veterans, conservatives, Judeo-Christian believers, and hard-working deplorables that Obama and Hillary said "cling to their guns and bible" were castigated harshly, and canceled. Many lost their livelihoods, families, and positions in society. The Democrats upheld the rioting and criminal marauding in

---

[59] Smith, Candis Watts. "The Making of a Mantra: Americans' Racial Ideologies in the Era of Black, Blue, and All Lives Matter." *Journal of Race, Ethnicity, and Politics* 8, no. 3 (2023): 371-396.

cities with law enforcement given the stand-down order by democrat city leaders. Ever wonder how many were charged with the rioting and destruction of cities and national monuments? Guess?

In today's society, the liberal democratic socialists claim institutional racism is rampant in society, whites have "white privilege," and they are labeled and blamed for every atrocity that happened in history. During the riots, gangs of blacks were going into white communities and giving notice that they were coming back to claim "what was theirs." It is a fact that liberal DAs stood down, law enforcement was ordered not to engage, and no significant measures were taken to stop the riots, public destruction, defacing of monuments, or enforcement of laws. Black Lives Matter, a Marxist ideology social activist group, caused riots, burned buildings, destroyed vehicles, including police vehicles, and chanted hate-mongering speech to "kill police (pigs)," "whites," and "political rivals." Cities burned, minorities and whites alike lost their businesses, and most cities to date have not recovered. Democrats and government officials have proposed the concept of "reparations for slavery" to exacerbate racial animosity and division in our society. This proposal, aimed at addressing the historical injustices of chattel and de facto slavery that started in the 1500s, is undeniably absurd. Those advocating for it must join a long queue of other proposals. Regrettably, the institution of slavery has existed in the world since ancient times, predating biblical history. In 1981, the Islamic Republic of Mauritania became the final country in the world to officially prohibit slavery. As late as 2007, it implemented legal measures to prosecute individuals engaged in this practice. Although slavery was formally banned, approximately 40 million people were still subjected to enslavement globally in 2019-20, with children accounting for 26% of this figure. Currently, more than half of enslaved individuals are working as coerced laborers, primarily in sweatshops and manufacturing plants owned by a country's private industry, catering to Western customers. Human trafficking is a modern form of slavery that occurs in developed countries, while debt bondage, which encompasses child soldiers, forced marriages, and captive domestic servants, is widespread in developing nations. The incidence of sexual slavery, allegedly endorsed by Islam, has increased in parallel with the global escalation of jihadism.

The media pushes narratives to label these "white males and Christians" as racist groups and haters of immigrants, especially Hispanic immigrants who presumably took away America's rights and were overpopulating their country. Following that line of reasoning, it is then justified to demonize whites, hold them accountable for everything, including slavery, and also discriminate against them, as Black and minority people can't be racist against the white culture. This ideology is prevalent among the younger generation, as witnessed in the media and college street interviews. This is yet another attempt to divide our cultures, segregate society, and drive wedges of hate between Americans[60]. It is time to set the record straight about national sacrifices and the "Evil White Christian Men" we are supposed to fear as minorities.

---

[60] Hackney, Jennifer K. "Hispanics and Extremism: A Double-Edged Sword."

Addressing the Hate of White America Rhetoric and Narratives Pushed by Liberal Democrats and Socialist Activists: Before we continue, In today's peculiar society, there is a particular fact and a point that needs to be driven home and that I need to address: I Identify as an American-of East Indian descent-Male-Heterosexual-Conservative-Immigrant-Veteran (I identify through fact, genetics, and affiliation, not whimsical feelings, or dress up), and I am disgusted with the widespread identity and gender politicking, liberal-wing Marxist-socialist-democratic ideologies that have weakened society and created a generation of ingrates oblivious to sacrifices of others so they can be "stupid." Christians, non-Christians, immigrants, men, women, Native Americans, and African Americans have all made significant contributions and sacrifices in defending the United States since its establishment as a sovereign nation. However, there is a group among them whose sacrifice is of even greater magnitude: the "White American Christian Male." To comprehend the significance of the situation and pay tribute to those who have made the highest sacrifice for our country in the name of "freedom and equality," one must assess the magnitude of this issue by observing or visiting our national military and veteran cemeteries as well as the foreign military cemeteries managed by the United States. Arlington National Cemetery and Gettysburg National Cemetery are the two United States National Cemetery System[61] cemeteries

---

[61] Wanger, Allison Lynn. *" These Honored Dead": The National Cemetery System and the Politics of Cultural Memory Since 1861.* The University of Iowa, 2015.

overseen by the United States Army. There are around 400,000 people buried in Arlington County, Virginia, covering an area of 639 acres. The 164 cemeteries in the United States and its territories comprise the United States National Cemetery System. The National Cemetery Administration of the United States Department of Veterans Affairs (VA) manages 148 national cemeteries. The Department of the Army supervises two national cemeteries: Arlington National Cemetery and the United States Soldiers' and Airmen's Home National Cemetery. The National Park Service (NPS) manages 14 national cemeteries associated with historic sites and battlefields[62].

We must also look at those honored patriots who gave their all but never returned to the homeland. They rest forever on foreign soil in cemeteries maintained by the United States American Battle Monuments Commission. We still honor and mourn the loss of our great patriots, who are not forgotten. Many of my readers might not be aware of these cemeteries filled with mostly "White Christian Men" who sacrificed so all races and religious backgrounds could be free in America:

1- The Suresnes American Cemetery is a United States military burial ground in Suresnes, Hauts-de-Seine, France. It is the burial site of 1,541 American soldiers who died in WW1.

2- St. Mihiel American Cemetery and Memorial are situated on the western outskirts of Thiaucourt in

---

[62] American Battle Monuments Commission. *American Memorials and Overseas Military Cemeteries*. American Battle Monuments Commission, 1985.

Meurthe-et-Moselle, France. The cemetery spans 40.5 acres and holds the graves of 4,153 American military personnel who died during World War I.

3- The Somme American Cemetery and Memorial in Picardie, France, is a cemetery managed by the American Battle Monuments Commission. The cemetery houses the graves of 1,844 American military personnel who died during WWI.

4- The Sicily–Rome American Cemetery and Memorial is a World War II American military cemetery in Nettuno, near Anzio, Italy. Adjacent to the pool lies a vast expanse of 7,861 headstones commemorating American military casualties from World War II.

5- Rhone American Cemetery and Memorial in France. The cemetery, named after the Rhone River, where the majority of those buried fought and perished, was established in 1956 and holds 858 American war casualties from World War II.

6- The Oise-Aisne American Cemetery and Memorial is a United States military burial ground located in the northern region of France. The site holds the graves of 6,013 American soldiers who perished in this region during World War I, with 597 unidentified. Additionally, there is a monument for 241 Americans who went missing in battles in the exact location and were never found.

7- The Normandy American Cemetery and Memorial in Colleville-sur-Mer, Normandy, France, designated a World War II cemetery and memorial dedicated to

American soldiers who lost their lives in Europe during the war. The area spans 172.5 acres and holds 9,388 burials.

8- The Netherlands American Cemetery and Memorial is a military cemetery dedicated to Second World War casualties. Just over 8,000 American casualties, whose exact number fluctuates due to identification and other factors, are buried, with most of them having died in battles nearby.

9- The Meuse-Argonne American Cemetery in France covers an area of 130.5 acres. The cemetery houses 14,246 American military personnel who perished mainly during the Meuse-Argonne Offensive, making it the most significant American military burial ground in Europe.

10-The Manila American Cemetery and Memorial is a military burial ground in Taguig, Metro Manila. It has the highest number of graves for U.S. personnel who died during World War II, totaling 17,206.

11-The Luxembourg American Cemetery and Memorial is a burial ground for American military personnel who died in World War II. It is situated in Hamm, Luxembourg City, Luxembourg. The cemetery holds 5,074 American war dead.

12-The Lorraine American Cemetery and Memorial is a burial ground for American military personnel from World War II near Saint-Avold, Moselle, France. The cemetery holds 10,489 American soldiers who were killed in action, making it the second largest

American burial site in Europe after the Meuse-Argonne American Cemetery, which has 14,246 World War I casualties.

13-The Henri-Chapelle American Cemetery and Memorial is a World War II American military cemetery located in eastern Belgium. The cemetery was established in 1960 and held the remains of 7,992 American soldiers.

14-The Florence American Cemetery and Memorial is approximately 7.5 miles (12 kilometers) south of Florence, Italy. 4,402 individuals interred here are primarily from the Fifth Army, who perished during the battles that ensued after the seizure of Rome in June 1944. Additional casualties occurred during the intense combat in the Apennines until May 2, 1945.

15-The Flanders Field American Cemetery and Memorial is a World War I burial ground located in Waregem, Belgium. The Flanders Field American Cemetery honors 411 United States Armed Forces service members.

16-The Epinal American Cemetery and Memorial is located in France. The 49-acre cemetery and memorial are situated on a plateau with a view of the Moselle River in the foothills of the Vosges Mountains. The cemetery holds the graves of 5,255 American military personnel who died in the campaigns from northeastern France to the Rhine and into Germany during World War II.

17-The Cambridge American Cemetery is located in England. The cemetery, spanning 30.5 acres and situated between the villages of Coton and Madingley, houses 3,809 headstones, plus the remains of 3,812 servicemen, including airmen who perished over Europe and sailors from North Atlantic convoys. The Wall of the Missing lists 5,127 servicemen who are unaccounted for, many of whom perished in the Battle of the Atlantic or the strategic air bombardment of northwest Europe.

18-Brookwood American Cemetery and Memorial is located in the British Isles. The only American Military Cemetery of World War I in the British Isles is situated in Brookwood, approximately 28 miles southwest of London. This 4.5-acre memorial cemetery is the final resting place for 468 American World War I service members, including 41 Unknowns.

19-St. James American Cemetery in France. Most of the 4,410 American soldiers buried at this 28-acre cemetery died during the Normandy and Brittany campaigns of 1944 in World War II. This site also commemorates the names of over 450 individuals whose remains were never found. Ninety-five headstones commemorate the graves of unidentified individuals, with two of these graves holding the remains of two unidentified individuals that could not be distinguished. There are 20 cases where two brothers are buried next to each other.

20-Ardennes American Cemetery and Memorial is in Belgium. This 90.5-acre cemetery and memorial are one of 14 cemeteries for American World War II dead located on foreign soil. It holds the graves of 5,329 U.S. servicemembers. Many perished during Nazi Germany's last significant attack in the west, the Battle of the Bulge, while others died during the advance towards the Rhine and across Germany. 60% of the individuals interred in this cemetery were American airmen.

21-Aisne-Marne American Cemetery and Memorial in France. The 42-acre WWI cemetery is situated in the foothills of Northern France and serves as the burial ground for casualties from the Battle of Belleau Wood and the Battle of Château-Thierry, where numerous Americans perished. There are 2,288 burials in the cemetery, with 251 of them having unidentified remains.

Point To Remember: The argument of sacrifice to the nation for the preservation of freedoms guaranteed under our constitution and the betterment of all Americans is that among the graves and memorials of servicemembers across the United States and abroad, some headstones do depict, in a lesser quantity, of equal importance, a representation of other faiths and racial constitution that made the ultimate sacrifice. **However, by an overwhelming and saddening number, the majority of the remaining graves bear the Cross (Christians), and the remains of white males, who comprise the majority ethnicity of the American service members laid to rest;**

and yes, as I referenced, other races are represented, but to a lesser extent and also never forget, many women are also represented in these honored fields of sacrifice. It would be an honorable task to see which racial makeup comes in second. May God bless and keep them all.

All patriots on these hallowed grounds are perpetually united for one purpose: the "defense and love of their homeland, families, and preservation of all American's freedom." Consequently, all individuals of every generation must recognize the dedication and sacrifices of these patriots, especially the most significant group that made such sacrifices—the "White Judeo-Christian Male"—who have been instrumental in safeguarding the freedom and sovereignty of the United States of America to the benefit of all over several generations, and alongside all represented races in America, they continue to pay that debt forward. It is because of this understanding of sacrifice, respect for our fallen comrades and America, our nation home, that overwhelming disdain is felt towards the masses of ingrate and disrespectful souls that seek to compromise our safety, embrace Islamism, divide, destroy, and reconstruct our American way of life and enjoyed freedoms guaranteed by our founding fathers in the constitution. This Political, Racial, and Ideological toxicity is counterproductive to preserving our American way of life and must come to an end.

Honoring the sacrifices of those who came before us, who entrusted us with the responsibility of continuing the fight to preserve the nation, is a monumental responsibility. This group, even though a product of their environment, is definitely not the "Evil White Christians" the liberal democratic socialist machine wants you to hate, are they? American whites and, to a lesser number, Black Americans and other race's heritage are filled with the blood of patriots. So, when you decide to go on a white-hating spree, tearing down our national monuments and destroying our cities, remember the veterans and patriots who are still alive and those who have sacrificed for the love of the country and the desire for freedom are watching and taking note. From the Civil War to today, white Christian Americans have been dying for our freedom and the nation. **"Thank you, America"**. This might be a more fitting sentiment before spewing your hate for America and ignorantly demonstrating in the streets under a false "social activism" smokescreen for an oppressive and murderous terrorist organization that intends to eradicate you and your freedoms in the West. It seems that many in this generation operate under a warped ideology, have the propensity to be ignorant, and enjoy being used as scapegoats by state and non-state actors with more nefarious motives in mind. Violence and hatred are not the way to national unity. It is advisable not to awaken the eagle. " This we will defend."[xxxiii]

Another narrative being circulated is the racism between Latin Americans[63], Caribbean, Asian, and Black Americans[xxxiv]. This is to counter the increased crossover of Blacks to the Republican party and the dissatisfaction

---

[63] Pirtle, Whitney N., Breanna Brock, Nonzenzele Aldonza, Kaline Leke, and Dallas Edge. ""I didn't know what anti-blackness was until I got here": The unmet needs of Black students at Hispanic-serving institutions." *Urban Education* 59, no. 1 (2024): 330-357.

and realization of Black America that they have been used for their votes only and are now being discarded. Black votes have been purchased over the decades by the democrats, social activists, and liberal elitists, offering "free phones, social handouts, and talking point promises." What has Black America gotten in return for their party loyalty, "lies, increased poverty, increased crime, lower economic earnings, lower home ownership, lower education, government dependency, victimhood indoctrination, and fewer opportunities." One of the latest PEW reports regarding African Americans in 2023[64] states that 50% of all Black Americans earned less than $50K per year, and a third (1/3) earned over $75K per year. Only 39% of Black Americans have married couple households, and of that, only 5% have men as heads of households. Regarding education, which is conducive to better salaries, only 26% of Black Americans above 25YO possess a bachelor's degree or higher, and only 42% graduated high school. Black American population in 2022-23 are reported at 47.9 Million, of which 2.9 Million are Black Hispanic, and 5.4 Million are Non-Hispanic Black. Homeownership for Black America stands around 45% in 2022-23 *(PEW. Lopez, Mark Hugo, and Mohamad Moslimani. "Key facts.. (2023)"*

Action Required: Americans have debated and argued for over a century regarding the existence of a correlation between criminal behavior and racial identity. Socioeconomic factors such as drug exposure, poverty, and residence in economically depressed areas are

---

64 Lopez, Mark Hugo, and Mohamad Moslimani. "Key facts about the nation's 47.2 million Black Americans." (2023).

identified as contributors to racial disparities in crime rates, according to research. In attempting to explain these disparities in crime rates between racial groups, several criminology theories have been proposed, including conflict theory, strain theory, general strain theory, social disorganization theory, macrostructural opportunity theory, social control theory, and subcultural theory. That is enough theories for one issue. Governments (Democrat/Republican), agencies, and organizations explore theories Ad Nauseam, but nothing happens year after year. How about eliminating all the fluff for once and getting the issue fixed? State the issue, identify the adverse resultant effects that are present, assess the operating environment and variables acting upon the issue that creates said resultant effects, and then mitigate each variable away. After mitigating all perceived risks of recurrence, propose safety measures or policy initiatives to maintain the desired outcome. It is now time for action and engagement with entities that can facilitate the recommended policy and secure resources necessary to effect change.

Regardless of the theories used to figure out what causes "Black" crime and getting bogged down in tons of useless data and years of debating, I would venture to say in a similar environment with comparable forces acting on the individuals that, the same would be for "White" crime, "Brown" crime, or just "human" crime. A crime is a crime; people are people, and reactions to insecurity are similar regardless of color schemes social scientists want to apply. I hope you are following my thought trajectory. We need to simplify and focus on the contributory factors that create an

223

environment conducive to criminal enterprise and remove those factors from play. Then, appropriately fill the void created by instituting safeguards to prevent reversion and opportunities for advancement and socio-economic stability, including human security (healthcare, judicial integrity, active policing, habitat infrastructure, housing access, education, employment opportunity, and community safety). The focus should be on providing residents with access to a good standard of quality of life, especially in high-risk crime areas, which are mainly saturated urban housing centers. I absolutely refuse to believe, based on knowledge and awareness, that the social, educational, and economic inequality faced by the African American and economically depressed subsection of our population cannot be corrected in short order if those in power were inclined to do so. The elitists do not want to relinquish the control and power held over this unfortunate segment of our society. Under a government that is not conducting social experimenting with our population, and where opportunities are available for all to benefit from, and access to these opportunities is across the board, we would have had better stats in the Black communities or any of the communities as a whole. It is indisputable that America is at its highest, most potent stage when all her individual cultures are aligned under one flag and recognized as one people, "Americans." The healing and understanding of the beast's true nature must start from within before change can occur. Individually as a race, together as a culture, and identifying under one flag makes us Americans, so we must come to terms with our individuality, shared belief structures, and defining purpose to forge ahead as a unified nation for change to occur for the better.

The elaborate question here is, which political party machine is pushing a destructive narrative for the nation? The Liberal Democratic Socialist Complex projects a revolutionary stance of (a). cancel culture activists, (b). bills targeting eradication of our constitution, (c). stacking the Supreme Court, (d). accession of more states to the union for party base dominance, (e). marginalizing Christianity and religious freedom, (f). disbanding the Electoral College, (g). changing voting laws and congressional rules to benefit manipulation, (h). open border with unrestricted entry to change voter demographics, thus securing a perpetual democratic party, (i). monocratic or autocratic ideology disregarding constitutional governance practices, (j). a deviation from a judicial system based on accountability and crime deterrence through punishment, (l). reconstructing our American social construct, erasing a Judeo-Christian belief framework, and replacing it with a Liberal Democratic Socialist World Order (k). beguile the African American base and employ cultural sabotage to maintain dependency, ignorance, and control (l). establishing a central bank digital currency to monopolize monetary functions, and last but not least, (m). the weaponization of government institutions to reinforce conformity of the citizenry and cessation to opposing ideology. I think we are in trouble, America.

Racial Manipulation by the Left: The level of destructive ideologies that instigate racial hatred within our American culture propagating racial bifurcation, reinforced through extreme disinformation campaigns in twisting the facts and reality of "Police killing Blacks," "Black Incarceration," "Systemic Racism," and "Racial Disparity in Society," has been highly influential in creating a victimhood syndrome in the culture. This psychological tactic of controlling complex social dynamics through herd mentality, agitation of the African American community, creating a false dichotomy, a call to action by activists, embedding mistrust of differing views, and most importantly, identifying a political doctrine and followers to direct and unload all the hatred and oppression toward (Caucasians). This purposeful disregard of the actual published statistics and facts surrounding the orchestrated decline of the African American culture for the past decades to date is unconscionable.

The Liberal Democratic Socialist Complex is aggregately responsible for the horrendous "Black on Black" shooting deaths, destruction of the inner cities support structures, institutional, social, and economic displacement of "Blacks," lack of economic opportunity, and the overall descent into anarchy. Here are some statistical facts published by many independent outlets, such as the Crime Prevention Research Center. Unfortunately, The FBI has admittedly not enough participation from law enforcement agencies, so their project statistics are inaccurate. The left-leaning organizations take the data and manipulate it to create a false perception for stoking the flames of racism in law enforcement. I suggest telling the Black community in the inner cities that there is no black-on-black crime, no drug epidemic, that the crime wave they live in daily doesn't exist, or that there is no money for opportunities, infrastructure, or support for their neighborhoods and see what the response is, especially since the myth of no funds for Inner-city revitalization has been busted wide open with the recent doling out of millions of dollars to repatriate illegal immigrants. Oh, how uplifting it would be if all those millions of dollars were used to uplift the inner cities, create opportunity zones, enable entrepreneurs' capital, improve transportation, education, and housing infrastructure, and institute proactive policing initiatives and residence programs. This should finally open the eyes of African Americans, and instead of giving their vote away, make politicians work to earn their votes.

Take your pick and do the research. In 2022-2023, the murder rate among blacks is 653% higher than the murder rate for whites. The murder rate for Hispanics is 65% higher than for whites. Nor are those numbers that much of an outlier. From 1990 through 2022, the black murder rate averaged 569% higher than whites, and the number for Hispanics was 57% higher. The majority of the black murder rate stems from black-on-black conflict involving inter and intra-gang rivalry, drug territorial claims, drive-by, and domestic violence. Local district attorney races have been the primary target of the Soros-backed renegade prosecutor movement, which has sought out, recruited, and funded candidates in these races.

Community safety is compromised as a result of the rogue prosecutor movement's support for criminal advocates who disregard the rights of victims. However, this movement ignores the requirements of those who are

227

actually victims, portraying criminals as victims and law enforcement as the perpetrators of wrongdoing. Many on the left are well aware of the devastation that has resulted from their liberal stance on crime in the cities where these policies have been implemented. A significant increase in crime rates, particularly violent crimes like murder, has been observed in communities where left-leaning individuals have adopted "progressive" measures such as the elimination of cash bail, reduction of police funding, non-prosecution of certain crimes, early release of convicted felons, and substantial decrease in the prison population. This correlation is supported by empirical evidence.

Liberal Democrat politicians and their followers recognize that under their watch, they have a volatile and mishandled foreign policy, escalating crime rates, particularly the occurrences of black-on-black shootings in urban regions including Chicago, New York, Philadelphia, the Democratic strongholds of the West Coast, and Washington DC, in addition to the pervasive infiltration of bad actors and illegal "gotaways" in the homeland, present a formidable obstacle to their electoral opportunities. The Democratic Party cannot run on its disastrous domestic, immigration, crime, economic, or foreign policy accomplishments, as there are no notable mentions. The party has no option but to spin the facts and spend millions of dollars to push false narratives attacking the Republican policy, congress, and, of course, demonizing white Christians before the elections. Oh, don't forget the identity politicking of race-bating and trans inequality and the pandering to fringe groups, with the public displays of eating more fried chicken, collard greens, and hot sauce, and now they'll have to include Mexican and Latin American foods. Well, at least they are eating good food.

A growing number of African American voters are becoming cognizant of the incongruous implementation of regulations and tenets affecting their communities. According to the results of recent polls, voters place a significant amount of importance on the issue of rising crime, which ranks second only to widespread inflation and the economy's poor performance. The electorate is seeing through the Obfuscation, finger-pointing, and shifting blame, which are long-standing political tactics that the Left continues to use, as referenced previously. Particularly in urban areas, where there was a convergence of unscrupulous prosecutors, advocacy for reducing police funding, failure to prosecute crimes, and the vilification and disheartening of law enforcement, the combined impact of these occurrences significantly influenced and largely established the circumstances that led to an increase in criminal activity throughout a significant portion of the nation. This was especially common in urban areas where rioting, destruction of public property, carjackings, and robberies have created a state of anarchy for hard-working, law-abiding residents. Crime rates have risen substantially in a number of categories, including drug trafficking, gang conflicts, and indiscriminate shootings that result in the loss of innocent lives in these cities and others where a combination of these detrimental factors exists. Particularly now more pronounced, in light of the realization that African Americans are socially, economically, and institutionally disenfranchised within their own communities by illegal immigrants, the majority of residents in these urban areas are experiencing fear of rejection and are beginning to voice their discontent with the Democratic Party's inability to address the issues.

Judeo-Christian Traditions in Politics: The motives of the left are evident; it is inconceivable to me that Americans would jeopardize their country and inflict harm solely for the sake of political gain and power. Judeo-Christian politics encompasses the political implications of the fundamental values and principles derived from Jewish and Christian religious traditions. Nevertheless, the term lacks a precise definition and has been employed to convey an ideological notion of equilibrium and inclusiveness: It is frequently employed to illustrate the shared ethical and moral principles of Western democracies like the U.S. and to contrast them with the tenets of communism, Islamism, or fascism. By doing so, we can combat antisemitism and prejudice and work toward a society where Jews and other religious minorities are welcome and accepted. This ideology has also been used in the past as a means of establishing the equitable superiority and inclusiveness of Western civilization, as well as to oppose the immigration and integration of cultures that are unwilling to assimilate, support terrorism, and repudiate the core values of a Christian society. These individuals generally practice some form of weaponized Islam (Islamism) and are determined to bring down Western democracies. It also aims to promote a conservative ideology and include logic and morality into the mix regarding social and cultural issues concerning such impactful topics as abortion, LGBTQ+ rights, traditional family values, and religious freedom.

Liberal Democrats Social Indoctrination: It is abundantly clear that the Liberal Democratic Socialists, with the backing of Islamists, Marxists, and other foreign actors, are practicing hyper-partisan politics and actively endeavoring to prematurely shape the left's narrative and, therefore, are the potential instigators of a "civil war trajectory" in the United States. Think for a minute: when the same schismatic messaging and key triggering phrases (racism, DEI, discrimination, white supremacist republicans) are consistently referenced in media, on a continuous play cycle week after month, individuals that fall into the "zombie electorate" sphere and other busy and easily indoctrinated in our society will believe these statements or ideological reasoning as gospel and for their survival. The destabilizing strategies implemented by these anti-capitalist, anti-conservative, and anti-democracy factions are consistent with actions advocating for a civil war. In the unfortunate event of a civil war, the Republican conservative nationalist political power base stands to lose everything. The core of the republican party is "one nation under god, with liberty and justice for all." If you want to comprehend the Liberal Democratic Socialist complex and the elitist vision, you should take a step back, observe, make use of your intellect, and apply fundamental common sense to the events that unfold on a national scale and the narrative embraced by the "Imperial Liberal Media." The messaging exhibits a striking level of consistency, with each disinformation campaign focusing on a core theme: the establishment of autocratic rule cloaked as democracy, intending to maintain perpetual control over the voting bloc by exploiting and manipulating detrimental social circumstances such as irregular migration, gender confusion, lack of civic knowledge, and a shifting societal framework that normalizes immoral behavior and politicizes it. Additionally, these campaigns show sympathy towards Islamism while opposing Christianity, capitalism, and the notion of personal accountability. One of the liberal media's key deception strategies is if the narrative is continuously repeated, then lies become the accepted truth in society. For those that have differing views on policy, vilification and discrediting lies are manufactured, and if you oppose liberal ideology, then you are a racist. There doesn't have to be any proof; the media machine will continue to keep on broadcasting the racist talking points, and you will be branded forever, especially by the illiterate and zombie electorate that cannot think for themselves.

Nevertheless, the American people will not stand idly by as their nation is devastated, their constitutional rights are undermined, law and order deteriorating, Judeo-Christian values are eradicated from society, Islamism gains ground, democratic processes are subverted, the government agencies weaponization against its citizens, and a lack of judicial integrity tainted with corruption proliferates our society. Americans must prioritize their awareness of global news and events and draw lessons from the errors made by other countries in order to avoid repeating the same path[65]. Brazil has experienced

---

[65] Akgemci, Esra. "Authoritarian Populism as a Response to Crisis: The Case of Brazil." *Uluslararası İlişkiler Dergisi* 19, no. 74 (2022): 37-51.

significant uprisings and protests within their country, opposing the oppressive and detrimental aspects of Socialism, Globalism, and Islamism[66]. Argentina has rejected Socialist indoctrination and instead embraced capitalism and freedom. The youth in Spain have rejected their country's socialist trend of over ten years and instead embraced capitalism, free market economies, and democracy. Europe as a whole has been experiencing conflicts with the excessive influence of the European Union (EU) and resisting the promotion of open borders and multiculturalism, which aligns with liberal ideology. Europe is continually grappling with the spread of this progressive globalist left-wing ideology and has been rejecting it. Implementing accommodating policies towards Islamic migration[67] and accepting irregular migration is counterproductive and financially unsustainable[68].

Is There Hope: From my perspective, I am convinced that despite the dominant social discourse and intentional efforts to sow discord among races and destroy our way of life, the American people will ultimately come together as a unified nation, uniting in opposition to the ideology of

---

[66] Burity, Joanildo. "Conservative wave, religion and the secular state in post-impeachment Brazil." *International Journal of Latin American Religions* 4, no. 1 (2020): 83-107.

[67] Casanova, José. "Transnationalism and religion: The European Union, from Christian-Democractic project, to secular cosmopolitanism, to populist 'Christian'neo-nationalisms." In *Religion and neo-nationalism in Europe*, pp. 27-48. Nomos Verlagsgesellschaft mbH & Co. KG, 2020.

[68] Nourbakhsh, Seyed Nader, Seyyed Abbas Ahmadi, Qiuomars Yazdanpanah Dero, and Abdolreza Faraji Rad. "Rise of the Far Right parties in Europe: from Nationalism to Euroscepticism."No. 68 (2022): 47-70.

destruction and hatred. Contrary to popular belief, the conflict at hand pertains to a confrontation between Americans and a detrimental ideology that threatens our ongoing existence as a democratically governed and free nation rather than a rivalry between different races. The disinformation campaign waged by the left of center is extremely destructive to our society's cohesion and advancement as a nation. America, without the corrupting liberal exclusionary and identity politics ideologies, will always seek to become a much more perfect union under one flag, respecting all without infringing on each other's rights. That's who we are, I think. Suppose the electorate becomes more informed and globally sagacious; in that case, any party's efforts at censoring and disinformation will be a moot point and will fail to control the masses.

PART IV

RELIGIOUS AND POLITICAL WARFARE

CHAPTER 11
KNOWING YOUR ENEMY - RELIGIOUS ACTORS

A Necessary Conversation: Let me be crystal clear: this is a viewpoint or topic of discussion that many have shied away from, as most in the West won't even denounce the actions of extremist Muslims and terrorist nations for fear of being labeled as bigots or islamophobes. That hands-off attitude and fear herein lie a significant part of the problem and why Islamist extremist ideology gains power and has been allowed to hijack the Islamic faith and spread its roots in American society, especially in our prison system, college campuses, and among younger Islamic migrants. Because of cultural ignorance, extremist views have been confused with true moderate Islam; conveniently, there is no coordinated Islamic leadership public pushback on the radicalization of their religion, so many in society are not aware, and the radicals have not been put on notice. Millions of peace-loving moderate Muslims continue to practice their faith freely in America, as they should. Freedom of religion speaks to who we are as a nation. To gain an elementary understanding of the motivations behind this religion, it is necessary to emphasize that within the Islamic faith, society, governance, economics, and politics are all regulated by Islamic religious principles[69]. Sharia law, which is

---

[69] Chang, Byung-Ock. "Islamic Fundamentalism, Jihad, and Terrorism." *Journal of International Development and Cooperation* 11, no. 1

interpreted as "the correct path" or "Fiqh," serves as the foundation of contemporary Islamic law and provides divine guidance on how to live a righteous life and develop a closer relationship with God. "Sharia Law" and "Islamic Law" are two terms that are frequently confused and misapplied in the written word. It is believed that only God can comprehend the immutable value system known as Sharia. Islamic law comprises a multitude of Sharia interpretations. This is one reason why the majority of Arab nations struggle to define "Moderate Islamic Practice" when attempting to position themselves in the geopolitical and geoeconomic landscape. The Western Hemisphere, America's backyard, and, in particular, the United States as a nation, is on a troublesome and dangerous trajectory as it relates to the proliferation of Islamic radicalization (Islamism). It has grave societal and political consequences that demand immediate attention, as is experienced with the Anti-Semitic, pro-terrorist movement present in our streets today. It is time to overcome our ambivalence, educate ourselves, and approach the matter of the proliferation of Islamist ideology in America objectively. America, if I am not mistaken, was founded on Judeo-Christian principles and also upheld the principles of being a religiously tolerant nation; however, it must not and does not adhere to Sharia law, and neither can the United States tolerate any form of Islamic radicalization. It must be stamped out immediately using whatever means necessary, or we will be doomed to follow the path of many European and Asian nations. It is irrelevant whether one holds this view or not; the conflict has been openly

(2005): 57-67.

declared against the United States, the "great Satan," which renders any disagreement regarding this matter inconsequential.

Formation of Islam: In its proper form, Islam[xxxv] is a monotheistic religion founded by the Prophet Muhammad, a religious, political, and social leader in the seventh century. At the age of forty (610 CE), Muhammad reportedly received his initial divine revelation from Gabriel. He began to preach at this time the concept that "God is One" and that complete submission (Islam) to God (Allah) was essential for attaining the correct path (Din) in life. Subsequently, he proclaimed himself to be a divine messenger and prophet. The foundation of the Islamic practice and faith is based on the "Five Pillars of Islam,"[xxxvi] which are the belief in Allah, daily prayers, fasting during Ramadan, giving alms, and pilgrimage to Mecca, as prescribed in the holy Quran. Traditional Islam has pushed a narrative of peace and used a non-aggressive interpretation of its ideology and teachings[70][xxxvii]. The question remains: how well have they as an institution been able to progress this moderate version of Islam, and what has been done to stamp out the subversion and hijacking of this religion?[71][xxxviii] This massively important question is, by itself, a loaded one and needs a lot more attention than a paragraph[72]. Regardless of the arguments

---

[70] Nasr, Seyyed Hossein. "The meaning and concept of philosophy in Islam." In History of Islamic Philosophy, pp. 21-26. Routledge, 2020.

[71] Ma'arif, Syamsul, Leonard C. Sebastian, and Sholihan Sholihan. "A Soft Approach to Counter Radicalism: The Role of Traditional Islamic Education." Walisongo: Jurnal Penelitian Sosial Keagamaan 28, no. 1 (2020).

[72] Rahman, Fazlur. Islam. University of Chicago Press, 2020.

presented, current trends would dictate that the effort to curb the radicalization of Islam has not been sufficient. It must also be emphasized that several moderate Islamic nations, which I have had the pleasure of visiting, i.e., Bahrain, Qatar, Oman, UAE, Kuwait, and Jordan, to name a few. They are very stable societies, accommodating, and economically prosperous nations.

Christians' Dark Era: In order to provide an accurate historical account of the earliest religious paths, it is necessary to acknowledge that Christians have also experienced periods of instability and troubled history, during which they harbored extremist ideologies against Muslims and retaliation for acts against Christians in occupation. The point at which so much blood has been and continues to be shed senselessly in the name of religion and God is a preternatural fact. We need not delve deeper than the Crusades for this. Following the Christians' initial crusades, the tables were turned, and subsequent bloodshed continued in the form of the Second Crusade and beyond. It is essential to recognize the presence of a turbulent past marked by ideological conflicts, ancestral animosities, and religious rivalries, in which both factions were complicit, vying for political and religious supremacy under the guise of God. We believe that occurred centuries ago and that it was a tragic aspect of the evolution of religions and ideologies. The animosity persists and has been progressively gaining momentum and prominence on a global scale. There is a concern that nations may once more find themselves embroiled in a religious and ideological conflict in the twenty-first century. This conflict would primarily involve non-Islamic religions, namely

Christianity, Judaism, and, to a lesser extent, Buddhism and Hinduism, which have all experienced conflicts with Islam throughout history, in addition to the Islamic faith.

Warped Doctrine: Welcome to the cruel mindset of Jihadism and Islamic Fundamentalists. To an extent, I will agree that traditional Islamic traditions and peaceful existence concepts have been hijacked and altered to reflect an ensuing and necessary battle of good over evil. Some of the orthodox Islamic teachings or ideas have been morphed or reinterpreted into a doctrine to support the indiscriminate killing and violence of those who oppose their view or are deemed the enemy of Islam. These doctrines are the important ones of mention: Takfir,[xxxix] Mufassala,[xl] Jahiliyya[xli], Hijra.[xlii], Istishad[xliii], and Jihad[xliv]. Terrorist leaders and extremist groups use these subverted reinterpretations to indoctrinate the illiterate and societally vulnerable to support terroristic actions and sanctified violence by brainwashed followers[xlv] against the greater and lesser Satan of the world (USA, Israel), as illustrated by them[73].

Brief Historical Review: In order to attain a comprehensive comprehension of the origins of Jihadist philosophies and their relationship to Islamic theology, it is imperative to examine the Umayyad conquests, which marked the initial documented expansion of the Umayyad caliphate into Hispania between 711 and around 718. The Visigothic Kingdom was annihilated, and the Umayyad Wilayah of Al-Andalus was established during this

[73] Watt, William Montgomery. *Islamic Fundamentalism and Modernity (RLE Politics of Islam)*. Routledge, 2013.

conquest; this marked the westernmost expansion of Muslim rule into Europe. The Almohad Berber Dynasty, an additional Muslim dynasty that arose in the 12th century, achieved complete conquest over North Africa and Libya. They, in conjunction with Al-Andalus, proclaimed an eternal Jihad against Jews and Christians. Prior to the Crusades, the Europeans divided the Islamic state's conquered territory into four kingdoms after recapturing a significant portion of it. Aside from the Egyptian Fatimids, almost no discernible effort was made to reclaim the Islamic territories that had been lost. With the advent of Zangi, the eminent ruler of what is now Northern Iraq, a transformation occurred. In an effort to reclaim territories, his leadership advocated for a resurgence of hostilities; he reclaimed Edessa, which ushered in the second crusades and a 47-year stalemate.

The resolution of this impasse was achieved in 1187 when Salah al-Din al-Ayyubi (Saladin) successfully captured Jerusalem (Horns of Hattin). It was throughout this forty-seven-year impasse that the majority of jihadi literature and its foundations were formulated and implemented in order to appease a regime intent on war. For the purpose of reclaiming territory lost during the first Crusades and enabling his forces to overcome the enemy with fear and, if necessary, fight to the bitter end, Saladin recognized the necessity of developing a doctrine that was both potent and unifying. Additionally, the principle was established that individuals who renounced the Jihad would beholden an irredeemable and perpetual transgression. This concise historical lesson will provide the reader with a starting point for their research and enable them to develop an opinion regarding the extent to which Jihadism is intertwined with Islamic teachings.

Summary of the Jewish Fight for Existence: Based on Jewish historical records[74], the period of significance known as the Jewish era begins around 1300 BCE (before Christ's era), predating the Age of Christ. Following this, around 1000 BCE, Joshua accomplished the remarkable feat of crossing both the Jordan River and the Red Sea, thereby establishing the kingdom of David, its capital being Jerusalem. Circa 957 B.C.E., the initial temple of Solomon was built in Jerusalem. This event occurred approximately 1600 years prior to the advent of Islam. Following the Assyrian conquest in 722 BCE, the Jewish diaspora was established under the Babylonian conquest in 586 BCE. The erection of the second temple of Solomon commenced in 515 B.C.E., subsequent to the initial temple's devastation. The occurrence in question is widely recognized as the Great Return. Judea came under the Roman dominion in 63 BCE and remained under their dominion until the Jewish uprising of 70 CE. At that point, Jerusalem was destroyed by the Romans. During the five years between 130 and 136 CE, Bar Kochba, a Jewish military leader, led a destructive rebellion against the Roman Empire that resulted in the establishment of an autonomous kingdom in the region.

In spite of their victory over the Jewish rebellion, the Romans renamed the region Palestine in 136 CE on purpose as an expression of contempt for the Jewish

---

[74] Brettler, Marc Zvi. *The creation of history in ancient Israel.* Routledge, 2002.

insurgents. It is critical to underscore that the appellation "Palestine" emerged approximately 1100 to 1200 years subsequent to the initial Jewish settlement in the Judean region. Moving forward, we shall examine the era in which Islam rose to prominence. The religion was established in the seventh century C.E., and by approximately 636 C.E., Judea had been successfully conquered, and the Jewish settlements had been subdued by Arab military campaigns. The Crusaders fought against the Islamic world and seized control of the territories between 1099 and 1291. Despite this, the Crusaders ceded control of the region to the Malmuk tribes in December 1291. Subsequently, in 1517, the Ottoman Empire seized control of the region as part of an expansionist conflict in the Arab world. It is imperative to acknowledge that the notion of Jewish occupation of the kingdom of Palestine is without merit, given the absence of historical records attesting to the existence of a designated Palestinian Kingdom. It is essential to recognize that Judea, particularly Hebron and Jerusalem, has perpetually been inhabited by Jews and that, in contrast to what some have claimed, the region was not devoid of Jews[75]. Conversely, it experienced a succession of power struggles among various ruling factions. In approximately 1882, the repatriation of Russian Jews to their ancestral homeland (First Aliyah) commenced. The inaugural Zionist movement was initiated by Theodor Herzl in 1897 in reaction to the pervasive anti-Semitism that characterized France and other European countries, most notably the Dreyfus Affair[76].

---

[75] Shindler, Colin. *A history of modern Israel*. Cambridge University Press, 2013.

Designation: The Balfour Declaration, enacted by Britain in 1917, declared the territory that is now recognized as Jordan to be the Jewish homeland. It is important to recognize that in the years that followed 1920, in particular, a significant number of Arab pogroms broke out, which were primarily instigated by the Jewish aspiration to meet for prayer at the "Western Wall." This contributed to the continued perception of Islam as an intolerant religion. By trying to assuage the fears of Arab revolt, the British made the mistake of appeasing Arab nations during their colonial rule. This strategic decision ultimately incurred significant financial costs for Britain and may have even led to the forfeiture of certain territories. This maneuver of appeasement appears to be one that the United States is presently employing in its foreign policy toward Iran. Ignore history, and it is repeated. In the years that followed, numerous acts of aggression and violence were committed against the Jewish community by various Arab factions. An individual of notable influence was Al-Husyni, who stoked the uprising and cultivated animosity towards the Jews and their presence in the region. Indeed, he engaged in discussions with Adolf Hitler regarding a definitive strategy to exterminate the Jewish populace from the area should Germany succeed in conquering it. Notwithstanding Hitler's defeat in World War II, England insisted on imposing restrictions on Jewish immigration to their designated homeland as a diplomatic gesture towards the major Arab states that bordered the region.

---

[76] Mayorek, Yoram. "Herzl and the Dreyfus affair." (1994): 83-89.

Olive Branch: The Israelis extended the Olive Branch to promote peaceful coexistence as it was a logical way forward for all parties. When the Israeli Declaration of Independence was issued in 1948, they extended an invitation for the Arabs to remain and actively participate in the process of establishing a unified and peaceful society. Notwithstanding this gesture, almost all of the adjacent Arab states chose to invade and completely destroy Israel. The undertaking ultimately encountered setbacks, and in 1964, in response to the division of Jerusalem, the Arab nations resolved to commence a propaganda campaign. Consequently, they financially supported the Palestine Liberation Organization (PLO), a surrogate organization they founded. The principal aim of this organization was to endure the conflict with the complete eradication of Israel and all Jewish settlers. During the Six-Day War in 1967, the Arab states undertook a substantial endeavor to eradicate the Jewish population entirely. Israel, however, detected this strategy and responded with a preemptive assault that effectively destroyed the numerous Arab forces on various fronts. Consequently, Israel reestablished sovereignty over the Sinai Desert in Egypt, Judea and Samaria, the Golan Heights in Syria, and the Gaza Strip. As stipulated in the Sinai agreement of 1979, Israel, as an act of reconciliation, returns the majority (excluding the strategically significant Golan Heights) or potentially the entire territory it had previously occupied.

War and Change: The Arab League Summit[xlvi] held in Sudan in 1967 resulted in the adoption of the three significant principles known as the **"No's"** (No-Peace, No-Recognition, No-Negotiations), which shaped the Arab doctrine until the Abraham Accords of 2020 during the republican administration. This agreement marked a significant and monumental change in the relations between Arab nations and Israel. It was the first instance where the Arab countries acknowledged that the dominance of Iran was highly destructive to the region and that Israel was not their adversary. This event was a significant milestone and, prior to the transfer of power in Washington (2021), was progressing towards achieving remarkable accomplishments. Regrettably, following the transfer of power, the Biden administration altered the course by returning to President Obama's vision of bolstering Iran's influence and backing their organizations and dominance through financial support for programs in Palestine, a region entirely under the operational control of Hamas. This was probably the most idiotic foreign policy decision of the Biden administration. This decision lends insight into the Biden administration's state of mind: empty, ill-informed, and "Geostupid." The Republican administration's approach towards Iran aimed to establish a stranglehold effect, to impede the financing of terrorism and campaigns of disruption, which were having a strategic favorable effect. Still, Biden lifted all the sanctions for them to accumulate funds and resume their terror campaign. Of course, Biden clearly is mimicking Obama's policy and possibly directives from the "shadows." In 2023, as cooperative negotiations with Israel, Saudi Arabia, and other Arab neighbors were on the verge of taking place, the Iranian proxy orchestrated the most violent attack on Jewish civilians since the holocaust. This act aimed to disrupt the ongoing efforts toward peaceful coexistence and the expansion of Iranian disruptive influences in the region. It can be strongly argued that it was the Biden/Obama reversal of the stranglehold policies placed on Iran to deplete their terror-supporting capability by former President Trump that gave Iran the means to engage in this brazen attack. The democrats, under the Biden leadership, have the blood of Israel on their hands, created instability in the region, emboldened Russia and China, and now we can only pray that nothing happens before the election. Hopefully, with the Republicans back in power, the geopolitical landscape and geostrategy will change in our favor, and peaceful coexistence will endure. Peace through strength and the concept of deterrence means a strong military and economy and a strong and savvy President at the helm to lead us.

Western Perspective and Blindness: Before continuing, one must understand a fact that is most often glossed over, and this misunderstanding frequently results in inadequate responses at the decision-making level in government. Individuals socialized in Eastern and Western psychologies perceive actions and issues entirely differently[77]. We must adjust our mindset and come to terms with personal perspectives and preexisting biases. Understand that our socialization and experiences are by design Western, and what we may call a humanistic and moderate approach to solving problems, by Eastern socialization norms, is often looked at as a weakness and a lack of purpose. Especially in America, a disposition of

---

[77] Brachman, Jarret M. *Global jihadism: Theory and practice.* Routledge, 2008.

arrogance is present; we tend to judge issues and apply standards based on our socialization, disregarding the fact that Eastern cultures, religions, and philosophies on life are markedly different from ours, not better or worse but steeped more-so in cultural and religious socialization[78].

The global dissemination of this distorted form of Islam's violent ideology and the loss of life, including that of Americans, at the hands of terrorism and indiscriminate acts of violence against nonbelievers worldwide over the last fifty years has been significantly accelerated by this "cultural ignorance," or whatever term you choose to ascribe to it. While it may be argued that this is a harsh assessment, you must understand the thoughts, drivers, framework, and methodology in order to defeat your adversaries. Subsequently, only then can the appropriate planning, countermeasures, and force be utilized to nullify a particular offensive action. Western leaders frequently promote the narrative that the war against terrorism is unrelated to Islam in an effort to avoid offending Muslim nations; this, in effect, amounts to the West pursuing an appeasement foreign policy. Does this sound familiar? We disseminate the narrative that the conflict is a struggle against malevolence. Jihadism and Islamic extremism do coexist and are joined at the hip; this may be true in essence; however, it is critical to recognize that they both stem from formative Islamic doctrine. This revelation serves as an initial stride towards recognizing the

---

[78] Tibi, Bassam. "The Islamist Venture of the Politicization of Islam to an Ideology of Islamism A Critique of the Dominating Narrative in Western Islamic Studies." *Soundings: An Interdisciplinary Journal* 96, no. 4 (2013): 431-449.

fundamentalist perspective and operational mindset that characterizes this conflict as a holy war with the ultimate objective of eradicating nonbelievers.

Jihadi, Islamist, Terrorism: If we were to analyze the origins of this jihad belief system, we could invariably distinguish political factors (such as the Arab-Israeli conflict), cultural factors (such as rebellion against perceived colonialism and Western cultural beliefs), and social factors (such as alienation and poverty) that the West eagerly ascribes to the instigation of terrorist activities. Irrespective of the underlying causes, it is undeniable that one is a derivative of the other. Jihadism has been bolstered, and the conflict with the West has escalated due to a policy of appeasement by Western leaders, a persistent "Islamic blindness" to current events, and the absence of resolute opposition. This complacent mindset has fostered an environment conducive to the infiltration of liberal organizations, social activists, and educational institutions in order to promote fundamentalist indoctrination programming[79]. One only has to look at the infiltration by Islamist ideology within the Democrat Party (Squad) and the flying of the Palestinian flag in the halls of Congress. Not to mention the Iranian double agent that advised the Biden administration and the withholding of ammunition from Israel, our trusted ally, while they embattle the terrorists that attacked their homeland. Yes, that was the Democratic Party trying to turn up the screws

[79] Hacsek, Zsófia. "Global Jihadist Terrorism. Terrorist groups, Zones of Armed Conflict and National Counter-Terrorism strategies: edited by Paul Burke, Doaa'Elnakhala, & Seumas Miller, Northampton, MA, Edward Elgar Publishing, 2021, 338 pp.,£ 105, ISBN 9781800371293." (2022): 1-4.

against Israel in favor of Hamas and Palestine terrorists/sympathizers. We have established an ideal environment conducive to the proliferation of dissent and the development of an extremist and hateful mindset within our government and society. This is currently very apparent in the Western world. It can only be surmised that the fundamentalist doctrinal infiltration is successful through observing the magnitude of the pro-terror, anti-Israel demonstrations that have occurred in America and around the world thus far.

Furthermore, political activists and sympathizers in the West propagate a prevailing social narrative that asserts that any support for Israel or an interpretation that attributes terrorism to Islamic religious and cultural factors renders one vulnerable to slander and Islamophobia, irrespective of the facts presented. This is done by sympathetic actors in an effort to stifle dissenting viewpoints. This is very similar to the arguments pushed in promoting Palestinians as innocent bystanders when they are actively intertwined within the Hamas regime. Any aid given to the Palestinians will go directly to Hamas and their net of sympathizers. Hamas[80] is a Palestinian armed group. Hamas, the most sizable armed Islamist organization in the Gaza Strip, exercises governance over the two million-person Palestinian territory. It is backed and armed by the Palestinians and other affiliated organizations. Initially, Hamas was embraced by a large proportion of Palestinians as the organization most willing

---

[80] Mishal, Shaul, and Avraham Sela. *The Palestinian Hamas: vision, violence, and coexistence.* Columbia University Press, 2006.

to resist Israel; some regarded it as less corrupt and better organized than the Palestinian Authority. However, as the lives of Palestinians have deteriorated due to conflict and years of Israeli and Egyptian blockade, discontent has increased, and a minority believes that the group's attacks have also harmed Palestinians[81].

Hamas maintains alliances with Middle Eastern nations such as Syria and Shiite Islamist organizations like Hezbollah in Lebanon, which are opposed to the policies of the United States and Israel. Iran, an ardent supporter, maintains a vested interest in the conflict with Israel. Hamas has received arms, technology, and training from Iran for decades in order to construct an arsenal of sophisticated rockets capable of penetrating deeply into Israeli territory. Hamas is intricately linked with the Palestinian people, who provide a strategic region for the organization's invasion of Israel[82]. Similar to how the American liberal left uses the racism card to obfuscate the truth, this is a standard maneuver by the anti-Semitic crowd. Strictly attributing Islamic terrorism to socioeconomic and political factors would be an inadequate representation of the profound influence that many in the Islamic world contribute to the Jihadis' extremist culture. To comprehend the motivating force inciting these acts and to draw up an effective strategic

---

[81] Knudsen, Are, and Basem Ezbidi. "Hamas and Palestinian statehood." *Where now for Palestine? The demise of the two-state solution* (2006): 188-210.

[82] Hannase, Mulawarman. "The Dilemma Between Religious Doctrine and Political Pragmatism: Study of Hamas in Palestine." *Religió Jurnal Studi Agama-agama* 10, no. 1 (2020).

strategy for a war against terrorism, it is necessary to understand the religious-ideological factors deeply embedded in Islam.[xlvii] Knowing your enemy is the first step to defeating them. Regardless of what the media pushes, the Palestinians are not the helpless, innocent sheep that they are portrayed as. A burning question on my mind, if the ruling party of the U.S. government goes to war, is America and her citizens at war? Yes. Then, if the Palestine ruling party legally elected government, Hamas, goes to war, are the Palestinian people at war? Yes. Well, has anyone explained the concept of war to all the protesters that "War is Hell on Earth"? Strategic objectives must be prioritized in war, and eliminating the enemy is paramount, regardless of where they are hiding. So, only engage in war as a last resort or suffer the consequences.

Ideology Let's briefly discuss the ideology of "ends justifying the means" embraced by fundamentalists, even though it may be a sensitive topic. Let's examine some common arguments. Debates have arisen among Muslim scholars in both Western and Eastern regions regarding the connection between Islamic Jihadism and Islamic teachings. Many Western scholars are reluctant to associate such actions with the fundamental principles of ancient Islam. This religion emerged during times of war, possibly due to concerns about being stigmatized. They tend to see Jihadism as unrelated to, or a distorted version of Islamic theology, which they perceive as a deviation from a peaceful and tolerant religion[xlviii]. As radical Islamism is a product of a more significant religious phenomenon (Islamic revival) that is sweeping the Muslim world, this argument is valid. It resides in the intersection of modern Islamic teachings and traditions, Islamic historical awakening, and prophetic charismatic leaders who profit from the widespread poverty and suffering in many Islamic communities. Thus, the Islamic religious reformation intersects with radical political ideology and social protest in three distinct ways. Religion occupies a fundamentally different place in Eastern societies and cultures than in the West. This distinction must be crystal clear to us moving forward. In Western societies, religion functions as a framework of convictions that provides direction for one's life through the observance of theological doctrines and confidence in the deliverance of God. Islam, in particular, is not distinct from existence, governance, economics, or way of life in the East[83]. Radical Islam operates on the same fundamental tenet: as a way of life and existence on this planet, guided by the teachings of Sharia law[xlix] and subject to the sovereign rule and law of God. This is a divinely ordained law for human beings to abide by, as supported by the Quran and Hadith; failure to do so will result in severe consequences. There are significant differences between fundamentalists and traditionalists in numerous aspects, with one notable distinction being the ideological pressure placed on the state to execute the fundamentalists' conception of itself as a divine instrument in the struggle against evil (as exemplified by the Iranian government structure). The concept of warfare to mobilize followers into activism has been drastically re-engineered. It removes the fine line between phrases in a context that symbolizes spiritual and moral battles, such as Jihad, and

---

[83] Johnson, Toni, and Mohammed Aly Sergie. "Islam: governing under Sharia." *Council on Foreign Relations* 25 (2014).

its modification to legitimize extreme violence and struggle to adopt an "ends justifies the means" ideology[l].

Defining Terrorism: The Federal Bureau of Investigation (FBI) defines international terrorism as *"Violent, criminal acts committed by individuals and/or groups to further ideological goals stemming from domestic influences, such as those of a political, religious, social, racial, or environmental nature."*[84] To the argument that Islam has been radicalized, it must be pointed out that when referencing Islamic terrorism, a distinction should be made between ideology and religion[85]. Radical Islamism is a term generally used in referencing terrorism, and the doctrine emphasized is a perverted version of Islam resulting from rebel charismatic leaders' interpretation and propaganda[li]. It has been sparsely stated that most practicing Muslims disagree with the premises of Islamism. Still, most will not publicly denounce this perversion of their religion for fear of retribution from within their community. Even though Islamism derives its core principles from religious material, its interpretations are riddled with political ideology, some of which resemble conspiracy theories, transforming Islamism to look more like a totalitarian ideology. As with other religions, the interpretation of orthodox Islam differs. Apart from the more publicized division of Sunni and Shia Muslims, multiple branches exist within and outside these two distinctions, all of which have incredibly varied characteristics[lii]. Violent

---

[84] Byman, Daniel. "Understanding, and misunderstanding, state sponsorship of terrorism." Studies in Conflict & Terrorism 45, no. 12 (2022): 1031-1049.

[85] Ghezelsofla, Mohammad-Taghi, and Mohsen Abbaszadeh Marzbali. "The Contending Hegemonies of Islamism: From Contextual Modernism to Reactionary Modernism."

Islamist extremism is most often connected to Salafism, which lies within the Sunni branch of Islam. All Salafists adhere to a literal interpretation of the Quran and the Sunnah, eliminating human subjectivity and creating a singular truth without pluralism[liii].

Similar to other extreme ideologies, Islamism works on three distinct levels: First, it identifies problems within the status quo and assigns blame. Secondly, it offers solutions packaged to support this ideology. Thirdly, it provides reasoning and justifies the decided-upon action, which is framed as a struggle[86]. Speaking broadly, Islamism's basic premise is the existence of a community of believers, the Ummah, which is threatened and subjugated by some global conspiracy against Islam. According to this narrative, the global injustices Muslims suffered, including Islam's perceived decay, can be blamed on the Western coalition of nations led by the US and Israel. Accepting these manufactured premises and injustices against Islam and God demands a duty to defend the faith and believers, thus continuing the struggle framed as Jihad or holy war[liv]. These ill-conceived premises provide the theoretical framework of Islamic terrorism and appear worldwide in the rhetoric and reasonings of radicalized individuals. This rhetoric is aimed at the victimization of one group and the demonization of the other[87][lv]. At the same time, the propaganda narrative by sponsor states (Iran) and the Imams pushes violence as the only means of effecting

---

[86] Hakim, Luqman Nul. "New Order and the Politicisation of Islam." In Islamism and the Quest for Hegemony in Indonesia, pp. 101-143. Singapore: Springer Nature Singapore, 2023.

[87] Al-Tarawneh, Alalddin. "The role of Quran translations in radicalizing Muslims in the west and misrepresenting Islam." Journal of Religion and Violence 9, no. 1 (2021): 101-122.

change, doing God's work, and whereby the act of Martyrdom is glorified.

Fundamentalists and Islamism: Islamist propaganda presents two major action pathways for recruits who are radicalized in the West[lvi]. On the one hand, is the perpetration of attacks against a wide range of objectives, and on the other, the immigration to various frontlines in the fight for global Jihad, either to participate directly as a combatant or support roles as in jihadi brides or sleeper cells waiting for the call. Currently, the porous US border creates a security deficiency in our threat prevention strategy, thereby facilitating the undetected deployment of sleeper cells and fighters into the American frontline[lvii]. Another pathway has emerged in the push to radicalize educated individuals in technical fields to modernize and diversify their operations. One crucial fact to note in the ongoing discussion is the impact of religious astuteness on the radicalization process[88]. Contrary to popular belief, several researchers, including terrorism expert Sageman[lviii], find that "religious formation prevents radicalization rather than promoting it" (Sageman, 2023). The reasoning is that religion provides arguments based on different interpretations of religious sources, which counter the Islamist narrative. These religious savvy individuals are not caught up in Islam's propaganda, misinterpretation, or misrepresentation[89].

---

[88] Bar, Shmuel. "The religious sources of Islamic terrorism." In *The Theory and Practice of Islamic Terrorism: An Anthology*, pp. 11-20. New York: Palgrave Macmillan US, 2008.

[89] Davis, Jessica. *Future of the Islamic State's Women: Assessing Their Potential Threat*. International Centre for Counter-Terrorism (ICCT), 2020.

Iran the Architect of Terrorism: As Qutb[lix] asserted, a global conspiracy exists between the Marxist Communism of the West, the Crusading Christian West, and World Jewry against devoted Islam, which must be vanquished at any expense. These three forces exemplify the worst of jahiliyyah; they are adversaries of God who perpetually devise schemes to destroy Islam. Aligned with the teachings of Qutb, the Supreme Guardian of the Islamic Republic of Iran, Iran, and Khomeini dismissed the United States and Israel as adversaries of Islam and Iran, referring to them respectively as "the lesser and greater Satan." There is a widespread belief in the Islamic world that the United States has caused Iran more harm than any other nation and that its arrogance and involvement in evil, betrayal, and murder merit the moniker "The Great Satan." The argument is advanced that the United States endorses the genocide against Arabs on a global scale due to its shady alliance with the Zionists and the Jews, the other two greatest adversaries of Islam. By defending the Jews and acting against Islamic states, the United States has committed crimes and sins against Islam through these acts of affiliation; they are explicit declarations of war against God, his messengers, and Muslims[90].

In this century, the war continues[lx], and we can thank Iran for orchestrating the evolution of their version of an Islamic crusade, steeped in a deep-set ideology of hate, revenge, oppression, and religious intolerance, into an actionable framework termed the "axis of resistance." The

---

[90] Cordesman, Anthony H. *Tracking the trends and numbers: Islam, Terrorism, stability and conflict in the Middle East*. Center for Strategic and International Studies (CSIS), 2022.

axis in question is an alliance that brings together antagonistic Muslim factions (Sunni and Shia), failed states (Iraq, Syria, Gaza/Palestinians, Lebanon), and terrorist organizations (Hezbollah, Hamas, Palestinian Islamic Jihad, Houthis). Its members are united in their objective to (a) eradicate the Jewish state, (b) oppose and diminish the influence of Western powers, and (c) propagate their interpretation of Islam in accordance with Sharia law. In order to establish and oversee this network within the framework, Iran employs the "Quds Force," a division of the IRGC (Iranian Revolutionary Guard Corps) that is supplemented with substantial funding and personnel. The Quds Force is responsible for mission guidance, funding distribution, and overseas training. It operates under the direct command of the Iranian regime. It is noteworthy to mention that additional benevolent sponsors contribute to the financial support of Hamas despite the organization striving to preserve a degree of autonomy and not acting as an official representative of Iran. The West appears to be less concerned about a development that worries me greatly: Iran's effort to unite the opposing forces under a unified framework of resistance. This development is cause for concern.

In contrast, modern Islamic fundamentalists, feeding off the Israel-Palestinian conflict, have developed a pernicious new form of anti-Semitism that sees all Jews everywhere involved in a sinister plot to destroy Islam[lxi]. Selectively using the same anti-Jewish sources of the Quran and Hadith as the traditionalists, the radicals effectively blur the distinctions between anti-Semitism and anti-Zionism. Islamists have studied methods of Western irrational fascist and Nazi ideologies to prop up and justify their racist anti-Semitism actions[lxii]. From all that has been explained in summary, the major groups of concern to the West, including the state of Israel, are Hamas, Hezbollah, al-Mulathamun Battalion (al-Mourabitoun), and the IRGC.[lxiii] They receive significant funding from Iran, which also supports and commands a powerful armed wing called the Izz ad-Din al-Qassam Brigades, operating out of Syria and Jordan with Hezbollah[lxiv]. Incidentally, Iran funds all of them, and they don't make much effort to hide this fact. I have always been skeptical of the United States' level of support for the UN and NATO alliances because of my exposure to their operations in Europe and Asia and what their ideology represents. This recent development after the Israeli slaughter has revealed that America finances many of these NGOs that give funding to terrorist organizations, as was just discovered in the Hamas attack on Israel. Approximately 12 staffers to date from the UN Relief and Works Agency (UNRWA) were involved in the October 7 terrorist attacks. Based on the investigation, close to 12% of UNRWA's 13,000 staffers are members of Hamas or other Palestinian militant groups. This is just a sampling and the tip of the iceberg. Our taxpayers' hard-earned dollars are currently going into the UN and other foreign coffers to fund the same anti-American hate groups that seek to destroy the West or are in opposition to our American way of life and want to erase our borders and threaten our National Security. This must stop. How senseless is this? More of our funding should stay in America to assist our own citizens' welfare.

PART V

Homeland Threat

Chapter 12

Homeland Infiltration - War Against The West

Homeland Threat: There has been a significant surge in concerns pertaining to national security in recent years. The menace of terrorism looms large over many nations as global interconnections intensify. Regrettably, the United States of America is not immune to this peril. Due to its prominence and international influence, terrorist organizations find the United States to be an appealing target in their efforts to sow fear and disorder[91]. Numerous elements contribute to the vulnerability of the United States, which cannot be disregarded or trivialized. From the outset, the United States has become an emblematic representation of Western ideals due to its steadfast dedication to safeguarding democratic principles and the inviolability of speech. As a result, extremist organizations perceive it as a primary adversary that requires degradation or annihilation. Through their deliberate focus on the United States and its populace, terrorists aspire to inflict damage upon democratic systems and instigate a global panic.

---

[91] Robillard, Michael. "National counter-terrorism responses: United States of America." In *Global Jihadist Terrorism*, pp. 212-232. Edward Elgar Publishing, 2021.

Furthermore, with regard to security, the immense landmass of the United States presents a substantial obstacle regarding defense. Islamist organizations, under the predominant influence of Iran, have refined and advanced their methods of infiltration within the United States. I fear that the methods used in the attack on Israel by Hamas (Iranian-sponsored), including motorized parachutes and desert bikes, would be an effective cross-border incursion tactic from Mexico into a U.S. border town, with great avenues of escape and a border to hide behind. This is very plausible given the icy relationship between both governments and a haven for terrorists to escape and evade U.S. forces.

Continuum of Terror: Iran is a critical component in the chain of terror directed at the Western world. Furthermore, Iran employs proxy actors to conduct its operations in the gray area. In addition, they have modified their operational strategy to capitalize on the crime-terror continuum by financing and expanding their terror projection through the use of criminal enterprises and networks. Its implementation has necessitated the DHS to modify its counterterrorism framework strategically. Nonetheless, crucial components of the framework that the administration must implement via effective policy are lacking. It appears to the average onlooker that the Biden administration is operating contrary to establishing a solid strategic framework. The DHS has been diligently striving to implement the revised Strategic Framework for countering terrorism and targeted violence within the country with its hands tied. This will demonstrate that the entirety of DHS is dedicated to combating attacks at home and violent extremism, just as we are committed to addressing the threat posed by international terrorist organizations. This holistic Strategic Framework enables our citizens, state, local, tribal, and territorial authorities, the private sector, non-governmental organizations, and community leaders to develop community-specific prevention frameworks to safeguard society. The objective remains to prevent terrorists and other hostile actors from entering the United States and denying them access to the nation's trade, immigration, and domestic and international travel system rules. To accomplish this, policies and laws must be supported and enforced at all levels of government. Active surveillance of groups and demonstrations with an Islamist slant to identify malicious actors and prevent domestic terrorism and targeted violence must be enforced, and enhanced community preparedness and infrastructure protections in the United States by empowering our homeland security enterprise must be put in play. In particular, the DHS must continue anticipating the evolution of threats in rural America as the illicit networks widen.

Regrettably, the administration has absolved itself of accountability by permitting unrestricted access to malicious actors through the opening of borders and the adoption of an appeasement policy concerning Iran. This policy reversal by the Biden administration, which represents a complete 180-degree turn from the approach taken by the Trump administration, has empowered Iran by granting it access to the United States through its porous border, acquiring the use of seized funds, and the ability to sell oil for revenue to finance terrorism and attacks against its adversaries. I anticipate that Iran, in the near future, will exploit these advantageous strategic errors committed by the Biden Presidency, or should I refer to it as Obama's OFA (organization for action) puppet masters? This could lead to an expansion of Iran's terror campaign in the region to acquire territory and influence (Syria, Jordan, Saudi Arabia) and potentially fund another direct assault on Israel or the United States through proxies, thereby consolidating its position as a more formidable threat actor. Even though most analysts disagree with this interpretation, it would be the most logical strategic move for the Iranian leadership to increase its influence.

Europe has been utilized for years as a testing ground to discover and modify intrusion techniques that are effective in indoctrinating and disrupting Western societies. They have come to comprehend the theory that one can control the future of a nation by exerting influence over the thoughts and ideas of its youth. It is by no mistake that Iran and China have been investing heavily in our educational institutions, where some schools at the elementary level are teaching Confucianism. Beijing utilizes numerous Confucius Classrooms to exert a personalized teacher-to-student influence campaign to shape American children's perceptions regarding the Chinese government, all under the pretense of providing Chinese-language, historical, and cultural programming.

Confucius Classrooms are lesser-known K-12 divisions of the Confucius Institutes, which have gained widespread and justified disapproval. Both programs are associated with the United Front Work Department of China, which supervises international operations and exerts ideological influence. Liu Yandong, the former vice premier of the People's Republic of China, managed the Confucius program. She later led "Hanban," which was an agency of the Ministry of Education in Beijing. This agency has now been renamed the Center for Language Exchange and Cooperation, all under the guidance of the Chinese Communist Party (CCP). It would seem that the Chinese and Iranians are working in cohorts, or they definitely understand the effectiveness of brainwashing the younger, more impressionable members of society to create a permanent foothold in America, changing our ideology and acceptance of their doctrine. Regardless, their intrusion tradecraft is very evident and at play throughout the United States.

Islamism is increasingly prevalent among the youth, misinformed, apathetic, and vulnerable members of our society. Sadly, our liberal educational institutions, Democrat ideology, and social activists have facilitated the spread of Islamist ideology in the United States. The liberalized educational system in the United States has facilitated the infiltration of Jihadism doctrine into secondary and tertiary levels of learning institutions with increasing momentum. The prevalence of anti-Semitic violence and the large number of pro-terrorist Hamas sympathizers who participated in campus demonstrations across the country served as clear indications of the extent of this indoctrination. Furthermore, Democratic Socialist organizations, some Democrat Congressional members, and grassroots social activist groups supported by Iranian-backed financiers and the Democratic machine have all contributed to its growth. The intentions of the Biden administration, the Socialist Democrat complex, and the Liberal Democrat Party Media Propaganda arm (Legacy Media) regarding the welfare and course of this great nation have been made abundantly clear through their actions. If the general public in the United States cannot recognize and comprehend the gravity of this situation, which is being played out publicly, then it is a sad realization that we might have already lost our nation. America is in need of an all-hands-on-deck "call to action." Our entire system has been turned on its head. Have you seen the statue of "Lady Justice" lately? She is standing on the broken scale of justice, sword pointed at you, and her blindfolds are off.

The arduous task of effectively policing each entry point is exacerbated by the presence of coastlines in both the Atlantic and Pacific Oceans and borders spanning multiple countries, not to mention when we have leaders that increase the risk to national security by rendering our border controls ineffective. The country's advantageous geographical location provides potential terrorists and other bad actors abundant opportunities to infiltrate without detection. Moreover, the diverse composition of the American populace poses an exceptional challenge. Although cultural diversity constitutes a notable strength of the nation, it concurrently fosters an environment that is conducive to radicalization. Disenchanted individuals may fall victim to extremist ideologies, which capitalize on their grievances by directing them toward perilous trajectories such as violence and terrorism. Furthermore, numerous extremist organizations have been incensed by the United

States military interventions and conflict in the world. The repercussions of these actions are felt on American soil, as they often provoke retaliation from those who perceive themselves as victims of aggression. Sadly, innocent civilians frequently bear the brunt of such retaliatory attacks, further highlighting America's vulnerability to terrorism[92].

In order to mitigate the imminent danger, the United States must effectuate a comprehensive strategy. Implementing robust counterterrorism measures, augmenting intelligence collaboration with global allies, and fortifying border security are all pivotal measures in ensuring the nation's protection. Moreover, promoting constructive discourse and comprehension among heterogeneous communities can serve as a preventive measure against radicalization and shield members from the influence of extremist ideologies. Consensus dictates that the United States must maintain a proactive and vigilant stance in its efforts to combat the threat of terrorism. By recognizing its susceptibilities and implementing suitable measures, the United States of America can reduce the likelihood of further acts of terrorism and safeguard its citizens. It is important to note that terrorism and crime go hand in hand as terrorist organizations are utilizing criminal networks (cartels) for transportation and access while supporting criminals with drugs, weapons, and funding. Transnational Criminal Organizations (TCOs) are very active on the U.S. southern

---

[92] Logan, Caroline, Randy Borum, and Paul Gill, eds. *Violent extremism: A handbook of risk assessment and management.* UCL Press, 2023.

border and down through Latin America. The open border policies of President Biden's Administration have seen a dramatic uptick in border infiltration, crime, and expanded drug distribution pipelines[93]. Many have forgotten about our northern border, which has recently seen a significant uptick in crossings and violations.

Let us Regroup: I have addressed highly contentious subjects and conducted an analysis of various theories. Nevertheless, this merely provides a superficial glimpse into the profound hatred and malevolence propagated by the fundamentalists—more precisely, the head of the serpent. Iran. To reiterate, I am of the opinion that the reciprocal association between traditionalist and fundamentalist tenets of Islam operates synergistically and that orthodox Islam has failed to adequately resist its transformation. This passivity has generated an environment conducive to operations and, in conjunction with this mutually beneficial occurrence, has facilitated the effortless assimilation of Islamic ideology into radicalism, which has been exploited to reignite the longstanding animosity that persists among the Jewish, Christian, and Islamic communities. The Islamic and Zionist empires are engaged in a holy war for survival; prior to formulating a winning strategy and course of action, the Western world must accept this reality. An overview was provided of the historical origins and radicalization of the theories of Da'wa, Mufassal, and Jihad, including their adaptation and re-engineering for military purposes, as well as the

---

[93] Celso, Anthony N. "The jihadist forever war: Islamic State innovations in terrorist propaganda, recruitment and organizational networking." *Terrorism and Political Violence* 32, no. 6 (2020): 1348-1355.

underlying causes present in the majority of Islamic communities that are utilized by charismatic and fanatical leaders to enlist soldiers for the Islamic state. We discussed Salafism and examined how the Eschatological concept of the relationship between God's kingdom, State Responsibility, and Societal laws are warped to indoctrinate the believers into identifying the enemies of Islam and fighting the final battle[lxv].

As previously mentioned, the purpose of this chapter was not to provide an exhaustive history lesson. Rather, it aimed to furnish the reader with a foundational understanding, prepare them for the subsequent deluge of information, and serve as a reference point for further research (refer to the endnotes for a list of references). I comprehend the sensitive character of these subjects and the manner in which specific individuals may respond to the severe and occasionally unorthodox methods of warfare. It is noteworthy to mention that the majority of contemporary and forthcoming conflicts will employ asymmetrical warfare, with urban areas and communities serving as the arena. It has occurred in numerous countries, including Israel and Ukraine, just recently. Please do not hold the erroneous belief that such an event is not possible or unlikely to occur in our nation. It may seem at times that I am advocating for war, being harsh in my assessment of Islam, and making recommendations steeped in extremely decisive actions, but let me assure the readers this much: we are facing an enemy that is determined, believe that they are doing God's will, have nothing to lose and all to gain, and any act of aggression upon the enemy is acceptable and favorable as taught in the Jihad, the "end justifies the means."[lxvi]

Awareness: As citizens of the United States, we don't need to forsake our virtuous and moral standards. Instead, we must increase our understanding of regional and global threats, rectify our naive perspective on matters, and recognize that our steadfast adherence to certain principles has not earned us universal acclaim and that "bad actors" are already present among us. Consider the extent to which political appointees who support terrorist actions and Hamas sympathizers are currently disrupting the American landscape, as well as the source of the funding that is being used to support this ideological shift in universities and social activism. For this reason, a robust national defense web, secure borders that enable subject identification and vetting, national awareness, a formidable military that generates the deterrent effect, and proactive and responsive law enforcement agencies that are exceptionally trained are all essential.

I implore my audience to reflect upon the following query: Does any individual believe that an incident similar to the one that recently unfolded in Israel on October 7th, 2023, is unattainable in the United States? 9/11 has been forgotten? As of November 2023, warnings have been issued by US law enforcement and counter-terrorism administrators regarding impending acts of terrorism motivated by Islamic fundamentalism and by Muslim sympathizers targeting the United States homeland. As a result of the Democrats' policy of maintaining an open border and permitting unrestricted entry for males and females of war age, Islamic origin, Chinese nationals, and other malicious actors seeking to cause damage to the United States, an attack on our homeland is inevitable; the question is when rather than if. Regardless of which political party is currently in power, how could this breach of national security be allowed to occur? Whether or not I am merely another patriotic ideologue, protecting the United States homeland must always take precedence. When do we, as a nation, reach the point where we determine that enough is enough? The days of ignorance of politics, current events, media censorship, our constitution, and national security issues are - over. Be responsible citizens and protect our own.

Christine Abizaid, the director of the National Counterterrorism Center (NCTC), issued a warning in January that the United States encountered a range of complex threats in 2023, including state sponsors of terrorism and lone wolf actors, in addition to foreign terrorist organizations like ISIS and al Qaeda. The most immediate peril to the United States homeland originated from individuals who were motivated by Islamist Jihadi organizations. However, the United States remained "extremely vigilant" regarding foreign terrorist organizations. In the wake of the Islamic Marxist Revolt of 1979, the Iranian regime, under the leadership of the mullahs, has consistently pursued the dissemination of its revolutionary ideology, Khomeinism, beyond the borders of Iran. An integral component of this approach has entailed providing financial assistance and backing to diverse terrorist organizations and militias worldwide. This analysis underscores the critical importance of the White House having a thorough understanding of the Iranian terrorist network and serves as an urgent cautionary message to them. The US seems to be engaging in an appeasement campaign with Iran, and this can be very dangerous. The United States government has designated Iran the "primary state sponsor of terrorism" due to its systematic development of terrorist proxy militias and organizations. This places Iran in an imminent threat category. The unwavering commitment to advancing its radical agenda via unconventional means has not only caused significant disruptions to the stability of the Middle East but has also posed considerable challenges to preserving global peace and security. Iran has conducted missile strikes against three nations: Iraq, Syria, and Pakistan. Additionally, it has extended support to proxy militant organizations that are actively involved in conflict with Israel and the pursuit of U.S. and Western interests. There have been raised concerns regarding the possibility of a conflict emerging in the Middle East, which possesses the capability to spread to neighboring regions. The significant assistance provided by Iran to proxy militias and terrorist organizations across the globe is a subject of considerable apprehension due to its potential ramifications on international stability. The proxies, which are backed by Iran in terms of equipment, training, and finances, consist of several prominent entities.

Hezbollah serves as the principal Iranian operative in Lebanon. Hezbollah is an organization with deep-rooted ties to Tehran. It conducts operations inside Lebanon's borders and poses a significant threat to Israel. Hezbollah is also the largest nonstate actor acting on behalf of Iran. The entity in question maintains a substantial arsenal of missiles and rockets that are distinctly aimed at the state of Israel. Since its establishment, Hezbollah has maintained a strong alliance with Iran. However, the group is also involved in a diverse range of aggressive, terrorist, and illegal activities beyond Lebanon that are equally crucial for comprehending the group as a whole. This encompasses the training of other Iranian proxy groups by Hezbollah, as well as the deployment of necessary personnel and military units to locations outside of Lebanon, specifically in Latin America and within the United States. These international activities, which surpass its domestic militia operations and conflicts with Israel, have prompted nations worldwide to assign their law enforcement and intelligence agencies the responsibility of combating Hezbollah's actions.

Hamas, the Palestinian Militant group, maintains a presence within the Gaza Strip and, notwithstanding intermittent divergences of opinion, adheres to the same ideological stance as the Iranian regime. Hamas and its armed faction have been consistently empowered by Iran's substantial financial assistance, which has enabled them to instigate a multitude of hostilities against Israel. Another critical factor for their success is the shielding, fighters, and interference the Palestinians provide for Hamas, and both are united in the hatred and destruction of the Israeli state. The Palestinians have a symbiotic relationship with Hamas, and separating them, especially the Palestinian youth, is going to prove difficult, as Israel has realized. Israel has no allies in the region to aid in the removal of Hamas. Unfortunately, aligning with Hamas has brought destruction to their doorsteps. The revolving door of violence is the age-old story for the region. Religious and ancestral hatred between these peoples will never cease until total annihilation is imminent. Rationale thought, and policy actions might just then emerge, purely out of the need for survival. Hamas is the official government of the Palestinians, and they have declared war, so all Palestinians are the enemy and at war. War is also hell on earth and should be the very last resort.

The Palestinian Islamic Jihad (PIJ), the second most populous faction in Gaza, is additionally supplied with weapons and training by Iran. This faction has engaged in numerous rocket attacks against Israel in conjunction with other Iranian-backed groups. Operating primarily in the West Bank and the Gaza Strip, the PIJ is regarded as one of the most extremist Palestinian factions. This Iranian proxy group has received terrorist designations from multiple nations, including the European Union and the United States. Historically, Iran and Syria have provided financial assistance to the organization, which maintains strong ties with Hezbollah. Al-Quds Brigades, its military wing, is actively engaged in offensive operations against Israeli targets. Training is also carried out by the Al-Quds members.

Kataib Hezbollah, According to the website of the US Director of National Intelligence (DNI), this is a Shia militant group that presents a significant danger to US personnel in Iraq and Syria. The Iraqi-based Shiite terrorist organization has received substantial support from Iran within the country. The group mentioned above has specifically targeted United States military personnel and their coalition allies, resulting in the United States administration imposing sanctions. In light of the ongoing Hamas-Israel crisis in Gaza, the leadership of that organization has recently made new threats against targets in the Gulf region and the Red Sea.

Asaib Ahl al Haq, Asaib Ahl al Haq is a Shiite militia established in 2006 with the support of Iran's Revolutionary Guards and Lebanon's Hezbollah. This insurgent Iraqi faction emerged with the explicit aim of resisting the American military's presence and control in Iraq. The organization still receives backing from Iran and has obtained official designation from the United States as a Foreign Terrorist Organization. Intelligence sources have detected a rise in communication activity involving Qais al-Khazali, the Iran-supported militia Asaib Ahl al-Haq (AAH) leader, and his supporters. This surge in activity suggests a heightened threat against U.S. troops.

Interestingly, al-Khazali has chosen to utilize a social media platform to communicate with his fighters and followers. He specifically shared a verse from the Quran that states, "Do not hesitate or feel sorrow." You are the ones who are superior. AAH-associated media frequently employ these verses to notify their followers of an impending significant decision, escalation, or attack. Khazali's post was most probably intended to provide reassurance and readiness to his followers in anticipation of an escalation.

Houthi Rebels: The Houthi Rebels, widely referred to as Ansar Allah, are a Yemeni faction that functions as a proxy entity for Iran. These rebels have been supplied with weaponry and training by the Iranian Republican Guard

Corps (IRGC). Under the direction of Iran, the Houthis are executing aerial assaults against commercial vessels in an attempt to disrupt the secure supply routes that the United States and coalition naval forces maintain. Furthermore, Iran provides financial support to smaller militias that have consistently launched unmanned aerial vehicle (UAV) attacks against American forces in Iraq and Syria from their base in Yemen. The ramifications of Iran's assistance to terrorist organizations transcend the Middle East and exert considerable influence in other geographical areas. Should the Houthis continue to threaten human lives, cause disturbances in the worldwide economic system, and obstruct the efficient flow of commerce through the critical waterways of the region, they will bear responsibility for the consequences that ensue. Iran has supplied weaponry to this faction for a significant duration of time during Yemen's vicious civil war. Subsequent to November, the Houthis have employed small assault vessels and unmanned aerial vehicles to engage commercial cargo ships in the Red Sea adjacent to the southwestern coast of Yemen. Currently, prominent commercial shipping companies such as Maersk are choosing to bypass the Red Sea and instead undertake a considerably more protracted and expensive voyage around the southernmost point of Africa, despite the fact that the U.S. Navy has effectively repelled the majority of these assaults. It is abundantly clear that Iran indirectly directed the Houthis to endanger maritime security in the Red Sea.

REGIONAL THREATS

Europe: A substantial Iranian proxy organization, Hezbollah, has established an extensive terrorist network throughout the continent. The network in question was found guilty of a deeply concerning bombing incident that took place in Bulgaria in 2012, with a specific target being Israeli tourists. The worldwide community was profoundly affected by this incident on account of the network's immense sway. Many Islamist organizations use Europe as a staging area, and due to the lax immigration and refugee programs in the past years, it would be impossible to flush out the embedded bad actors in their society. Incidences of violent extremism (VE) and terrorism are increasing. It is my belief that VE poses a more significant threat due to the proliferation of liberalist ideology in society and government, which is fueled by numerous resultant factors that the major media outlets refuse to report on. Additionally, the cycle is driven by a profound fear of losing national identity, the spread of Islamist doctrine, and mistrust of elected officials. Apprehension exists in a space where government support for irregular migration, Islamism, multiculturalism, and open borders is generating an unsustainable influx of migrants that bring about the collapse of the social system of the receiving country and eventually erase the conservative population and their national identity. Islamic migrants in Europe defy the laws and fundamental tenets of the countries that granted them entry and demand that those countries conform to their Islamic standards. In reality, this is an additional clandestine method of propagating Islam and upsetting Western societies.

Nevertheless, this viewpoint will not be investigated by liberal leaders or the media complex due to its incongruity with their destructive ideology. Legal citizens of the host nation are consequently disenfranchised due to the lack of access to resources allocated to them by taxes, exposed to an increase in gang warfare and criminal activity, the degradation of their environment, the transformation of cities into slums, and a general deterioration in safety and quality of life comparable to that of a dictatorship in the third world. However, the mere mention of these facts provokes widespread condemnation from the left, including accusations that they are racists, white supremacists, and anti-Muslim haters. Their propaganda-supported media outlets further amplify these accusations. Extensive documentation exists in Europe regarding this situation, which has since spread to the United States, yielding similarly catastrophic consequences. Our struggle for the preservation of the American identity is comparable. When we speak of terrorism, we are merely scratching the surface; these organizations employ a variety of methods to sow havoc on the society of the host nation. It is critical to acknowledge that the potential consequences for citizens and the integrity of democracy could be far more severe than one might anticipate, with violent extremism posing a greater threat than terrorism.

Latin America: The emergence of Hezbollah in Latin American nations has generated concern due to mounting apprehensions regarding potential assaults and the organization's growing sway in the region, particularly in the Northern Triangle Region (Guatemala, Honduras, El Salvador). The nations of Latin America are impacted by the peril of terrorism that is financed by Iran, and indoctrination of the vulnerable, underserved segment of their societies is in full swing. Hezbollah's networks in Latin America remain intact. An important focal point is the Tri-Border Area of Argentina, Brazil, and Paraguay, where individuals who provide financial support to Hezbollah and those who endorse them have historically engaged in the illegal activity of money laundering. The region, characterized by its permeable boundaries, serves as an ideal sanctuary for both criminals and terrorists, granting them the opportunity to avail themselves of valuable resources. Furthermore, a sympathetic populace, stemming from the sizable Lebanese expatriate community of 30,000 (+) individuals and the accessibility to three nations hosting U.S. and Israeli diplomatic missions and substantial Jewish populations (such as Argentina and Brazil) further enhances their advantages. In Brazil, the lenient government of Luis Ignacio Lula da Silva has permitted Hezbollah and Iranian fronts to discreetly grow without facing any significant investigation from authorities. In Chile, the Palestinian diaspora is highly influential and politically extreme. Iranian operatives and Hezbollah networks have successfully infiltrated various sectors, including the government, media, and academia. Additionally, they are involved in operating illegal financial networks. Additionally, they possess a robust presence in the geographical region known as the Northern Triangle, which encompasses the area surrounding Honduras.

Ultimately, Iran and Hezbollah are polluting the source of information by spreading exaggerated and inflammatory messages. Iran operates a satellite network called

HispanTV, which broadcasts misleading information to Latin American viewers. Additionally, Hezbollah utilizes the Al Mayadeen Espanol platform to disseminate its message. Iranian operatives have formed alliances with pro-Palestinian organizations and leftist groups to provoke opposition against American interests. Iran's cultural centers and academic institutions are actively recruiting individuals, both on and off campuses, through cooperation frameworks to radicalize them and transform them into supporters of terrorism. The combination of illegal financial networks with the ability to mobilize resources and their close collaboration with criminal syndicates indicates an increasing level of risk. There is a significant and widespread mobilization in support of the Palestinian cause throughout the Americas, primarily driven by the Iran-backed dissemination of false information, opposition funding, and collaboration with liberal factions. For decades, it has maintained the ability to carry out acts of terrorism against Israel and America. Now is an opportune time to create destruction and disorder in order to further Iran's goals. Washington should enhance its security protocols in Latin America and the Caribbean, as this region is being utilized as a strategic location for planning and executing terrorist attacks on the American mainland.

Africa: Hezbollah and other Iran-backed factions have increased their presence in the continent, thereby contributing to the expansion of Iran's global terrorist network. Their activities across this diverse continent serve to underscore the far-reaching repercussions that result from Iran's support for terrorism. Many different state and non-state actors act within this space, which ties in with mining, mineral rights, and access. Almost all young military-age men in the African region are indoctrinated by one of many actors, and their belief systems and hatred of the West are embedded within their psyche. It is worrisome that many have reached our southern border and are unaccounted for in the United States. The media and democratic machine are quick to push the "statistics narrative," referencing no attacks in America in the past and relying on historical data to incorrectly dispel concerns and raise the anti-immigrant flag. Unfortunately, this is a political deception and a flawed method to predict the probability of attacks and the threat level assigned to each group. Instead, we need to look at the alignment of many threat-related factors, the current politics of the region, and the influences they were exposed to, which will shape their ideology. It will be a sad but curious day after the next attack on the homeland to see how vicious the fingerpointing and assignment of blame will be.

Asia: The deployment and operation of Iranian paramilitary factions in Syria, including the Zaynabiyoun Brigade and Fatemiyoun Division, demonstrate the extent of Iran's global influence. Comprising individuals engaged in combat from both Afghanistan and Pakistan, these factions operate throughout Asia, thereby exemplifying the considerable sway of Iran. This development raises concerns. There have been recent tensions between Iran and Pakistan, with both countries conducting airstrikes against each other. Pakistan launched airstrikes inside Iran, allegedly targeting militant hideouts, which resulted in at least nine casualties. This was in retaliation for Iran's earlier strikes on Pakistan, which escalated the conflict between the two nations. The situation has drawn international concern, with calls for de-escalation from the United States, China, and the United Nations. Asia is a hotbed for grooming terrorists; it is a hornets' nest we must shy away from. America has a unique gift throughout its history of "backing the wrong horse," we must get out of the regime change game. For example, we have botched up the Middle East and the LAC (Latin American and Caribbean) region. It's time to put that doctrine to bed unless highly necessary due to National Security developments that pose an imminent threat to the homeland.

Difficulties and Repercussions: This is undoubtedly a matter of importance for global security. The substantial financial, military, and technical support that Iran extends to terrorist organizations and militias worldwide presents substantial obstacles and apprehensions for the state of global security and is a direct threat to the national security of America and Western interests. Iran has mastered the art of operating in the grey zone using non-state actors to extend its reach and project force far beyond its borders. These challenges encompass a wide array of matters that necessitate careful consideration. Support for proxy groups by the Iranian regime has been instrumental in sustaining and instigating instability in the already turbulent Middle East. Iran plays a substantial role in the ongoing conflicts in Syria, Yemen, and Iraq, contributing to the escalation of tensions and the encouragement of violent outcomes. Hezbollah and Hamas, two prominent proxies of Iran, are presently presenting Israel with an urgent threat. Armed factions with a formidable arsenal of rockets and missiles routinely employ them to target Israeli population centers, thus exacerbating regional tensions. Possibility of Escalation: Hamas' recent orchestration of the October 7, 2021, massacre, which was followed by attacks from Iranian-backed groups, has substantially escalated regional tensions. These developments underscore the potential for more protracted regional conflicts that could encompass a multitude of nations and actors.

The unwavering support that Iran provides to renowned global terrorist organizations like Hezbollah gives rise to the unsettling potential for terrorist assaults to extend beyond the confines of the Middle East. Constant vigilance is essential for the international community to effectively monitor and counteract these threats. Because of the waning influence of militias backed by Iran, the sovereignty of states in the Middle East has been considerably weakened. These militias often operate independently from the central governments in nations such as Iraq and Lebanon, exacerbating state authority's decline. The humanitarian ramifications of Iran's support for proxy groups are immense, as the ensuing conflicts have taken a considerable toll on human lives and general welfare. The conflict has resulted in the displacement of countless civilians, loss of life, and infliction of unfathomable suffering on those caught in the crossfire. The myriad of intricate challenges underscores the critical nature of global collaboration in addressing the pervasive security risks engendered by Iran's significant support for terrorism. It is of the utmost importance to take decisive action and implement diplomatic solutions in order to guarantee regional and global stability.

Defensive Posture: A comprehensive understanding of Iran's terrorist network should be of the utmost importance for the White House and the U.S. Army to efficiently confront the imminent and critical risks it poses to regional and global stability. Addressing these challenges necessitates a resolute and unified international effort. Addressing the challenges emanating from Tehran and working towards a future marked by peace, stability, and the advancement of human rights necessitates the absolute necessity of global unity. In contrast to the threat that Iran's support for terrorism poses to international security, this issue can solely be resolved through concerted international effort and an unwavering dedication to justice. Tehran serves as the operational hub of this global terrorist network, which underscores the critical nature of taking decisive actions to dismantle it. In order to establish long-lasting peace and stability in the region and beyond, it is critical to eradicate the principal entity, represented by the head of the snake, that is accountable for the organization and maintenance of these detrimental endeavors. In addition to suppressing the aspirations of the Iranian people, the "religious octopus" in Tehran promotes violence and anarchy on a global scale. It is critical to blind the eye of this octopus, disrupt its malicious operations, and hold accountable those responsible for state-sponsored terrorism. The subsequent decline of the corrupt Ayatollahs and the overthrow of the mullahs' government ought to be celebrated as a triumph for modern civilization. Iran's actions are a destabilizing force in the Middle East, Asia, and the West. An international forum comprised of the Great Powers and other influential partners must unite in a message of force to "cease and desist," or overwhelming force politically, economically, and militarily will be brought to bear.

If the United States were to elect a President who possesses a deeper understanding of how to effectively establish deterrence through strength and negotiate skillfully within a diplomatic framework, the outcome of this situation could be significantly different for all involved parties. As an example, during phase one, the United States could establish a cooperative hegemony with President Xi Jinping of China, dividing control areas and engaging in trade with mutually advantageous agreements. During phase two, China and the U.S. would agree to exert pressure on Russia to collaborate on mutually beneficial issues while also reaching a separate agreement for President Putin to restrain Iran. An era characterized by both strategic peace and growth is within our reach. If Iran agrees to stop sponsoring terrorism against Western countries and reaches an agreement on nuclear issues, phase three could potentially offer additional benefits. This could involve gradually including Iran in normal diplomatic relations, including trade with all partners. Successfully achieving this objective would be challenging and necessitate a capable and astute president to strategically navigate the complex geopolitical landscape in America's favor while pursuing three specific objectives. (1) Ensuring economic well-being for all parties involved, (2) Avoiding any hostile or confrontational power-plays aimed at gaining dominance, and (3) Collaboratively working towards establishing regular trade, eliminating food insecurity, and promoting effective governance in their respective areas of control to prevent failed nations from developing. This fosters global stability as transnational criminal organizations are forced to relinquish their control over individual nations. Each major nation that competes for power has a midpoint and a red line that cannot be crossed; the challenge lies in navigating within that range, with the ultimate focus being the welfare of one's own nation. Choosing this alternative is preferable to engaging in a nuclear confrontation between dominant global powers.

Embedded Iran: The successful implementation of authentic regime change requires unwavering determination and shrewd judgment, as opposed to merely supporting a corrupt faction that seeks reform or a self-interested clique motivated by individual benefit. Iran supplies military training and weaponry to factions active in the given regions. In the Gaza Strip, Iran offers assistance to the Palestinian Islamist organizations Hamas and Islamic Jihad. The assault that occurred on October 7th, which initiated the protracted conflict in the Middle East, was carried out by Hamas, the governing organization of the Gaza Strip. Iran projects an image of unwavering support for the Palestinian resistance in its perceived struggle against the Israeli occupation. At present, Hamas and Israeli forces are involved in armed hostilities in the Gaza Strip, which is an integral part of Israel's military intervention in the region. Iran maintained diplomatic ties with Shiite insurgents in Iraq, which it extended support to throughout the duration of the U.S. occupation. The Popular Mobilisation Forces (PMF) is a coalition of paramilitary factions in Iraq that has received official recognition. It comprises a staggering 150,000 (+) members. The coalition predominantly comprises experienced and well-equipped factions demonstrating allegiance to Iran and upholding strong ties with its Revolutionary Guards. In Iraq and Syria, the PMF factions have launched a multitude of assaults against American military installations.

In retaliation, the United States executed retaliatory airstrikes that specifically targeted the elimination of a commander stationed in Baghdad. Syria plays a pivotal role in facilitating the movement of Iranian proxies between Iraq and Lebanon. Following the commencement of the Syrian civil war in 2011, Iran extended a humanitarian aid package to President Bashar al-Assad. This required the mobilization of Guards-affiliated advisors and combatants from Pakistan, Afghanistan, and Iraq. These factions were allies of the Lebanese Hezbollah, which existed to protect the Assad regime. They maintain a presence throughout Syria. Hezbollah is the most steadfast militant ally of Tehran in Lebanon. Since its formation in the 1980s with the intention of resisting Israeli forces in Lebanon, this organization has amassed a considerable quantity of rocket stockpiles amounting to tens of thousands. It also maintains a skilled cadre of fighters who have participated in prolonged confrontations against Sunni Islamists in Syria. Hezbollah conducts recurrent assaults against Israeli forces along the Israel-Lebanon border. Since capturing a substantial portion of Yemen in 2014, the Houthi group has been embroiled in a power struggle against the forces backed by Saudi Arabia to establish its authority in the Gulf nation embroiled in conflict. At the outset, Tehran extended an offer of aid to the Houthis in their confrontation with their Gulf adversary, Riyadh. Presently, the Houthis, alternatively referred to as Ansar Allah, are employed in activities that encompass the deployment of ballistic missiles towards Israel, alongside the deliberate targeting of oil tankers and merchant vessels in the Red Sea. In pursuit of Houthi objectives in Yemen, military airstrikes have been executed by the United States.

The "Axis of Resistance," a coalition backed by Iran and comprised of Tehran and its allies, asserts that its recent actions, which commenced on October 7th, are an immediate retaliation against the aggressive assaults and invasion of Gaza by Israel. Other factions, including the Houthis and Hezbollah, have declared their intention to cease hostilities exclusively in exchange for Israel ceasing its offensive against Hamas. The Houthis persistently engage in intentional assaults against maritime vessels in the Red Sea, thereby impeding global shipping and impacting American interests. In the preceding quarter-century, they have launched a grand total of 143 assaults against American military installations situated in Iraq. In recent times, Russia and Iran have established a more robust alliance, spurred by their shared past experiences of international isolation due to U.S. sanctions and their joint opposition to the hegemony of the United States on the global stage. Unmanned aerial vehicles (UAVs) are being supplied by Iran to Moscow in support of the latter's military operation that targets urban regions in Ukraine. Both countries were engaged in military intervention in Syria in an effort to protect their shared ally, President Assad. Russia has conveyed concern over the escalation of hostilities between Pakistan and Iran, urging both Islamabad and Tehran to resolve their differences diplomatically. Analysts and Western and regional officials are largely of the opinion that Iran's primary aim is to evade a direct military confrontation with Israel or the United States. However, Iran remains prepared to utilize its proxies as a means to confront the military forces of these adversaries in the surrounding area. An unintended attack by Iran and its allies, on one hand, or the United States and its allies, on the other, posing a significant risk of escalation, is exemplified by the intentional killing of American military personnel. Iran has truly mastered the art of waging war in the grey zone using nonstate proxies.

Chapter 13
Leadership Failures – Funding Terrorism

Questions to Ponder: I find that continually asking the reader about the most pressing questions that face us as a nation keeps the reader focused as they navigate through the myriad of information thrown at them to digest. So, are our National Security issues being tackled with fervent vigor, and our projection of power being strategically manipulated to prevent a domestic attack and proactively avoid warfare and sovereignty incursions globally? Are we perhaps projecting weakness with our foreign policy and less than optimal handling by our government concerning global and national security? How many attacks on our citizens, soldiers, and interests will we sustain before taking decisive action? Is our political and military stance with Russia regarding Ukraine - Iran regarding Israel - Hezbollah regarding Israel, and - China regarding the South China Sea sovereignty incursions firm enough and being handled with the correct mix of soft and hard power? Are the use of proxies by Iran, Russia, and China being addressed with enough strength to deter their use against our forces? Last but not least, are we funding and engaging in destructive foreign policies by supporting the countries and groups that sponsor terrorism and seek to do us harm? The ideology practiced by the democratic party, which is heavily influenced by a liberal world order and socialist ideology, has weakened our resolve and placed

America in dire straights. It must be noted that the Republican party has also been guilty of many of these policies that have propped up America's enemies. Are our elected governments (Democrats/Republicans) ensuring that the countries we provide aid to are utilizing it for infrastructure development, improving human security, countering food insecurity, and not funneling it to elements hostile to the United States? Do we have good government oversight of foreign nation program approval, execution, assessment benchmarks, and desired outcomes? As Americans, we need to know where our taxpayer funds are going and what these foreign nations are utilizing these funds for. Most Americans haven't got the foggiest about who their tax contributions are supporting or where it is going, and all this while we are burdened with so many socio-economic issues in our nation. We cannot continue to fund countries, i.e., Pakistan[lxvii], Syria, and Yemen, who support terrorism and actions advocating the destruction of America[94]; it is asinine. We also support refugees and immigrants from these nations, but instead of gratitude, they assemble in the streets of Michigan chanting "Death to America." Why are they not rounded up and deported? We do not need that type of Islamist insurrection in our nation. Islamist ideology must be stamped out immediately as one would address cancer.

---

[94] In fact, a federal audit reveals that for years the government has "lacked a framework to manage fraud risks in humanitarian responses," in Syria. The culprit is the United States Agency for International Development (USAID), the State Department offshoot with a $40 billion budget that annually doles out gigantic sums to foreign causes, including a multitude of leftist groups around the globe. (MAY 12, 2022. JUDICIAL WATCH

U.S. Gives Terrorist Nation $15 Billion in Humanitarian Aid Despite Fraud, Abuse)

Is proper research being done to ascertain what organizations, especially those under the humanitarian guise, use US funding for, and not just rely on what their websites push as the global narrative, but actually where and who their distribution channels lead to? I can assure you there is no great effort to do oversight, as the information at hand is quite troubling[lxviii]. Are these organizations aligned with America's shared global goals, and are the funds being used for humanity's betterment or promoting our enemies' actions? The American political machine is famous for giving out money without instituting suitable accountability measures and ensuring the monies are spent for the purpose indicated[95]. Is any of the funding given to the UN being funneled into organizations supporting Iranian proxies and terrorists, i.e., Hamas and Hezbollah?

Some recent and publicly announced foreign relations blunders include the Biden administration's decision to transfer $235 million in "humanitarian aid" to the Palestinian state, which shows geopolitical ignorance and naivety regarding Gaza's power structure. Hamas stifles Gazan civic society and controls all monetary functions. Since 2007, the Islamist organization has dominated the 2 million populace with an iron fist. From water and power to education and healthcare, Hamas controls everything. It runs the local judiciary under restrictive Islamist laws. The administration of Joe Biden cannot be so daft as not

---

[95] Shahzad, Umer, Suleman Sarwar, Muhammad Umar Farooq, and Fengming Qin. "USAID, official development assistance and counter terrorism efforts: Pre and post 9/11 analysis for South Asia." Socio-Economic Planning Sciences 69 (2020): 100716.

to recognize that one of the world's most violent Islamist groups runs Gaza as a terror state. What could possibly be their motive when even Israel is advising against this, and they know the regional power dynamics very well? The answer is the liberal new world order, liberal activists, and Islamist doctrine have infiltrated the administration (Rob Malley) and Congress as in the members of the squad and their cohorts. (IRAN-The-Ayatollahs-Hidden-Hand. Nov-14-2023 PDF (www.nationalreview.com). In addition to supporting Hamas, the Biden administration and previous administrations of the Republican Party have deliberately contributed to the financing of terrorist organizations in countries hostile to American interests, including Afghanistan and Pakistan. They have been channeling funds to Afghanistan, which is under the control of the Taliban, and are all too familiar with the power brokers who control the funds. The Biden administration established a $3.5 billion fund "for the benefit of the Afghan people" one year after a humiliating retreat. This was yet another waste of taxpayer funds, but it was done to wipe the administration's hands of the egg on their faces, and the Taliban were extremely grateful for the funds and the equipment left behind. In an effort to dissuade terrorist organizations such as the Taliban, Hamas, Hezbollah, and others from targeting American interests, we engage in dialogue with them and exert pressure on our ally Israel to facilitate the release of prisoners. This appeasement of Arab-backed sponsors of terrorism over our military and industrial allies was popular with the Obama administration.

The United States also provides financial support to adversaries outside the Middle East. Recent research by "Open the Books" and Sen. Joni Ernst (R-IA) revealed that over the past five years, federal agencies have given over $1.3 billion to organizations in Russia and China, with $2 million going to the Wuhan Institute of Virology, the origin of COVID. Despite the ongoing conflict between the Ukrainian government and Russia, your tax dollars are being used to pay salaries and other government expenses. Thousands of Ukrainians' salaries will continue to be funded by American taxpayers despite the threat of a government shutdown at the end of September. Following Russia's invasion, the United States has provided Ukraine with a total of $113 billion in financing cycles since then. President Joe Biden recently unveiled a $325 million aid package for Ukraine, which coincided with the visit of Ukrainian President Volodymyr Zelensky to the United States. There are numerous instances of absurdly funded projects involving nations and organizations that have no strategic relevance to the United States.

During a congressional review, the acting directors of the Office of Management and Budget (OMB), Shalanda Young and Antony Blinken, revealed that the President's 2023 Budget allocated approximately $2.6 billion to foreign assistance endeavors promoting worldwide gender equality. This signifies a surplus of over twofold compared to the allocated funds for gender-related initiatives in the prior fiscal year. I wonder if these funds could have helped our city's wounded or homeless veterans or homeless residents. I guess not because we didn't have a Chinese dignitary visiting, as in California, where this was so evident. Oh, don't forget that the critical petition for transgender protections in Bangladesh is included in this budget. That is certainly not how Americans envision their hard-earned tax dollars being spent, but if we don't take notice and be informed, this is what happens. We, the people, have allowed the politicians to do this, so embrace that thought and let us correct it.

Biden's foreign policy has miserably failed in a multitude of instances. Their policies predominantly follow a template to appease and accommodate America's adversaries with the hope of them not furthering their hostile interests. The Democratic Party administration is guided by an ideology that promotes appeasement and a withdrawal from demands and compliance. This approach uselessly aims to defuse tensions and ensure peace by engaging these adversarial nations in dialogue. However, anti-American extremists in the growing Eurasian axis do not want a negotiation as the aim is to reduce the extent of American influence in the region and globally. The absence of strategic long-term planning and leadership in administration policies is evident in their actions, which illustrate how the Biden liberal New World ideological approach to foreign affairs has replaced a legitimate foreign policy strategy in favor of anarchy.

Recently (2023-4), the administration attempted this strategy with Mexican President Obrador and was ridiculed, as Obrador out-negotiated President Biden's staff and instead sent the United States packing with the following demands: over $20 billion, work permits for 10 billion Hispanics, an end to the Cuba blockade, and

Venezuela sanctions. Imagine that Mexico is now dictating American foreign policy. Every one of our adversaries has detected the undeniable weakness of the Biden Administration, their lack of resolve, and like sharks, sense blood in the water and are en route to attack us. President Biden is a laughing stock; just listening to the comments when we travel to Europe and Central America is embarrassing but valid. Foreign news outlets do very revealing, uncensored reporting of the Administration.

Latin America and the Caribbean (LAC): Here are some sobering yet sad realities that exist in our region of the Americas. For decades, the United States has consistently increased the "trust deficit" gap between itself and the nations of the Western Hemisphere to its own detriment. Most nations in the LAC region trade and tolerate America because of necessity, not through goodwill as neighbors. For strategically insignificant reasons, the U.S. has invested more sweat equity and funding in obscure regions of the world rather than in the LAC region, including Mexico. Latin America and the Caribbean have struggled to develop their trade markets and fully capitalize on globalization in an increasingly interconnected world. This has led to a state of stagnation in the region, consequently leading to the emergence of weak and failed states.

There are numerous factors that we can ascribe to this development. Factors such as inadequate governance, ineffective state and regional leadership, socioeconomic inequality, informal economic practices, and lack of human security all contribute to the situation. However, an important yet neglected factor is the absence of regionalization, which refers to the limited exchange of money, trade, and knowledge within Latin America[96]. The current opportunity resides here, and China has seized the opportunity to challenge American hegemony and competitive advantage in the region. Latin American countries have the potential to harness the economic and commercial vitality that has fueled growth and prosperity in other regions of the world if they can establish and enhance their connections with each other in the evolving global landscape of the 2020s. Implementing these changes will necessitate substantial reforms in sectors such as education, automation, and public investments, and in certain nations, a shift in mindset. The United States has consistently failed the region over the past 4-5 decades by excessively engaging in regime change and frequently supporting the wrong leaders, resulting in regional instability.

The majority of U.S. involvement in the LAC region has been short-term and strategically shortsighted, without a focus on long-term infrastructure development, human security, food insecurity, effective governance, and economic growth. As a result, the region is not adequately prepared to withstand political, environmental, and social shocks. The absence of American regional guidance and leadership has resulted in a void of power, leading to political instability, corruption, and the flourishing of illicit markets such as drug trafficking, human trafficking,

---

[96]Why Latin America Lost at Globalization—and How It Can Win Now. https://www.americasquarterly.org/article/why-latin-america-lost-at-globalization-and-how-it-can-win-now/

weapons trading, and organ trading. Currently, the United States is faced with the costly consequences of having neighboring nation-states that are weak and have failed. This vacuum also facilitated the infiltration of Transnational Criminal Organizations into governments (Cartels), enabling them to expand their national, regional, and international networks to facilitate illicit activities and support terrorism. The presence of regional insecurity exacerbates crime rates, irregular migration patterns, and political instability within the United States. The irregular migration has also crippled cities and taken an economic and social toll on American society. An additional consequence of this monumental breakdown in U.S. foreign policy has been the facilitation of substantial Chinese influence in the area via infrastructure, economic, and market expansion, thereby contesting U.S. hegemony and competitive advantage in our immediate vicinity. Less than one-fifth of trade in Latin America takes place within the region. These nations have grown more slowly than many other emerging markets that have stronger commercial ties to their neighbors, which is no coincidence.

The LAC region has long recognized the importance of market alignment and integration. However, despite numerous endeavors to establish free trade agreements (FTAs), they have all fallen short due to a multitude of factors, with leadership deficiency being the most significant. To further elucidate the issue at hand, in the absence of robust leadership from the United States, "too many chefs are gathered in the kitchen." Additionally, the region's preferential trade agreements (PTAs) and free trade agreements (FTAs) are feeble or riddled with bureaucratic exceptions, which hinders their ability to deepen regional flows. When the United States entered into FTAs, trade with its new partners increased compared to non-treaty nations. In the same way, the establishment of the European Economic Community and, subsequently, the European Union boosted regional trade in Europe. Nevertheless, trade agreements in Latin America have had little impact on the expansion of regional commerce, either in absolute terms or in comparison to relations with other countries. It is not coincidental that despite facing comparable challenges, a number of Asian countries have narrowed their wealth gap with the developed world. In contrast, Latin America has remained stagnant, partly due to failed U.S. foreign policy and a lack of leadership spanning many administrations. Consequently, Latin America and the Caribbean should not become complacent. They must address the integration gaps, specifically those pertaining to the largest economies, which should include Mexico, establish a robust leadership framework, and foster convergence among the pacts. This approach would inevitably culminate in establishing a viable Latin American and Caribbean Free Trade Agreement (LAC-FTA).

This course of action is pragmatic and necessary; however, it becomes even more so when considering the protectionist backlash emerging in certain developed nations and the increasing prominence of mega-trade pacts progressively shaping the global landscape. Consider the Comprehensive Progressive Trans-Pacific Partnership and the Regional Comprehensive Economic

Partnership, which is currently under the leadership of China, or the deliberations aimed at establishing an African Continental Free Trade Area. Given that a fully-fledged LAC-FTA would be only half the capacity of the Chinese market, one-third the size of the EU excluding the United Kingdom, and one-fifth the size of NAFTA, being a small PTA in Latin America is a precarious position. Regardless of all the options to consider, one constant remains. The United States must take charge of the region, or China will control it, with Russia and Iran having greater access. This is not a scenario that needs to play out.

Domestic Policies: Are our American domestic policies and enforcement concerning the US/Mexican border lacking and contributing to America's insecurity? Is the expansion of transnational criminal enterprises and drug trafficking across the southern border, along with the drug epidemic in the US, affecting our citizens' safety and security? Is our lack of enforcement and prosecution of criminal activity, reduced support and funding for law enforcement in cities across the US, and the demonizing of police action an emboldening factor for the increased criminality plaguing our streets? Are the liberals, socialists, and social activism groups, which are directly funded by the democratic party machine sponsors in the US, responsible for the multitude of social disruptions, i.e., a) anti-Semitic tensions, b) religious attacks, c) racial tensions, d) inner city looting, e) pro-terrorism demonstrations, f) indoctrination in our education institutions, and breakdown in law and order in society? These are all overt actions and factors present in society on full display. No interpretation is necessary; watch the news stations, including FOX and foreign stations, to include the Spanish feeds. We must answer these questions. YouTube is a good platform for foreign news online feeds. Get informed with truth, America.

Leadership: At this juncture, we shall scrutinize the fundamental and interconnected elements that constitute the majority of government failures. The chain of command is strengthened when leaders manifest leadership qualities such as integrity, respect, intelligence, tenacity, and truth through their actions. Additionally, with the current Biden presidency, another component enters the conversation: cognition must be entertained based on public displays of incoherent thought, garbled speech, frailty, and frequent vacant gazes during communication. Irrespective of the magnitude of an organization, deficiencies in any of these elements lead to vulnerability, unethical conduct, attention diversion, internal conflict, inefficiency, and disorder. In the case of a nuclear country's leader, that could create too many missteps, placing the world in jeopardy of a nuclear conflict. A proficient and unwavering leadership structure functions as a pragmatic illustration and prototype for all subordinate components to imitate. Military circles are cognizant of the historical validation and substantial value attributed to the principle of "leadership by example" as it pertains to effective governance. A series of historical and contemporary examples of leadership deficiencies that have contributed to the current state of our nation and the erosion of societal integrity, respect, and impartiality are presented in the book. The deterioration of all aspects of this country directly results from our elected officials' ineffective leadership and unclear objectives. In another troubling series of events, a breach of the National Command Authority has transpired, jeopardizing the safety and security of the United States during a time of heightened danger. The lack of consistent information or intelligence exchange between the White House and the Department of Defense for at least one week, and most likely for a longer duration, compromised the integrity of the nuclear threat deterrence system (December/January 2023-4). This failure to communicate was in reference to the absence of primary and subordinate personnel responsible for directing the Department of Defense (DOD), who were absent from their posts for medical procedures and vacation. This oversight disrupted the flow of information, a violation of security protocol regarding the "nuclear football," and a critical disconnect between the DOD and the White House. At the time, American military personnel were involved in a multitude of conflicts. Furthermore, it is apparent that a minimum of two weeks elapsed without any security updates or communication between the President and the DOD officials, which transpired once more during a period of active engagement, as evidenced by the extended duration of the MIA (missing in action) incident.

This demonstrates that a breakdown in protocol and inadequate leadership occurred from the highest levels of administration downward. By consistently employing unethical practices to attain their goals, these behaviors serve to reinforce a pervasive mindset that undermines ethical principles and established protocols and regulations within the administration. In addition to this debacle, it seems that numerous government institutions have been refocused from external threats, weaponized and employed to attack political opponents, spreading a particular ideology, and willing to bring to bear any methods required to attain their objectives. This is evidenced by the Justice Department's focus on law-abiding citizens, religious organizations, lawfare, and election interference. Fueled by apprehension regarding potential conflict with Iran, the absence of consistent strategic military engagement against the Islamic Revolutionary Guard Corps (IRGC) represents a monumental error in strategy. Others will soon follow Iran's lead and employ proxies to wage war against the United States, causing American casualties without incurring significant retaliation or suffering losses to the home sponsor.

With respect to the U.S. so-called retaliatory attacks, the Houthi rebel encampments are merely disposable assets; the ruling Mullahs are not significantly affected by the destruction of equipment and manpower. Iran is executing an exceptionally successful stand-off combatant campaign against the United States. Iran's comprehension of the extent of military destruction it would endure in the event of an American strike, which would render futile its efforts to promote political Islamism, could be discerned through a strategic examination of historical, military, social, and internal political data. Such a development, coupled with strict economic sanctions and covert support, would render them susceptible to an internal party revolution, ultimately leading to their political and religious disintegration. Their oppressive regime and the Persian people's subjugation would eventually come to an end with this strategy. By all internal indications, the Persian people are ready for a return to moderation and peace.

Permit me to furnish a brief overview of the present crisis. Iran strives to obstruct the peace process with the aim of impeding the political reconciliation between Israel and Saudi Arabia and undermining the Abraham Accords peace plan, which was formulated during the Trump administration. In addition to hindering the pursuit of diplomatic tranquility in the Middle East by the United States, the Gaza/Israel conflict's violent unrest will inevitably destabilize any Arab-Israeli agreement. Iran's principal aim is to consolidate its status as the preeminent power in the region and the authoritative leader in pursuing Islamic reform. Globally, a time of perpetual turmoil and change is currently in effect. Through terrorist attacks, irregular immigration, and Europe's self-imposed multicultural crisis, Islamists have contributed to unrest in Western nations. Crossing over to the United States, Islamists have been actively subverting stability on the domestic front. Withal, from a strategic standpoint, Iran can benefit from the "ethnic cleansing" of Armenian territory in the Caucasus by Azerbaijan, the potential escalation of hostilities in the Middle East, the incursions into the South China Sea, and the Ukraine conflict in Central Europe. In conjunction with a prisoner exchange, the Biden Administration discharged $6 billion of assets that had been seized from Iran during the previous administration. In doing so, the administration eased the implementation of sanctions and adopted an appeasement policy toward Iran.

Although publicly supporting Israel with strings attached, the Biden administration has been covertly trying to limit the country's military policies regarding Palestine and eliminating Hamas. The Biden administration has recently recommended regime change in Israel, then in another statement a few days later, Biden says he is behind Israel but not any offensive military operations. Talk about confusing and mixed messages from the white house. In what world is this acceptable? Why is the Biden administration involved in recommending regime change against our most trusted ally in the Middle East? It is clear, as a 200W halogen bulb, what side of the coin the administration supports, and this should scare the dickens out of everyone, regardless of party affiliation. Our administration is backing the enemy of our nation; no other explanation exists. In the wake of the Hamas terrorist assault on Israeli citizens, the United States has implemented tactics to undermine Israel's endeavors with the dual purpose of protecting its territory and eliminating the ongoing threat to its populace. Sanctions have been imposed by the administration on Israel to compel the country to cease its offensive operations against Hamas, which is considered a substantial threat to Israel's sovereignty. Even after an all-out assault on Israel by Iranian rockets, missiles, and drones, the administration haphazardly defends Israel's right to self-defense. This move was taken in an attempt to appease the pro-Hamas Anti-Israeli voter base in the United States, especially the democratic constituents in Michigan, Virginia, Georgia, Arizona, and Pennsylvania, while throwing our trusted ally under the bus in their time of need. This strategically incompetent calculation, along with the botched withdrawal from Afghanistan, the border debacle, and a host of other actions, characterizes the helter-skelter policies, ineptness, and lack of loyalties of the administration. I wonder how we would have reacted as a nation after 9/11 if Israel, our trusted ally, tried to sabotage our efforts to retaliate.

The national security crisis has reached a definitive conclusion: the Defense Department and the Commander-in-Chief, or whoever controls the organization, exhibited a lack of discernment, disregarded strategic military analysis, and reacted indifferently to more than 140 attacks on American troops. To date, these assaults have claimed the lives of five Americans, and the administration has failed to establish effective safeguards to protect our military assets against aggressors and attacks while on foreign soil. This can be succinctly summarized using a single word or acronym: "Incompetence or FUBAR." Readers should undertake further research regarding the significance of this acronym. In stark juxtaposition to the preceding administration, the current government exhibits a manifest and verifiable deficiency in aptitude, military strategy, leadership, and administrative acumen.

Takeaway: I hope the reader acknowledges the varying perspectives and ruminates over the many trains of thought presented. Hopefully, many questions have been created to this point in the book. I urge you to fervently seek out the facts, not just rely on mine or other opinions, and make good decisions at the voting booth, as our country and democratic freedoms depend on us, the electorate, to change the trajectory of our country. The shared information and thoughts should not be the gospel you follow but an encouragement to seek out the truth and make an informed decision. I don't see it as my or anyone's job to convert someone's political beliefs and party choice. However, I ask that the reader get excited about their role in upholding democracy, make the party work for your support, and get engaged, fully armed with the truth. I also want my readers to start holding their elected officials' feet to the fire and get involved with correcting the epic failures our politicians have allowed to flourish[97] [lxix]. Americans, in general, have become slaves to politics (mental/political slavery); this is not the correct order of operation. Politicians and politics are merely our elected members and the policies used to represent our (people's) views and direction for the country. Let us take back the reigns of this schizophrenic horse that has escaped the burning barn, return the power to the people, and place America back on track for success.

---

[97] Wiarda, Howard J., and Esther M. Skelley. The crisis of American foreign policy: the effects of a divided America. Rowman & Littlefield, 2006.

PART VI

GEOPOLITICAL

WAR

CHAPTER 14
NATIONAL SECURITY AND HEGEMONY

Geopolitical Threat: Nations across the globe are encountering difficulties in maintaining democratic structures and preventing the rise of autocratic regimes, partly due to the assistance that autocratic-minded leaders receive from countries such as Russia, China, Iran, and North Korea to further their vision of world dominance. The challenges often encompass diminished socioeconomic performance, pervasive corruption, the adverse effects of climate shocks, and the propagation of extremist ideologies through insurgent and terrorist organizations. A decline in global democracy, tensions in U.S. partnerships, weak U.S. governance, and threats to established international standards have impeded the ability of the United States and its allies to address transnational issues over the past decade. Voter discontentment with the inability of governments in Latin America and the Caribbean to improve living conditions will continue to fuel protests against incumbents and intermittent outbreaks of unrest through 2030. Domestic insecurity and violent incidents have been exacerbated by Haiti's ineffective government. Persistent gang-related violence, political instability, deteriorating economy, and health problems have further complicated the humanitarian crisis. This is also true in Mexico, which is primarily controlled by the Cartels. Hopefully, the new law and order female candidate for president can win the elections and change things around from the previous corrupt administration.

The global order is collapsing due to the absence of defined American and Western leadership and a clear guiding principle to follow. The other dominant global powers, unchecked, compete for strategic advantage in the geopolitical space, including the four domains (Air, Space, Land, and Maritime), and exert their influence against a weak U.S. foreign policy. Amidst the shifting geopolitical landscape, the key determinants are the relative power and dominance of the United States and China, as well as the mutual relationship between these countries. Undoubtedly, the United States and China hold the primary positions as key actors, and their respective influence and interaction will undeniably exert a dominant influence in shaping the international landscape in significant regions worldwide. The relationship between the United States and China will perpetually lack complete cooperation due to substantial ideological disparities between them. It will oscillate between "net sum" and "positive sum" outcomes. By collaborating with its allies and partners, the United States possesses the capability to wield additional leverage over China. Nevertheless, accomplishing this objective necessitates active participation from multiple nations and carefully evaluating the advantages and disadvantages of endorsing a global order led by the United States instead of one led by China or without any alignment. The United States must alter its foreign policy perspective towards developing nations, including its commitment to participate in infrastructure development and nation-building efforts. China is gaining favor and support from many nations because of its extensive infrastructure enhancement policies in developing countries, which are improving their domestic capabilities.

China has been using the same economic statecraft to expand its influence in Latin America and the Caribbean, while the United States remains somewhat passive and observant. Over the past few decades, the U.S. has been more involved in Band-Aid foreign policy and short-term investments geared toward drug enforcement and regime changes in the LAC rather than long-term infrastructure, trade, and economic viability investments to elevate the region and prevent its decline into a weak and failed region status. The prevalence of weak or failed states in our Western hemisphere results in a significant influx of irregular migration and transnational crime, which has a detrimental impact on the United States. The decline of the Western hemisphere can be attributed to the lack of strong leadership from the United States and the prolonged failure of its foreign policies from both sides of the U.S. political aisle. In my view, based on the strategic positioning of our power competitors, the most likely scenario for the global order in the next decade would not involve a single dominant power or a rivalry between two major powers akin to the Cold War. Instead, it would entail a loosely dispersed power framework characterized by multiple centers of influence acting within the geopolitical and domain space. The relative power of the United States and China would be counterbalanced by the impact of the security and foreign policies of India, Japan, Germany, France, the United Kingdom, and other countries as they exert influence in their respective regions. A destabilizing element arises from the escalating array of threats to U.S. authority and sway, predominantly stemming from the influence or hostile deeds of Russia, Iran, and North Korea. The deployment of advanced military technology is a subject of concern, but I expect it to be mainly characterized by gradual changes over a period of time. However, it is important to acknowledge that the potential for unexpected technological advancements should not be disregarded. The key technologies to monitor, prioritized based on their likely strategic importance, include conventional and nuclear hypersonic weapons, autonomous systems, and synthetic biology. The occurrence of a strategic surprise and the ability to counteract its effects is of significant concern to the U.S. Defense Department. It is predicted to likely occur in the outer space domain due to increased gray zone competition, strategic importance, and the increased potential for military conflict and gaining the upper hand.

This situation may necessitate reevaluating strategic stability and initiating discussions on arms control, or it could potentially escalate into a military confrontation. Another anomaly that needs to be cautiously observed is the employment of nonstate actors to escalate gray zone activities in various situations. Their objective is to reduce the likelihood of conventional or nuclear conflict while attaining geopolitical goals in regions where the United States has encountered challenges in its response. Analysts at a leading think tank were asked the question, "What or who currently represents the most significant geopolitical threat to the United States?" Without pause, the clear response was China. However, based on my analysis, I have concluded that Russia, China, Iran, and North Korea are not directly culpable for our demise; rather, they are just advancing the geopolitical strategies of their respective nations and ideologies. We would bear the responsibility for our own downfall and insignificance on the global platform by the destructive trajectory we find ourselves on. Our society is currently being threatened by our adoption of appeasement policies and liberal ideology, coupled with a lack of effective governance and political corruption. Should we persist in viewing politics as a form of entertainment and fail to address the problems that have been brought about by the elitists and a president who persistently undermines truth, justice, and trust, we will probably be confronted with significant irreversible consequences. As witnessed in other nations, if political and unchecked power corruption and poor governance overtake the American political landscape, we are doomed as a nation. The Democrat Party's utilization of race and identity politics as a divisive strategy and the President's ineffective governance are leading to extensive political, ideological, cultural, and societal polarization within our country. This is a very destructive trajectory for any nation to be on.

In light of the escalating dangers presented by air and missile assaults, this differentiation is of the utmost importance. A multitude of actors, including non-state organizations like the Houthi insurgency groups, utilize advanced air and missile systems. Participating nations are Iran, Russia, China, and North Korea. The astounding capabilities of these developments, including fractional orbital bombardment systems and hypersonic weapons, are cause for concern. Although not every assault on North America will inevitably entail strategic nuclear confrontation, such a scenario is exceedingly uncommon. Potentially limited air and missile assaults by our adversaries against vital infrastructure could jeopardize our capacity to mobilize forces and execute operations in distant areas[lxx]. The financial difficulty associated with separating air and ballistic missile defense missions arises from the need to allocate resources more efficiently for one goal at the expense of the other instead of considering them as a cohesive mission and pursuing solutions that benefit both sectors.

A sufficient air and missile defense strategy is not in place at the Department of Defense to meet the needs of each combatant commander. Congress must allocate adequate and dependable financial resources to support a comprehensive strategy for air and missile defense sensors, command and control systems, and missiles, emphasizing competitive development, exhaustive testing, and sustainable manufacturing. A recent report recommending a reduction in competition and funding for the NGI to achieve cost savings is perceived as a sly strategy that could compromise the interceptor's military efficacy. The developments in Ukraine and the Middle East demonstrate the expanding complexity and scope of the air and missile threat. There are capable Air Forces in more nations than previously, and no country possesses an arsenal of excessive air and missile defense capabilities. Countering these threats with a unified air and missile defense system is the most efficient course of action, especially counter-drone defenses and GPS scrambling to confuse targeting systems.

The Department of Defense and Congress must work conjointly to strategically develop and finance a comprehensive air and missile defense strategy. This policy would aim to facilitate seamless integration with our allies and partners while equipping combatant commanders with critical capabilities to protect the nation and American forces deployed overseas. This is a contentious and intricate inquiry that might lack a conclusive response. Nevertheless, drawing from many sources of information, I can offer some discernment and viewpoints regarding the present and forthcoming perils that threaten the United States homeland. Terrorism, both domestic and international, continues to be the foremost menace to the Homeland, according to the 2024 DHS Intelligence Enterprise Homeland Threat Assessment. However, the threat landscape is becoming progressively crowded with other potential dangers. Illicit drugs, foreign disinformation, espionage, border and immigration concerns, transnational criminal organizations, environmental-financial-infrastructure-medical-facilities cyber attacks, and economic manipulation are just some examples of other security threats faced. Additionally, the DHS report predicts that the risk of violence posed by radicalized individuals in the United States will continue to be significant, albeit largely unaltered. This threat will be characterized by lone attackers or small-scale attacks that transpire unexpectedly. Terrorist organizations with international ambitions, such as al-Qa'ida and ISIS, may attempt to incite or direct attacks against the United States or its interests abroad in an effort to rebuild.

Furthermore, the DHS report cautions that cybercriminals, nation-states and their proxies, and transnational criminal organizations are employing intricate and malevolent strategies to compromise vital infrastructure, pilfer innovation and intellectual property, conduct espionage, and threaten democratic establishments. Annual cybercrime damages will have already surpassed the $6 trillion spent in 2021-22. The White House issued the National Strategy for Homeland Security in 2023, which delineates the overarching vision and key objectives pertaining to safeguarding the lives and means of subsistence of the American populace. It mandates that the United States implement strategies to discourage acts of terrorism, reduce its susceptibility to both man-made and natural disasters, and mitigate the potential repercussions of an attack or catastrophe. Additionally, the strategy underscores the importance of a comprehensive approach encompassing all levels of government and society. This entails the active participation of private sector, public, tribal, territorial, and federal partners to bolster the Homeland's resilience and security. The local and state law enforcement agencies are still not receiving the training resources to develop an effective dragnet to counter threats. In conclusion, numerous changes in the threat landscape threaten the United States homeland, and the nation must continuously innovate and adapt to defend against them. Although future predictions are inherently uncertain, the United States possesses a comprehensive and resilient framework to evaluate, avert, safeguard, react to, and recuperate from any tangible or potential damage inflicted upon its citizens, values, and interests. It is the early detection and prevention phase that must be improved up and down the line.

Russia: Russia has been accused of developing and conducting space-based nuclear anti-satellite weapon tests. This action may compromise the capabilities and space assets of the United States and its allies. Furthermore, Russia and Ukraine are embroiled in a conflict that has attracted the backing of both NATO and the United States. The presence of tens of thousands of Russian military personnel and apparatus in close proximity to the Ukrainian border has increased the likelihood of a significant escalation or invasion. The full-scale invasion of Ukraine by Russia, which was carried out without any provocation, demonstrates that nation-state competition and conflict are still prevalent in the modern era. In addition to exerting pressure on global norms and potentially posing a threat to its neighbors, China is a formidable competitor. Across a wide range of domains and regions, it possesses the capacity to alter the existing global order. The aggressive territorial war that Russia is currently waging is posing a challenge to the United States of America as well as certain international norms.

The military action that Russia is taking in Ukraine is evidence of its revanchist nature. Russia is seeking to retaliate against Washington both domestically and internationally in order to regain what it perceives to be a sphere of influence, and it is doing so without regard for the interests of its neighbors. Local and regional powers, in addition to strategic rivals, frequently attempt to expand their spheres of influence at the expense of neighboring nations and the international system. While North Korea will continue to strengthen its capabilities to produce weapons of mass destruction and cause significant disruptions on both the regional and global levels, Iran will continue to pose a threat to the region through activities that extend beyond the scope of its regional influence with its coordinated activities with Russia. Iran has been coordinating with Russia on drone technology, and I suspect Iran will build its own drone factory for mass production. They have been supplying some drones for Russian deployment in Ukraine, which will be their testing ground.

China: China's rapid and significant expansion of its military and economic influence in the Indo-Pacific region and other areas threatens both U.S. interests and its allies. China has implemented various strategic measures to strengthen its conventional military capabilities, upgrade its nuclear weapons arsenal, and make progress in advanced technologies like hypersonic weapons, artificial intelligence, and quantum computing. China actively asserts its territorial claims and engages in maritime disputes in the South and East China Seas while also expanding its operations and influence in the Arctic, Africa, and Latin America. China's leadership will likely continue implementing interventionist economic tactics to decrease reliance on foreign technologies, enhance military advancements, and maintain economic growth. These policies, however, could hinder the increase in household incomes and the advancement of China's private sector. Beijing recognizes the fluid and significant geopolitical changes in the escalating competition between the United States and China. It asserts that the United States' diplomatic, economic, military, and technological efforts are intended to impede China's advancement and present a threat to the authority of the Chinese Communist Party. Beijing is enhancing its conventional military forces, power projection, territorial defense, and unconventional warfare capabilities to match the West's and India's posturing within the region. In addition, Beijing is increasing its economic, technical, and diplomatic influence beyond its borders in order to project CCP power, protect its perceived sovereign territory and dominance in the region, and expand its global hegemony.

String of Pearls and Belt Road Initiative: This geopolitical theory was put into practice, and China constructed a series of economic hubs and military installations beginning at the southern tip of China and extending throughout the South China Sea. This will undoubtedly expand their influence and establish a claim to the extensive natural gas/crude oil reserves and fishing resources. The Belt and Road initiative will leverage land and sea routes to establish economic and trade dominance in the Eurasian region, as well as to displace the US competitive advantage. This will result in the acquisition of protected markets. The proposed Silk Road is supplemented by the China–Pakistan Economic Corridor. The theory of China's String of Pearls strategy is in alignment with the Maritime Silk Road. These practices are currently in play, even though a slowing of the Chinese economy has placed a few constraints on expansion.

China Expanded Military Policy: The Chinese government may successfully attain its objectives by capitalizing on its influential position in vital global supply chains, including rare earth minerals. However, this achievement will undoubtedly entail substantial expenses and Western blowback. The CCP leaders' goals are likely to be hindered by a multitude of economic, domestic, and global obstacles that China is currently facing. The present circumstances are shaped by several factors, such as a progressively aging population, significant corporate indebtedness, economic disparity, and increasing opposition to China's assertive conduct in Taiwan and other nations. The current trajectory of the Chinese government (CCP) policies shows it will persist in enhancing its military capabilities to counter the perception of U.S. military superiority, safeguard its sovereign territory, establish regional hegemony, and project influence worldwide. Beijing is accelerating the development of essential capabilities that it deems necessary for the People's Liberation Army (PLA) to confront the United States in a prolonged and comprehensive conflict. China has also adopted import substitution strategies to strengthen its domestic defense production capabilities for sophisticated conventional weapons and weapons of mass destruction. To prevent what Beijing deems a U.S. injection of its Western ideology in a domestic crisis between the two sides of the Taiwan Strait, Beijing plans to establish a sophisticated stand-off military force by the year 2027 to make it tactically costly for U.S. forces to intervene in

Taiwan's defense. The People's Liberation Army possesses the region's most extensive air and naval capabilities. China consistently adopts innovative platforms to enhance its air superiority capabilities and extend military strike capability beyond its initial archipelago and into the Indian Ocean choke points.

The PLA Rocket Force's conventional systems, which include short, medium, and intermediate-range weapons, can potentially threaten American forces and bases in the region. Beijing demonstrates a disinterest in agreements that impose limitations on its goals and declines to engage in negotiations that give advantages to the United States or Russia. Beijing is effectively constructing a "deterrence through strength" framework to put in play as it aspires to gain more operating space and achieve global hegemony. Beijing's increased confidence in its nuclear deterrent will strengthen its determination and intensify conventional conflicts. China is currently constructing numerous Intercontinental Ballistic Missile (ICBM) silos. China is continuously advancing towards becoming a leading space power and aims to equal or exceed the United States by 2045. It is extremely probable that China will achieve world-class status in space technology by 2030. China's primary objective in its space initiatives is to enhance its international position and offset the United States' dominance in economic, military, technological, and diplomatic domains.

PLA military campaigns have a strong dependence on counter-space operations, with China possessing counter-space weapons that are specifically designed to target satellites belonging to the United States and its allies. The People's Liberation Army (PLA) currently deploys advanced anti-satellite weaponry capable of destructive and non-destructive actions in space and ground operations. China has deployed various ground-based counter-space capabilities, such as electronic warfare systems, directed energy weapons, and ASAT missiles, intending to disrupt, damage, and eliminate target satellites. China has showcased its ability to operate potential space-based counter-space weapons through orbital technology demonstrations. However, it is important to note that these demonstrations do not constitute actual tests of counter-space weapons. China's persistent challenge to the technological competitiveness of the United States stems from its focus on critical sectors and its exclusive possession of commercial and military technologies acquired from the United States and its allies. The Chinese government is enacting more stringent measures to promote domestic innovation and achieve self-sufficiency.

China Market Leverage: China leverages its extensive market penetration and authority over vital supply chains to apply pressure on foreign governments and corporations, compelling them to grant authorization for the transfer of intellectual property and technologies. China holds a significant role in international supply chains that span numerous technology sectors, such as pharmaceuticals, critical minerals, semiconductors, batteries, and solar panels, among others. In April 2020, Xi declared his intention to heighten the international supply chain's reliance on China to exert control over critical supply chains and potentially utilize them to sever or coerce relations with other countries in times of crisis. Regardless of political or economic motivations, the manufacturing and consumer sectors of the United States and Western nations could be significantly threatened by the Chinese government's effective utilization of its dominance in these markets. Presently, China is at the forefront of the construction of new semiconductor chip factories. By late 2024, it aims to have established a multitude of semiconductor factories, focusing on the production of established older technologies.

The extraction and processing of various critical materials, such as rare-earth elements under China's control, pose a significant vulnerability for the United States. China could manipulate the markets for critical minerals for economic gain or as a negotiating strategy in the event of a political or commercial dispute by imposing quantity restrictions. Prolonged supply disruptions caused by China may lead to production shortages that have a negative impact on the Western nations and the United States civilian and defense manufacturing sectors. Additional sectors that merit consideration include manufacturing solar panels, pharmaceuticals, and batteries. By 2025, it is projected that 65 percent of the lithium-ion battery market will be controlled by PRC-based companies, with China leading in every aspect of the supply chain.

Presently, China produces forty percent of active pharmaceutical ingredients (APIs), which are critical components of medications. Moreover, at each stage of production, China has already captured over 80 percent of the global market for solar panels; this proportion is expected to surpass 95 percent in the near future. Without question, China's cyber espionage threat to U.S. private and public sector and government networks is the most extensive, dynamic, intrusive, and persistent at this moment in time. Should Beijing maintain the perception that a significant confrontation with the United States was imminent, it would almost certainly employ aggressive cyber attacks that specifically target American-owned military assets and critical infrastructure across the globe.

The strike would aim to disrupt American military operations by impeding the decision-making processes, generating widespread public panic, and paralyzing the deployment of American forces. China may possess the potential capability to carry out cyber assaults that could cause significant disruptions to critical infrastructure services in the United States, such as oil and gas pipelines and rail systems. Beijing aims to enhance its covert influence and global intelligence strategy to promote the CCP's political, economic, and security objectives more efficiently. China is actively pursuing strategies to cast doubt on the United States' leadership, erode democratic values, and increase its own sphere of influence, specifically in the East-Asian and Western-Pacific regions, which Beijing considers to be within its sphere of influence. The primary goals of Beijing are to exert influence over U.S. policy and foster a positive public perception of China in the United States.

At times, nevertheless, it has intervened in specific campaigns for office that involved politicians deemed to hold anti-Chinese views. Beijing employs a sophisticated combination of covert, overt, legal, and illegal tactics to mitigate United States censure, sway the perspectives of American power centers regarding China, and exert sway over decision-makers at all levels of government. Likely, leaders of the People's Republic of China (PRC) hold the belief that a bipartisan consensus in the United States that opposes China hinders their capacity to exert direct influence over U.S. policies concerning China at the national level. Beijing has stepped up its efforts to increase its influence at the state and local levels in an attempt to sway U.S. policy in its favor. It believes that local officials are more receptive to pressure than federal officials.

Iran: As a regional adversary, Iran poses a substantial threat to the security and stability of the United States and its allies in the Middle East. Iran has continued its quest for a nuclear program with the capability of producing nuclear weapons in defiance of the 2015 Joint Comprehensive Plan of Action (JCPOA) agreement, which sought to restrict the country's nuclear aspirations. Proxy organizations and militias supported by Iran have also launched attacks against U.S. and coalition interests and forces in Syria, Yemen, Iraq, and other regions. Iran's development and testing of ballistic missiles and drones have the potential to pose a threat to American and allied forces and bases located in the region. This threat could extend to the United States. Tehran has employed strategies to achieve its objectives by expanding its nuclear program, engaging in diplomatic maneuvers, employing conventional, proxy, and allied forces, conducting military transactions and acquisitions, forming partnerships, and conducting increased proxy operations. The issue that bothers me the most is either side misreading the strategic landscape, escalating operations, and engaging in a full-blown attack on military infrastructure. The constant attacks on Israel by Iranian proxies will result in a regional skirmish and could involve battlefield nukes.

Notwithstanding its perception of a fundamental conflict in its relationship with regional allies and the United States, the Iranian government persists in its quest for regional dominance. The Iranian objective for the region is to develop its hegemony and network footprint in satellite nations. Their other immediate focus is to displace the ruling mechanisms in Jordan and close the operating space between Iran and Israel. Iranian generals are developing and directing attacks on Israel from Syria. To disrupt the attacks and leadership infrastructure against Israel, these proxy strongholds and Iranian TOC (tactical operating centers) outposts at their embassies need to be neutralized. The governing Iranian administration participated in prolonged negotiations lasting more than a year with the objective of extending the Joint Comprehensive Plan of Action (JCPOA), which had expired in 2015. Due to the belief of senior Iranian officials in Washington that the United States is incapable of delivering or sustaining the benefits of a renewed JCPOA, they have been unable to finalize the agreement. In the Middle East, Iran will persist in presenting both direct and indirect dangers to the United States. For more than a decade, Iran has endeavored to achieve its goal of establishing proxy networks within the United States. Based on observed actions coming out of Iran and its political climate, I worry that Iran is becoming more brazen and willing to create a catastrophic event in the United States through its grey zone operators.

Actors operating under the banner of Iran may attempt to initiate attacks against United States personnel and forces in Iraq, Syria, and potentially additional nations and regions, such as Jordan and Israel. The United States will continue to face challenges in the region from Iran as a result of its hybrid warfare strategy, which combines conventional and unconventional capabilities. Iran has been working on drone technology with the Russians and, to a smaller extent, China. With regard to enhancing Iran's military capabilities, the IRGC will remain an essential element. Recently, there has been increased activity coming from the Quds Force, an Islamic Revolutionary Guard Corps (IRGC) elite clandestine division, which is primarily tasked with training proxies and conducting foreign operations. They have been staffing out their generals to proxies, especially in Syria, to coordinate attacks against Israel. According to reports, Iran is allegedly procuring sophisticated conventional weapon systems, such as attack drones, helicopters, fighter aircraft, trainer aircraft, main battle tanks, and para-naval patrol ships. However, financial limitations and budget deficits will hinder the pace and extent of acquiring these systems. The United States and its allies in the Middle East face a significant risk to their military and commercial assets due to the persistent missile, UAV, and naval capabilities of Iran. Tehran strategically expands its regional influence by employing irregular warfare operations and a network of militant allies and proxies. Iran's ballistic missile programs pose an ongoing threat to nations in the Middle East due to the continent's largest stockpile of such missiles. Utilizing its pursuit of innovative fuel for its reactors, Iran acquired this enriched metal uranium.

Under the JCPOA, uranium metal production, a critical component in nuclear weapons, was strictly prohibited. Despite the JCPOA, Iran has continued to augment the volume and concentration of its uranium stockpile. The increasing sophistication of Iranian cyber operations and its propensity for aggressive behavior present a significant risk to the security of networks and data belonging to the United States and its allies. The opportunistic strategy employed by the Iranians has exposed owners of critical infrastructure in the United States to the risk of coordinated cyberattacks. This becomes abundantly clear whenever Iran identifies a new domain in which it may pose a threat to the United States.

Biden gives Iran Lifelines: One of the worst strategic moves America could have made in this Biden administration is the switch to a more docile stance on actively enforcing Iranian sanctions and allowing funding to be available for them to access indirectly. This appeasement strategy has given Iran strategic operating space to escalate its regional game plan. This misreading and policy direction will encourage Iran to take increased action in the near future. I foresee an impending Israeli-Iranian military action and intensified covert actions between these nations. America is delaying action to assist Israel, which could result in Israel using other than conventional means or corralling actions in Gaza to eliminate Hamas and terminate hostilities with the least damage to their homeland. Suppose Hezbollah and Iranian main forces engage Israel simultaneously, and America doesn't assist in offensive operations because of Islamic, anti-Israel domestic pressure in America. In that case, the Biden administration and America will lose credibility on the world stage. Iran still needs to assert dominance in the eyes of its followers by striking a blow on the American homeland. I suspect that is in the works. The Democratic Party's southern open border policy is giving all bad actors the necessary access to our homeland. It is inconceivable to me that any American political party would place the nation and its citizens in mortal danger. What is the democrat's motive, you ask?

North Korea: North Korea is classified as a rogue state due to its refusal to comply with international sanctions and pressure to terminate its nuclear and missile programs. North Korea has carried out a total of six nuclear tests and dozens of missile launches, some of which have demonstrated the ability to reach the U.S. mainland. Furthermore, North Korea has instigated provocations, infringed upon human rights, and launched cyberattacks against Japan and South Korea, both of which are critical regional allies of the United States. Investing in specialized capabilities to deter external intervention, cover up ongoing weaknesses in conventional forces, and advance political objectives through coercion are all ways in which the North Korean military will continue to pose a significant threat to the United States of America and its allies. Kim Jong Un, the leader of North Korea, is steadily increasing the country's conventional and nuclear capabilities, intending to go after the United States of America and its allies strategically. A strengthening of North Korean and Russian alliances is on the horizon and must be watched closely.

North Korea will be able to engage in intermittent acts of aggression to reshape the security dynamics of the region to its advantage if it is able to acquire this capability. There is a high probability that Kim Jong-un is actively working to improve North Korea's standing in a global context that he considers to be favorable to his highly authoritarian regime. Consistently, North Korea demonstrates public support for the foreign policy goals that are being pursued by Moscow and Beijing. Kim probably believes that nuclear weapons and intercontinental ballistic missiles (ICBMs) represent the highest available level of security for his autocratic regime. The fact that he is certain he will eventually be recognized globally as a nuclear power is why he has no intention of discontinuing these programs. In the year 2022, Kim strengthened his position by carrying out a series of intercontinental ballistic missile (ICBM) tests. The purpose of these tests was to improve North Korea's ability to carry out offensive maneuvers against the United States of America. In addition, he made modifications to the nuclear legislation of his country, which resulted in a greater emphasis being placed on the nuclear arsenal as a fundamental component of North Korea's national security. As the most important component of his national security strategy, Kim continues to maintain his unwavering commitment to increasing the size of the nation's nuclear arsenal and maintaining nuclear capabilities and capabilities.

A public declaration has been made regarding the enhancement of North Korea's capability to threaten both South Korea and the United States by threatening both countries. North Korea is presumably making preparations to carry out a nuclear test in order to advance its military modernization goals and to facilitate its efforts to engage in tactical nuclear endeavors. A piece of legislation was passed by the government of North Korea in September 2022 that ratified the country's self-proclaimed status as a nuclear power, established indefinite durations for nuclear utilization, command, and control, and rejected the concept of denuclearization. In spite of the fact that North Korea's CBW capabilities continue to pose a threat, the International Criminal Court is concerned that Pyongyang may use them in a covert operation or during a conflict.

North Korea's cyber program presents an agile and sophisticated threat in the areas of cybercrime, cyberespionage, and cyberattacks. The cyber forces of Pyongyang have achieved an exceptional level of expertise in achieving a wide variety of strategic goals against various adversaries. These adversaries include an expanded roster of targets within the United States government. Espionage operations have been carried out by North Korean cyber actors with the intention of compromising multiple organizations. These operations are in addition to the cybercrime activities that Pyongyang has orchestrated. The discourse makes reference to a variety of entities, including academic institutions, the media, defense companies, and governments representing a variety of nations. The North Korean government continues to engage in cyber espionage activities, most likely with the intention of acquiring technical data that would enhance the capabilities of its military and weapons of mass destruction (WMD).

Global Terrorism: The enduring and intensifying menace that terrorism poses to the United States and its global interests continues. The United States faces a threat from both domestic and international terrorists who may be swayed or driven by extremist organizations or ideologies. Notable terrorist groups, such as al-Qa'ida, ISIS, and their associated factions and partner organizations, present a significant danger to the United States of America. The United States is facing the danger of domestic violent extremists, Islamist sympathizers, anti-government militias, and political/religious/ideological radicalized individuals who may target government officials, law enforcement, minorities, or individuals who are perceived as adversaries. This was very evident in the spat of political, social activist-infused race riots in the past few years. The United States faces several significant military challenges that require continuous vigilance and readiness. The United States and its allies collectively employ diplomatic, economic, and military strategies to discourage, counteract, and mitigate these threats. Due to these threats' complex and ever-changing nature, developing new and creative strategies and solutions may be necessary.

In the coming year, terrorism will continue to be a persistent and increasingly diverse threat to American individuals and interests, both domestically and internationally. The United States faces substantial risks from terrorist organizations such as ISIS, al-Qa'ida, and the transnational Racially or Ethnically Motivated Violent Extremists (RMVE) movement, which pose significant dangers to individuals, buildings, and national interests. Both Iran and Hezbollah are firmly dedicated to carrying out acts of terrorism and may potentially attempt to do so within the United States. After 2021, there was an increase in ISIS and al-Qa'ida restructuring, and both of these groups persist in exploiting regional conflicts and political instability to advance their objectives. This was evident as the U.S. policy towards Iran loosened. Despite the elimination of several prominent ISIS figures, the group will continue its insurgency in Iraq and Syria to restore its capabilities and bolster its membership. ISIS is anticipated to continue being the predominant menace to American individuals, structures, and interests in areas where the organization is actively engaged.

The ideology and propaganda of ISIS are expected to persist in inciting acts of violence in Western countries, including the United States. Interstate conflict, the instability of states, and challenges in governance present risks to the interests of the United States domestically and internationally, as well as to our allies and partners. The escalating tensions arising from heightened strategic competition have manifold implications for the national security of the United States and its allies. Countries that increase their military operations in critical areas are at risk of unintentionally escalating tensions and triggering conflicts between nations. It is noteworthy to understand that a shift in policy towards appeasement and not showing strength coupled with effective diplomatic missions has caused increased attacks on our servicemembers and interests. An area of concern regarding the crime-terror nexus is the Iranians utilizing Hezbollah and other LAC (Latin America and Caribbean) converts to develop forward staging camps with the cartel's infrastructure and networks in Mexico for attacks on the American homeland. Their drone technology would be perfect for this strike package to be highly effective.

White Supremacy: At this moment, it would be irresponsible of me not to highlight an exemplary instance wherein the media industrial complex, in tandem with the Biden administration, disseminated white supremacist propaganda with the intention of confusing, diverting attention, and inciting racial animosity between Blacks and Whites, and other minorities. Fear not; only "common sense reasoning" will be necessary to decipher this sophisticated disinformation strategy. It is referred to as the "wrap-up smear," and prominent Democratic Party leader Nancy Pelosi described it well, as referenced earlier. In all candor, she initially tried asserting that this was a Republican tactic to start with. However, I implore you, the reader, to scrutinize the methodology and extrapolate it to the widespread misinformation strategies currently being employed by the Democrats, which are replicated by their weaponized agencies and media surrogates. It is playbook perfect. One could counterargument this line of thinking by claiming that Republicans also employ it, but current actions say otherwise. I concur that the notion that every politician has likely engaged in some form of deceit is highly plausible.

Hence, a historical assessment of the political and media landscape over the past three and a half years is necessary. Presently, I request that the reader don their critical thinking caps and impartially analyze the prevailing political information environment in the United States, including the favored groups and the propagandized ideology. Consider whether this administration is currently engaging in anything resembling the political misinformation, slanders, smears, pandering, election interference, voter demographic fixing, and politicking that is occurring. Pelosi provides an analysis of this strategy in the subsequent quotation. "You disseminate false information and smear someone, and then you sell the smear. After that, you compose it, and if they see it, the press will report that it is this, this, this, and this. You fabricate an allegation, have the media cover it, and then proclaim that everyone is writing about this charge" (Pelosi, 2017). This playbook sounds all too familiar to me.

The democratic machine propagates the fallacious narrative that "white supremacy has reached an all-time high in a racially fractured America, surpassing even the threat of terrorist attacks." Furthermore, it asserts that the white culture in the country is becoming more anti-government, anti-trans, anti-Islamic, and anti-transgender and that these individuals are Republican party members who support "MAGA" and candidate Trump. It is interesting to note that these Republican rallies are peaceful, and some news reporters have even called it a love fest, as in the massive New Jersey and Bronx rallies. Federal agencies are influenced by the elected leaders and elitists of the ruling party to present supporting narratives and skewed statistics that bolster talking points for mass consumption. Subsequently, the talking points are distributed to the propaganda arm of democratic media, social activists, and talk show repeaters; "one manufactured narrative" is broadcast almost verbatim across the airwaves.

This constitutes a rudimentary strategy whereby the same message is repeatedly disseminated through the airwaves and ultimately evolves into a manufactured truth. The public will now accept as gospel truth any argument substantiated by manipulated "factual statistics" published by perceived "reputable federal agencies and aligned think tanks," allowing any talking head to legitimize their position. This is marketed to the "zombie electorate," which consists of the uninformed, ignorant, and slothful members of society who refuse to think independently and blindly follow orders. This is a severe characterization of a cross-section of our society. Still, it must be discussed because the United States is in a downward spiral, and social irresponsibility cannot be embraced at any level. The label "white supremacist" is applied to every violent act committed by a Caucasian. Furthermore, endorsement of Israel is considered anti-Islamic, and any discourse that challenges Islamism, transgenderism, liberalism, illegal immigration, border security, or conservative viewpoints is promptly stigmatized and linked to white supremacy. Oh, don't forget the catch-all phrase, racism, which all are included in the "wrap-up smear" strategy utilized to discredit such speech or dissenting opinions.

Border Infiltration: It is in total disbelief that I watch the attitudes, answers, lack of information, and arrogance that government-appointed officials display during congressional hearings. Absolutely no regard for the constituents they serve or the harm they cause to our nation. The open-border policies implemented by the Biden administration and carried out by Alejandro Mayorkas, the Secretary of the Department of Homeland Security (DHS), involved reversing effective border security measures and his refusal to enforce laws passed by Congress, are matters that extend beyond the scope of legal discussion. Instead, the administration's decision to permit millions of undocumented immigrants, cartel agents, convicted criminals, gang affiliates, potential terrorists, and foreign adversaries to enter the United States through its borders has led to significant, measurable, and devastating outcomes that are impacting every state, city, and town in the nation. The fentanyl crisis, exacerbated by the administration policies, persists and continues to inflict severe consequences on families and communities nationwide. The men and women engaged in safeguarding the border and protecting the homeland are experiencing a growing sense of neglect from their Washington leadership. Furthermore, states are being exposed to perilous situations due to the policies implemented by Mayorkas and other officials. The effect of this situation on Border Patrol agents and other law enforcement officers has been unparalleled.

Due to Biden's policies, there has been a growing number of undocumented immigrants who are engaging in criminal activities in the United States and are not being caught when they enter the country. Due to the criminal intentions of undocumented immigrants, Americans often experience injustices such as sexual assault and physical violence. Furthermore, a substantial portion of the American population has been victims of homicide perpetrated by illegal immigrants residing in the United States. Moreover, illegals who drive in a careless and lawless manner are transforming our streets into perilous zones. Mayorkas' decision to open the border under the administration's directives, driven by political motives and executed with careful calculation, has resulted in even those who choose to make the journey and enter the country illegally becoming victims of the decision. Countless individuals have endured violence, degradation, and abuse perpetrated by these merciless organizations. Simultaneously, numerous individuals have either died or been abandoned to their fate in the jungles and deserts during the journey. This is due to the fact that a vast number of individuals have entrusted themselves to cartels and smugglers as a result of their desperate desire to undertake the journey towards the Southwest border. Transnational criminal organizations (TCOs) can potentially undermine the legal systems in partner countries and jeopardize the integrity of the international financial system. These actions significantly threaten the public safety of the United States of America and its allies. These challenges greatly affect the national security of the United States as they directly contribute to concerns related to unauthorized migration, incitement of criminal activity and violence, and the advancement of the goals of certain bad actors in the United States. Transnational criminal organizations (TCOs) engage in a diverse array of illicit activities that have a direct impact on the United States of America. These activities encompass the manufacturing and distribution of narcotics, the transportation of individuals for illegal purposes, the illicit transportation of people, illicit financial activities such as the laundering of illegal cash, and criminal activities conducted through computer networks. TCOs classify operations in human trafficking, encompassing smuggling, sex trafficking, and forced labor, as highly profitable and low-risk crimes that are exploited easily. These organizations present a menace to the well-being and security of a substantial portion of the American population and facilitate the increased operations of criminals and individuals engaged in corruption.

The United States' lenient border policies have empowered these organizations and facilitated their growth and establishment of extensive networks within our states. Fentanyl is believed to be the primary cause of the majority of the 100,000 deaths that occur each year in the United States due to drug overdoses. Law enforcement agencies across the United States are confiscating a growing amount of fentanyl, even in previously regarded safe rural towns. Mexican multinational corporations employ mislabeling techniques on unregulated dual-use chemicals in order to evade international regulations and distribute them globally. China is the main supplier of the precursor chemicals necessary for the manufacturing of fentanyl. These chemicals are acquired through chemical intermediaries, predominantly of Mexican and Chinese origin. Presently, Mexican transportation companies and their competitors are involved in intense territorial disputes regarding the routes utilized for the transportation of migrants and narcotics, often resulting in violent confrontations. The participation of transnational criminal syndicates in illicit drug activities is a major contributing factor to the escalating homicide rates in Colombia, the primary producer of cocaine worldwide, and the cartel expansion in Mexico. Unlawful financial activities endanger global financial systems by allowing the laundering of billions of dollars of illicit funds through financial institutions in the United States and other countries, and some of these funds are earmarked to fund terrorism. Oftentimes, transnational criminal organizations (TCOs) employ shell corporations as a means to obscure their authentic identities. Furthermore, individuals may seek the aid of professionals who serve as gatekeepers or money launderers in order to obtain entry into legitimate financial systems. The professionals encompassed in this category are accountants, lawyers, notaries, and real estate brokers. Transnational criminal organizations (TCOs) facilitate the movement and concealment of illicit funds through various means, such as acquiring real estate in the United States, employing structured deposits, engaging in trade-based money laundering, conducting wire transfers, and smuggling significant sums of cash. Regardless of the avenue or income stream, these funds go to either expand illicit operations, reward bad behavior, corrupt the judicial and political system, or fund acts of terrorism.

Overall Threat Theater[98]: The United States will be confronted on many fronts, and although both domestic and international terrorism continue to pose the greatest risk to national security, the threat environment is expanding to include additional perils. It is expected that the level of violence threat presented by radicalized individuals in the United States will remain substantial, albeit with minimal modifications, throughout the course of the subsequent year. Occasional attacks carried out by small groups or individuals acting alone will constitute this threat. Terrorist organizations from around the world, such as al-Qa'ida and ISIS, are expanding their operations globally and possess support networks that could potentially enable them to launch attacks against the United States. Officials anticipate that the primary cause of death for Americans will continue to be the trafficking of illegal drugs from Mexico to the United States. In contrast, terrorism will continue to pose a continuous overarching threat. Involvement in the mixing and pressing of fentanyl by traffickers based in the United States has increased over the past year, resulting in the production of increasingly lethal drug mixtures. It is anticipated that in the coming year, both domestic and international adversaries will target our critical infrastructure out of concern that it will negatively impact American industries and way of life. Unfortunately, the Biden administration has not taken a tough stance on China to curb Fentanyl exports to the Americas. Also, the administration has not held Mexico's

---

[98] Cao, Lansheng, Ming Gu, Ding Jin, and Changyan Wang. "Geopolitical risk and economic security: Exploring natural resources extraction from BRICS region." *Resources Policy* 85 (2023): 103800.

feet to the fire in controlling the cartel operating space within Mexico and at the border. Just these two issues and their inability to receive direct action from the U.S. Government, even with the amount of American fatalities attributed to their continued operation, is unforgivable and reflects the true nature of the Democrat party's protection for its citizens.

On other fronts, the persistent prevalence of cyber assaults targeting networks for military, financial, or strategic objectives, as well as critical infrastructure, has experienced a discernible surge in physical assaults over the past year. This cyber vulnerability could have cataclysmic consequences as the collapse of society and our support systems could render America inert and irrelevant on the global stage. Many analysts fear that orchestrated acts of violence and external interference targeting our election systems, procedures, and personnel could have a substantial impact on the 2024 election cycle if allowed to occur. We are already witnessing demographic voter manipulation and an attack on the democratic process by enforcing candidate suppression using federal agencies to wage "lawfare" and do the bidding of the elitists, with total disregard for the people's choice for presidential representation. It's the old adage that we know more than you do, so we will make the decisions for you. I think that is called autocracy shrouded in democratic clothing to deceive the people.

Due to the dynamic nature of our security environment, it is imperative to change the CBRN and CWMD (Chemical Weapons of Mass Destruction) strategy to effectively address the current and persistent challenges and other immediate and long-term threats. The United States must enhance its ability to conduct large-scale cooperative military operations in a CBRN battlespace. This is crucial for effectively addressing the challenges posed by the current and future security environment. Furthermore, the Department of Defense's operations, activities, and investments must consider the ever-changing variables to thwart potential adversaries from gaining an unjust advantage in various types of conflicts, including asymmetrical warfare scenarios. The possession of weapons of mass destruction (WMD) and chemical, biological, radiological, and nuclear (CBRN) weapons by China and Russia presents substantial challenges to the United States of America. However, it is crucial to prioritize dealing with the current regional dangers presented by nations like Iran and North Korea, especially considering the increasing presence of non-state actors operating in the grey area. There are ongoing concerns about the potential for both governmental and non-governmental organizations to develop or improve programs related to weapons of mass destruction (WMD). The swift advancement of technology, encompassing various domains like life sciences, artificial intelligence, automation, nanotechnology, hypersonic delivery systems, and defensive structures such as fortified and deeply buried facilities, has intensified this concern.

Some actors along the southern border exploit established supply chains and networks to procure unauthorized materials while concurrently fabricating domestically manufactured components. This is an additional cause for worry, especially considering insufficient security and lack of accountability at the southern border. Espionage and the misappropriation of intellectual property are two further elements that contribute to this situation becoming more severe. The challenges of preventing proliferation are exacerbated by the interconnectedness of global supply chains, the use of front companies and cryptocurrencies to enhance anonymity, the availability of dual-use materials and knowledge, and the lack of universal export controls on critical items. Enormous volumes of data, artificial intelligence, and genomic modification are all potent technologies that can greatly influence the CBRN landscape. These technologies offer the potential for creating enhanced military and civilian solutions that are simultaneously more efficient, resilient, and cost-effective. However, they also create the potential for unforeseen risks from both governmental and non-governmental entities. Potential adversaries can utilize the same scientific advancements in biology and chemistry that have been applied to develop medical countermeasures, thus enabling them to create new or improved hazardous substances. A significant amount of information and testing that could be utilized to develop a biological weapon was obtained due to the COVID experiments, including the presumably accidental release of the experimental virus and the dispersal rate. This information could be used to assist in the development and dispersal of a biological weapon.

Given the prevailing challenges to America's homeland, it is anticipated that the People's Republic of

China (PRC) will capitalize on this and diligently employ assertive economic strategies in an effort to surpass the performance of our military, financial, and industrial base. The People's Republic of China is expected to continue to manipulate markets, conduct economic espionage, employ coercive economic strategies, and acquire our technologies and intellectual property without authorization. The advancement in artificial intelligence platforms and advanced software application tools will undoubtedly augment the strategy employed by our adversaries if we are not proactive in developing counter strategies. Nationalist entities employ artificial intelligence to generate and disseminate misinformation to erode confidence in democratic procedures, governmental establishments, and societal cohesion. By developing new entry points and tools, cybercriminals can compromise more targets and execute extensive, effective, and difficult-to-detect cyber assaults. International terrorist organizations persist in interacting with their digital adherents for the purposes of fundraising, disseminating information, and inciting violence. In contrast, their counterparts in Africa, Asia, and the Middle East prioritize objectives specific to their respective regions. Following the withdrawal of the United States from Afghanistan, ISIS-Khorasan, a regional affiliate of the organization, has gained prominence due to a series of noteworthy attacks executed in foreign nations and English-language media releases that sought to disseminate the group's regional concerns to Western audiences. Terrorists with ties to the United States may gain entry into the country through well-established travel routes and permissive immigration loopholes.

Russia will probably continue to exploit clandestine websites, social networks, online bots, trolls, and conventional media to amplify pro-Kremlin discourse and maintain sway in the United States. In order to bolster their public relations endeavors, it is anticipated that China, Iran, and Russia will continue to engage in transnational repression within the United States, which will undermine American laws, norms, and individual liberties. Several citizens in the United States have attracted the attention of adversaries who perceive them as authentic dangers to their statecraft. This includes political dissidents, journalists, and members of religious and ethnic minorities. To stifle dissenting viewpoints, agents of these regimes employ physical aggression, threats, harassment, defamation, rendition, and manipulation of international law enforcement personnel and procedures. China and Iran will probably remain the most aggressive nations toward the United States in employing their disruptive statecraft.

Special Edition Chapter

Why Did It Happen?

Witnessing the circumstances that have developed since the original version was printed is a highly disheartening experience and warranted the addition of this special edition chapter. The realization that the events that have occurred in our society are even being normalized as they unfold is incredibly devastating, as it demonstrates the extent to which our nation has sunk into immorality and corruption. It also embodies the corrupted and toxic political climate awash with disinformation, slander, mistruths, and outright contempt for any opposing political views.

I am alluding to the following: (a) The assassination attempt and shooting of former President Trump at a political rally in Pennsylvania on July 13th, 2024, (b) The killing of the former fire chief from the area and two other critically injured individuals attending the rally, (c) The utter disgust of the democrat surrogates media complex that has engaged in blaming President Trump and the Republicans base for causing the incident, and (d) The questionable breakdown of the most basic of security and protection protocol that allowed this shooter to gain access to the

HVP (High-Value Protectee) protectee. Given the obloquy climate that has engulfed the former President, the harsh rhetoric and condemnation that the current President (Biden) has dispensed towards Donald Trump over time, and the weaponization of the Justice Department against the former President, it is reasonable to question the integrity of the leadership of his protective detail.

The venomous attacks on Trump originate from within the Washington bureaucracy, which some individuals refer to as the 'deep state' or the 'swamp.' It is a significant error to exclusively link these individuals with the Democratic Party. They are integral to a significantly larger and more significant entity than the Democrat Party, and the elitist industrial infrastructure is largely just as subservient to them. Foreign governments provide funding and support to various social activism groups, universities, and democratic agencies, which has created a covert means to weaken society and foster political and social divisions, ultimately diminishing America's global strength. Islamism, Antisemitism, Socialism, anti-Christianity, Chinese intellectual and tradecraft interference, and mass social rioting and unrest are all consequences of these intrusive foreign operations, which are facilitated by the democratic complex.

However, in my view, the primary motivation behind the Democrats, intelligence agencies, and federal law enforcement targeting Trump is his ability to attract the support of genuine nationalists who possess a deep love for America and are committed to safeguarding our way of life and liberties, not to mention an opposing view of the

348

power exerted by the Military Industrial Complex in prolonging wars to make a profit. These individuals comprehend the existing threat and are actively disseminating the message that our government is under the control of external forces, and they desire to take action to rectify this situation. Therefore, Trump must be annihilated. Unvanquished in a political contest. The current punishment is insufficient to effectively convey the intended message. It is imperative that he be eradicated using any means required. There is no speculation or guesswork involved; please analyze the evidence independently.

Creating a Toxic Political Environment: The utilization of talking points and political rhetoric has long been a part of American politics. However, it is uncommon for the White House, the President, the media complex, and other behind-the-scenes operatives to exhibit such skill and cynicism in their deployment of vitriolic language. The animosity, defamation, legal harassment, and incendiary remarks from the Democratic Party and its supporters have collectively played a role in the assassination attempt on Donald Trump, a former President, political adversary, and leading figure within the Republican Party. Well, is anyone surprised at the attempt on the former President's life? After all these years of political smears, character assassination, and outright lies, "America," what did you expect to happen? I argue that this was a deliberate tactic to eventuate a particular result, in addition to the questionable failure in security that occurred.

Blame Game Strategy: It is incredible that liberal Democratic party commentators and their media proxies are trying to pin the blame squarely on the Republican base and on Trump himself. The American people will hopefully not put up with being lied to; how can the ruling elitists possibly think that? I have an easy answer: the people who actually vote for these politicians put up with their incompetence, ignorance, and lack of accountability for their actions. Thus, we convey an air of unrestricted liberty. The idea that the Democratic Party's harmful and destructive politics is completely innocent or that years of hate speech wouldn't lead to this outcome is completely ridiculous. It seems to me that this is just another planned effort to set the stage for that kind of scenario to happen. It is critical to recognize the executive branch's failure to lead, its condoning of actions and negative influence, and its descent into corruption and dishonesty. Although some readers may see my statements as paranoid or conspiracy-minded, it is worth considering every possibility in light of these circumstances. The liberal media and the Democratic Party's fallacious political rhetoric come straight out of the White House, and I despise parroting it.

Media Role: The media machine spreads toxic narratives via various surrogate media news reporters and talk show hosts in an effort to confuse, disorient, and distract the public from important issues that affect their daily lives. Rather, they keep the masses fixated on lies that cover their political aspirations or attempt to deflect criticism from their own shortcomings. Nancy Pelosi gave an interview outlining the democrat's playbook for misinformation as detailed in a previous chapter. By controlling the narrative, the Left seeks to delegitimize any executive, journalist, academic, public official, or court that does not support the administration's agenda. Unfortunately for America, they are succeeding

False Narratives: Most notable of these toxic trumped-up statements are President Biden's campaigns that accuse former President Trump of attempting to revoke the results of an election and that he and his followers stormed the capitol building to stop the victor from taking office and is an existential threat to America. Democratic Party leaders publicly campaigned that Trump's presidency was not legitimate and that he represents an existential threat to democracy, which in turn threatens American society and democracy. Some political figures have accused Donald Trump of racism and said that African Americans will be oppressed by his government. The fact that Republicans demand proof of identity to secure our voter eligibility and accountability in order to cast a ballot has led to unfounded claims that they are trying to suppress minority votes. A small number of influential political figures have compared President Trump to Hitler and his followers to fascists. The media has posted pictures of a beheaded Trump, and Hilary Clinton demonized Trump's followers as "Deplorable Americans." Obama referenced these same Americans as some insignificant cross-section of America that clung to their bible and guns.

President Trump allegedly has a deep-seated hatred for immigrants and plans to deport them all. They state that social programs like Medicare will be cut by

351

President Trump. The former president is facing accusations of sexism and opposition to women's rights, according to some. The president was also accused of being involved in a conspiracy with foreign leaders, namely Russians, who plotted against the United States, only to be exposed as a Democrat Party ploy involving the Justice system. Also, don't forget the narrative pushed by prominent figures in the media viciously and vehemently accusing Trump of destroying the world's good things and causing all its bad things to occur. He is also accused of ruining Christmas family gatherings and blighting dating scenes for single adults looking for love. I guess the left disregarded the fact that under the Trump presidency, we had no declared "wars" and that Middle-Eastern peace was prospering with the Abraham Accords, and geopolitical strategizing was being advanced, especially with the great powers in play.

Lawfare against Trump: When the narratives did not affect the Trump base, the Biden administration embarked on weaponizing the justice system to manipulate the law and prosecutorial processes in order to bring fallacious charges. The highly organized campaign to oust President Donald Trump from all official positions is being carried out through an extensive range of legal proceedings and investigations aimed at him, his campaign, his transition team, and his associates. From a legal standpoint, the numerous lawsuits filed against Trump appear to be completely arbitrary, much like the outcome of rolling a dice. Conservatives argue that Trump's opponents will exploit any chance to disqualify him from running for president. All options are being considered. I have to insert a thought here; based on the declined cognitive abilities demonstrated by Biden and the many reports from his own administration supporting his decline, coupled with the frequent consultations with Obama's circle of influence, it is very evident who the puppet and the puppet masters are.

The term "lawfare" refers to the increasing prevalence of legal actions that resemble warfare, combining elements of both law and warfare. Lawfare is a strategy that involves using the legal system to achieve a public relations victory, undermine or harm an adversary, or seize their resources. These actions have been very evident to the nation. This legal campaign is a result of the organized resistance against Trump that developed after his surprising victory in the 2016 election, where he defeated the highly favored Democratic candidate, Hillary Clinton. The orchestration was carried out by the Democratic Party apparatus, employing the propaganda division, namely the media complex, and receiving support from left-wing activists, democrat-backed non-profit organizations, and affluent democratic socialist foundations. There is a publicly available list of investigations that have targeted individuals and entities associated with "President Trump's world." These investigations are being conducted by federal, state, and local prosecutors. Just to refresh your memory:

(a). Robert Mueller, the special counsel, conducted an inquiry into a variety of matters, such as the potential for obstruction of justice, the influence of Middle Eastern powers on the Trump campaign, the actions of Paul Manafort, the former campaign manager for Donald Trump, the abandoned Trump Tower Moscow project,

353

communication between the Trump campaign and transition team with Russia, and Russian interference in the United States elections. The Hilary camp was the source of the majority of the influences that were examined. Nothing has been established to date that would implicate Donald Trump.

(b). Geoffrey Berman, the U.S. attorney for the Southern District of New York, engaged in an inquiry into the financial affairs of the Trump Organization, alleged campaign conspiracies, funding for the inauguration, financial support for Trump super PACs, and foreign lobbying activities seeking desperately to find a crime.

(c). Jessie K. Liu, the U.S. attorney for the District of Columbia, conducted an investigation into the National Rifle Association (NRA) and Maria Butina, who was accused of being a Russian spy. Incidentally, it was discovered years later during the Boden administration that Iranian assets were active within their office.

(d). The United States attorney for the Eastern District of Virginia, Zachary Terwilliger, was conducting an investigation into allegations of wrongdoing, while Elena Alekseevna Khusyaynova had served as chief accountant at the Internet Research Agency.

(e). The investigation also encompassed an analysis of the impact of Turkish influence on Trump and his associates. The allegations are partially outlined in Michael Flynn's plea agreement, who previously held the position of national security adviser. Needless to say, the threats of going after his family by the justice department were absolutely criminal.

(f). The attorneys general of other predominantly Democratic states, as well as New York City and New York State, conducted investigations into a variety of tax-related allegations. According to The New York Times, Trump gained financial benefits from tax strategies amounting to over $400 million. Trump's tax payments were also investigated by city officials and the New York State Tax Department. We are all aware of the outcome of that disastrous situation.

(g). The DC and MD attorneys general, Karl A. Racine (D) and Brian Frosh (D), have issued subpoenas to seize the Trump Organization's and its hotels' financial records in an effort to uncover illicit transactions. These subpoenas are related to the difficult-to-prove claim that the president is violating the Emoluments Clause of the United States Constitution. Designed to protect American democracy, the provision forbids government officials, without Congress's consent, from accepting gifts from foreign monarchies and states. I guess this clause does not apply to our current President (Biden). So much inconsistency and corruption.

(h). The recent example of the in-your-face New York Attorney General-elect Letitia James (D) is a prime example of the frightening consequences of this the-ends-justify-the-means mentality. James put it succinctly: She was determined to secure an election in order to devote herself entirely to the confiscation of Trump's assets and the pursuit of his businesses. This is in direct opposition to the concept of justice. Fani Willis and her motivation in the

Atlanta case also express a similar sentiment. Coincidentally, they all went to the white house several times to coordinate efforts.

New York: You don't want to have a government that picks a target first and then figures out what for afterward, as in New York, Alvin Bragg, under James, manipulated and resurrected a charge that was past the statute of limitation, endorsed and supported by a disclosed Trump-hating Democrat Judge, with numerous incidents of prosecutorial inconsistencies, and violation of protected rights and procedures. This case has bewildered legal scholars and, all in one swoop, delegitimized the protection and integrity of our judicial system. It is also destined to be overturned on appeal due to the many inconsistencies.

Atlanta: Fani Willis and the Atlanta court case is falling apart on several fronts, including conflict of interest and procedural misconduct involving the prosecutors. In my opinion, the Supreme Court decision sinks this case. So many politicians on the democratic ticket voice complaints and are very confrontational in accusing republican counterparts of winning constituents, but nothing is said of that. The double standard in play, I guess.

Florida: The U.S. District Judge Aileen Cannon dismissed former President Donald Trump's classified documents case on July 15, finding that special counsel Jack Smith's appointment was unconstitutional. The Superseding Indictment is "dismissed" because Special Counsel Smith's appointment violates the Appointments Clause of the United States Constitution, the order reads.

Supreme Court: On Monday, the United States Supreme Court issued a 6-3 ruling exonerating former President Donald Trump from prosecution for specific "official" acts performed in the course of his presidential duties but not for "unofficial" acts performed while in office, such as those done in his personal capacity or while standing for reelection. Delaying trial in the federal election interference case, the district court will have to go through the motion of classifying Trump's actions as official or unofficial. The judge presiding over Trump's trial in Fulton County, Georgia, may also need to make comparable rulings in that case, which could cause a delay in that trial as well.

All in all, these frivolous and far-reaching attempts to destroy former President Trump and his bid as the front runner to be the next President of the United States are unbelievable for a nation that is not a "Banana Republic" and prides itself on the integrity of governance. America no longer has the moral high ground to exert its influence on developing nations regarding corruption, integrity of office, and effective governance. The damage to our system is yet to manifest itself. From confronting numerous legal challenges to subsequently attempting to remove President Trump's name from the ballot, it is evident that the Left has weaponized our judicial system against the former President. However, the reality that Americans observe in real-time is that an unbridled lawfare campaign is unraveling while the rule of law remains in place. Just weeks after, the Supreme Court served as a counterbalance to the Left's weaponization of the judicial system.

This is a significant victory for our Constitution, the rule of law, and equal justice. It is our hope that this marks the commencement of a movement to restore the integrity of action and the proper application of jurisprudence. It is worth mentioning that the problems and dangers to our democracy as we experienced with the Biden administration, as well as their assault on our highest court and plenty of unrest, were never present during Trump's presidency. There is nothing but the relentless hatred-mongering and winning tactics of the left. At every opportunity, they undermined the Trump presidency and the administration's operations by the ruling party, completely disregarding the primary event. The nation's financial health, welfare, and security were thriving. So, how curious it is that when all attempts to stop the former President from winning the next election are failing, a sniper attempts to take his life, narrowly missing by the grace of God. Is it just a horrible coincidence? The Kennedy tragedy comes to the surface, and the government's reluctance to release the report to family members, notably Robert Kennedy Jr, a Democratic presidential candidate. Again, am I delving into the realms of being a conspiracy theorist, or is my suspicion warranted based on all the facts available and what has transcended our political climate over the years?

Assassination Attempt Denial: Democratic Party members constantly spread divisive rhetoric. As we have seen, words have power, so if you were a mentally ill or easily influenced person and you kept hearing things like "Trump is a dictator" and "Trump is a threat to democracy," you might interpret this as a rallying cry. Political behavior in the modern era is characterized by a complete lack of decorum and honor. The only acceptable behavior is to destroy and defeat one's opponent using any means necessary, even if it means resorting to illegal and unethical tactics. The liberal news outlets continued to downplay the assassination attempt on live broadcast, promoting the idea that he received justice and even going so far as to tweet that people should improve their shooting skills to avoid missing the next time. According to CNN, "Trump falls" during the rally. The Washington Post said they heard "loud noises," while NBC said they heard "popping noises" for a time. No one wanted to label it as an assassination attempt. The fact that CNN still characterized it as an interruption after viewing the footage says it all. The false narratives of the assassination attempt continue with circulation by left-leaning surrogates on social media, categorizing it as a "Hoax," irrelevant that one person died and two others are critical. The other narrative being circulated on the major democrat media outlets is that Iran has made threats, and the chatter is way up. They want to distract from the fact the shooter was following a leftist ideology and even donated to a liberal progressive organization. It is likely that pressure from family made him register as a Republican against his desires, based on some witness statements. However, these are second-hand opinions and have not been verified by any independent source.

Security Failure, Unintentional or Orchestrated: With the attempted assassination at the rally in a rural working-class area of Pennsylvania and the reporting of the sequence of events, specific questions come to bear. I will lead off by thanking the Secret Service and other law enforcement agencies for their continued honorable and necessary service to the nation. However, as in any AAR (After Action Report), it is essential to identify all positive and negative factors involving a particular action or operation. A look in the mirror, if you may. This assessment will most definitely entail an examination of the procedural, leadership, communication, personnel, training, access, environmental, and equipment failures or anomalies at a minimum. The effectiveness of the chain of command, communication, and external agency coordination will also be addressed, along with existing protocols and procedures for conducting the operation. The military force protection workups are very similar to those of our law enforcement counterparts.

The big question that we all should be asking is, "How did a hostile shooter breach the layers of security and get within 150 meters of unobstructed line of sight of the high-value protectee, with enough time to establish a perch, and successfully fire several rounds at the target before being neutralized." For this to occur, multiple failures had to be present and contributing. The other big question on the minds of many, including myself based on the hostile political landscape is "was this somehow orchestrated," or a "colossal failure." Another element to consider is the leaders' training proficiency and operational experience with the current administration's overwhelming funding and focus on DEI (Diversity, Equality Inclusion) initiatives government-wide versus training dollars and a system of meritocracy where the best of the best are selected regardless of sex, gender, or race.

Analysis: Caveat - It is unproductive to quarterback an operation without full access to tactical data. Some assumptions will have to be made based on various streams of available reporting, eyewitness accounts, and personal knowledge base. Remembering that hindsight is always 20/20, I will approach this analysis, as with any AAR, to tease out possible avenues of failure and how it could have been prevented and lessons learned.

Leadership Experience: The Director of the Secret Service bears the overall responsibility for the failures under her watch. Based on an initial assessment of her career, it seems very light on operational field experience and more on administrative support and planning. I cannot assess her tactical proficiency in the field, which would enable her to make sound operational decisions and set standards for the field leaders to accomplish the mission. There are some speculations that this was not an appointment of merit but of friendship with the Bidens. I cannot confirm or deny these assumptions. I hope a congressional inquiry might shed more light on her competence.

Leadership Failures: I have no confidence in the Director of the Secret Service or her subordinate field leaders' ability to manage the situation, as evidenced by the ABC interview. Some of her statements and rationale were nonsensical and lacked tactical and operational knowledge. She referenced the fact that the environment was intricate and saturated. This is not accurate, as supported by the images on the website. The Director of the U.S. Secret Service also stated during an interview with

ABC News that the agency was aware of the security vulnerabilities posed by the building from which the shooter ascended to a sniper's position to target Trump. Why didn't the on-site manager take measures to mitigate these vulnerabilities? This is troubling. If the manager was relying on the sniper team on the roof behind the stage, then why was the response so delayed that the shooter got off several rounds? Things are just not adding up.

The director admitted that the building in question had a sloped roof at its highest point, and therefore, a safety concern existed for the operators, so the high point with a clear line of sight, under 150 meters away from the protectee, was left unsecured. This failure falls in the category of gross negligence. Somehow, the genius decision was made to secure the building from the inside. This statement is as incompetent as ever and speaks to the evaluation of her experience level and the on-site manager's failure to develop a sound operational plan. How can a high-ground vulnerability be mitigated by officers enclosed within a building, with no oversight of all access points to the roof? According to local law enforcement reports from Butler, Beaver, and Washington counties, the sniper element was tasked with crowd overwatch and would not concentrate on roof access. Incidentally, other agency snipers in the protection detail were stationed on identically sloped roofs, dispelling the argument for sloping roofs' safety concerns.

Additionally, a sloped roof does not serve as an operational obstacle to securing a site. Operators are instructed on how to establish and manage exceedingly challenging positions. This entire operation reeks of leadership failure, which is also concerning, as it bears the hallmarks of ineptitude, which will carry over to other operations. The cluster of buildings surrounding the shooter's perch, which is claimed to be challenging to control, could have been reduced to negligible levels by posting a sniper element on the tallest building in the cluster to eliminate high-ground vulnerability from that sector, as indicated by the available site pictures. This was an effortless resolution, and it would overlap with other overwatch teams.

Communication Failure: The media and bystander reports all document a timeline of between 5-30 minutes where the shooter was spotted with a range finder, then observed and recorded climbing onto the roof and even pointing a weapon at an investigating officer while he peeked over the roof edge. Law enforcement was aware of the possible threat at least 5 minutes before the first shots were fired by the shooter. This was critical information, and local law enforcement claimed it was passed up the chain. Questions I have are: (a) Did the threat report make it up to the TOC (Tactical Operations Center) or command post? (b) Was the threat report received by the Secret Service Operations Command? (c) Why was the protective detail not instructed to secure the HVP (high-value protectee) as soon as a threat was identified? (d) Was an emergency channel incorporated into the communication package, where all agents and local law enforcement could announce imminent threats, which would have alerted the protective detail to secure the protectee immediately?

If this was in play and the local officer's reports of "gun" and "shooter on the roof," which they claimed to have reported, were broadcasted on the emergency channel, then the protective detail would have been monitoring, responded to secure the HVP, and the sniper elements would have engaged the shooter based on their threat response protocol. A critical aspect that must also be covered, probably one of the most essential operational requirements, is the operations briefing. The more detailed it is regarding local departments' exact roles and zones of responsibility, threat identification and reporting, emergency channel broadcast, converging on and isolating threats, security gaps, and overwatch zones as a minimum, it creates a coordinated unit and minimizes the cone of confusion during escalation. It also eliminates duplication of resources and identifies areas that have insufficient coverage.

These basic operations for security site surveys, force protection planning, personal protection, and force protection mitigation strategies should be basic knowledge for the Secret Service Agents and their superiors. I don't expect the local law enforcement to be versed in these specific security operations, so comprehensive briefings and areas of responsibility are vital for mission success. The Secret Service pointing fingers at the local law enforcement partners shows a lack of leadership in the agency. The overall responsibility is theirs. One of my concerns is whether we have the most qualified individuals as leaders or whether these positions are filled under the DEI mandates. Critical failures can be costly and must be addressed. The shooter had explosives staged in his vehicle and a detonator on his person. This situation could have been worse. I still find it improbable that this bad actor didn't have external assistance and motivation. I also find it extremely hard to believe that so many simple mistakes, which resulted in a complex failure of protocol and procedures, were allowed to occur without someone questioning the operation. I fear a colossal coverup will continue, and having the white house and Justice Department investigate the failures is like asking a fox to investigate missing chickens in a hen house. America, we are in trouble. In my opinion, this is the result of the democrat party leadership gone awry. Irrespective of my views, it falls to you, the electorate, to decide the future of our   beloved   nation.

FINAL THOUGHTS

In closing, I will reiterate that the primary purpose of my current books, Oh Say Can You See "Destroying the Homeland," my previous book, Oh Say Can You See "America," the "Special Edition," and persadbooks studio, Eagle Rising Podcast is to awaken the electorate to America's trajectory.

America needs us to be there for her, so buck up and do your duty, or she will be lost to us, our children, and our future generations. America was founded on Judeo-Christian principles, which also allows latitude for other religions to incorporate their belief structures. Morality, integrity, hard work, family, service, sacrifice, civility, and personal responsibility are the bedrock beliefs in our nation, and they have served us well. To make America strong, we must all unite under one flag, under God (General Concept of a Creator), with respect for all. *Note: I say respect, not to be confused with the pushing and acceptance of controversially immoral and unnatural actions on society as a whole by fringe elements practicing identity politics. Private lifestyle choices must remain as such private choices.

In moving forward, it is essential to determine which political party or presidential candidate is a threat to our democracy. Place your personal biases aside; it is unimportant when your family and country are at stake, and the cost of living exceeds income. Effective policy and good governance is what matters. Now engage common sense reasoning and: (a) Ask yourselves which party censors freedom of speech by using liberal media surrogates that demonize everyone with an opposing voice. (b) Which party is collaborating with the media complex to control the messaging and information to the masses, therefore manipulating the people as in a socialist regime? (c) Which regime is eliminating Christianity in society while advocating the acceptance of immoral and vulgar activities and organizations in schools to indoctrinate our children? (d) Which Party supports Islamism and has members of their government flying terrorist flags in their offices? (e) Which party demonizes Law Enforcement while labeling mass rioting, burning of buildings, and destruction of small businesses as peaceful demonstrations? (f) Which party has engaged in "Lawfare" using whatever means necessary to imprison and eliminate opposition presidential candidates as dictatorships do? (g) What party has weaponized its intelligence and federal agencies to spy on, harass, and incarcerate American citizens with manufactured facts? (h) What party politicians and liberal advocates lobby heavily against the Second Amendment, want to change the Constitution, and pack the Supreme Court? (i) Which one of the political parties wants to change our democratic election process and encourage fraud by eliminating checks and balances (voter ID, mail-in periods, ballot stuffing), ballot integrity, demographic rigging, and eliminating the Electoral College? As I alluded to earlier, you don't have to be a genius to figure things out. Why are there so many geopolitical hotspots and wars popping up globally, and why has the U.S. not been successful in containing the threats for the past 3.5 years in the Biden administration? A historical landmark agreement (Abraham Accords) by the Trump administration was never followed up on and discarded for policies appeasing Iran, which angered many of the influential Middle Eastern nations. Why continue with the Obama "Blame America" tour? These questions must be asked. Many more issues in play have caused turmoil, limited our freedoms at home, changed our social construct, and relegated us to irrelevance on the world stage. At this stage of our space in time, we, the people, need to get engaged. We can no longer afford to be depicted like the "three monkeys, who were blind, dumb, and deaf."

These books are written to awaken the intellectual and rational being within the reader, then apply good old "common sense" to everything. Citizens and legal residents, native-born or naturalized, we have the honor and privilege of inheriting one of the world's most incredible countries to call home. We must protect her and secure our way of life for generations to enjoy. There are internal and external forces at play that seek to destroy our great nation and indoctrinate many among us to hate what we, as Americans, stand for. So, as long as you were legally admitted into our country, regardless of your circumstances or if you were born here, this nation will cover you under her protective veil equally. Native Americans, African Americans, Caucasians, Asians, Caribbean, Latin Americans, Hispanics, and any other ethnic classification, if legally admitted under our laws, we all belong here and call

America home. She has opened her arms to all legally admitted residents for generations. Still, basic ground principles and the rule of law must be adhered to so as to protect our freedoms and way of life. Even though America's history has been imperfect and more challenging for some among us, we must continually strive to develop that perfect union and equality of opportunity for all racial classifications.

Not all readers will share my informed opinion or interpretation of the facts, which is quite okay. I urge you to ask the hard questions and not allow anyone, including this book's author, to tell you what to believe in. Formulate your own opinions by getting accurate and truthful information, then use common sense deduction to determine your position. Hold politicians accountable, and exercise your right to vote. The order of life should fashion some similar social stratum as in God, Family, Country, Humanity, and then Politics. Politics and politicians must never be allowed to occupy our head space and divide us as a nation. Democrats or Republicans, we are still Americans. Preserve our nation. We are extremely too polarized to think rationally; politicians must work for us and do our bidding.

Call to Action: It is clear that our nation is being destroyed by our own Democrat Party and the Shadow Government Elitists. It is time to wake up to the realities of our affairs. This is not the civil-minded Democratic Party that many remember. It would behoove all members of Congress and the House, as well as other elected members, to remember their oath of office and ready themselves to be held accountable if they break their promise to the nation. "We the people" must exist in a space above party politics. Let us motivate our leaders to get back to healing and growing America into being the most politically influential, technically and economically savvy, united, and morally upright nation-beacon in the world while understanding the intricacies of peace through strength deterrence concepts. Also, a humble request to all veterans and American patriots is to be especially cognizant of what transpires so that we may be ready to stand up, speak out, and protect our nation if the need arises. Remember the oaths of office many of us have taken either in service to the nation or immigrating to the nation. Participate actively in the democratic process and hold our elected officials accountable. My oath to this nation as an officer and soldier has no expiration date attached. It is authorized by statute "Section 3331, <u>Title 5, United States Code</u>. Naturalized Citizens of this great nation also take an oath through the "Pledge of Allegiance." Federal Officers and Law Enforcement Officers also take a specialized version of the oath. The protection of our nation, our Judeo-Christian principles, and the preservation of our rights and freedoms are paramount to being "The United States of America." Freedom isn't free; don't squander it. Too much of our national treasure has been spilled on foreign lands in defense of these great "UNITED STATES OF AMERICA." May God (Our Creator) continue to bless and keep us all safe through our growing pains and our desire to be a more perfect union.

MILITARY OATH[99]

"I do solemnly swear that I will support and defend the Constitution of the United States against all enemies, foreign and domestic; that I will bear true faith and allegiance to the same; that I take this obligation freely, without any mental reservation or purpose of evasion; and that I will well and faithfully discharge the duties of the office on which I am about to enter. So help me God."

THE OATH OF ALLEGIANCE[100]

"I hereby declare, on oath, that I absolutely and entirely renounce and abjure all allegiance and fidelity to any foreign prince, potentate, state, or sovereignty, of whom or which I have heretofore been a subject or citizen; that I will support and defend the Constitution and laws of the United States of America against all enemies, foreign and domestic; that I will bear true faith and allegiance to the same; that I will bear arms on behalf of the United States when required by the law; that I will perform noncombatant service in the Armed Forces of the United States when required by the law; that I will perform work of national importance under civilian direction when required by the law; and that I take this obligation freely, without any mental reservation or purpose of evasion; so help me God."

---

[99] Tillman, Seth Barrett, and Josh Blackman. "Offices and Officers of the Constitution Part III: The Appointments, Impeachment, Commissions, and Oath or Affirmation Clauses." *S. Tex. L. Rev.* 62 (2022): 349.

[100] Jones, Jeffrey Owen, and Peter Meyer. *The Pledge: A history of the Pledge of Allegiance.* Macmillan, 2010.

BIBLIOGRAPHY

1. Nasser, Noelani. "American Imperialism in Hawai'i: How the United States Illegally Usurped a Sovereign Nation and Got Away With It." *Hastings Const. L.Q.* 48 (2020): 319.

2. Feldmann, Andreas E.; Maiju Perälä (July 2004). "Reassessing the Causes of Nongovernmental Terrorism in Latin America." *Latin American Politics and Society.* **46** (2): 101–132. doi:10.1111/j.1548-2456.2004.tb00277.x. S2CID 221247620.

3. Crafton, Lance D. "U.S. Supported Corporations and Modern Imperialism: America's Takeover of Hawaii." (2015).

4. Ceaser, James W. "The origins and character of American exceptionalism." *American Political Thought* 1, no. 1 (2012): 3-28.

5. Ninkovich, Frank. *The Wilsonian Century: U.S. foreign policy since 1900.* University of Chicago Press, 1999.

6. Sachs, Jeffrey D. *A new foreign policy: beyond American exceptionalism.* Columbia University Press, 2018.

7. Kinzer, Stephen. *The brothers: John Foster Dulles, Allen Dulles, and their secret world war.* Macmillan, 2013.

8. Alnawafleh, Ibrahem Mohammad. "The Phenomenon of War in the Post-Cold War Era." *J. Legal Ethical & Regul. Issues* 24 (2021): 1.

9. Pedi, Revecca, and Anders Wivel. "What Future for Small States After Unipolarity? Strategic Opportunities and Challenges in the Post-American World Order." *Polarity in International Relations: Past, Present, Future* (2022):

10. Syed, Aamir Aijaz, Muhammad Abdul Kamal, and Assad Ullah. "Do shadow economy, institutional regulatory framework, government stability, and corruption affect non-performing banking loans in emerging market economies: A dynamic common correlated effect (DCCE) approach." *International Social Science Journal* 72, no. 246 (2022):

11. Maihold, Günther. "Shadow supply chains and criminal networks." In *Geopolitics of the Illicit*, pp. 53-82. Nomos Verlagsgesellschaft mbH & Co. KG, 2022.

12. Poznansky, Michael. *In the shadow of international law: Secrecy and regime change in the postwar world.* Oxford University Press, USA, 2020.

13. Nelson, Anne. *Shadow network: Media, money, and the secret hub of the radical right.* Bloomsbury Publishing USA, 2019.

14. Carnegie, Allison. "Secrecy in international relations and foreign policy." *Annual Review of Political Science* 24 (2021).

15. Walldorf Jr, C. William. *To shape our world for good: Master narratives and regime change in U.S. foreign policy, 1900–2011*. Cornell University Press, 2019.

16. Osiewicz, Przemyslaw. *Foreign Policy of the Islamic Republic of Iran: Between Ideology and Pragmatism*. Routledge, 2020.

17. Combs, Jerald A. *History of American Foreign Policy, Volume 2: From 1895*. Routledge, 2017.

18. Smith, Tony, G. John Ikenberry, Thomas J. Knock, and Anne-Marie Slaughter. *The crisis of American foreign policy: Wilsonianism in the twenty-first century*. Princeton University Press, 2008.

19. Pitruzzello, Salvatore. "Trade Globalization, Economic Performance, and Social Protection: Nineteenth-Century British Laissez-Faire and Post–World War II US-Embedded Liberalism." *International Organization* 58, no. 4 (2004):

20. Michael Eisenstadt, *Iranian Military Power* (Washington, DC: The Washington Institute for Near East Policy).

21. *The Fraught Politics Facing Biden's Foreign Policy | Brookings*, 2017

22. Haar, Roberta. "The Biden administration's incompatible views on multilateralism." *Atlantisch Perspectief* 45, no. 5 (2021): 20-24.

23. Li, Wei. "Indo-Pacific Economic Framework: Biden's New Institutional Instrument in the Asia-Pacific Region." *East Asian Policy* 15, no. 03 (2023).

24. Malik, Kenan. "What is wrong with Multiculturalism?." *A European Perspective with* (2012).

25. Banting, K. G., Daniel Westlake, and Will Kymlicka. "The politics of multiculturalism and redistribution: Immigration, accommodation, and solidarity in diverse democracies." *Handbook on migration and welfare* (2022): 210-229.

26. Mathieu, Felix. "The failure of state multiculturalism in the U.K.? An analysis of the U.K.'s multicultural policy for 2000–2015." *Ethnicities* 18, no. 1 (2018): 43-69.

27. Malik, Kenan. "The failure of multiculturalism: Community versus society in Europe." *Foreign Aff.* 94 (2015): 21.

28. Chin, Rita. *The crisis of multiculturalism in Europe: A history.* Princeton University Press, 2017.

29. Noury, Abdul, and Gerard Roland. "Identity politics and populism in Europe." *Annual Review of Political Science* 23 (2020): 421-439.

30. Reno, R. R. "Anger-Politics on the Right." *First Things* (2021): 1-17.

31. Sowell, Thomas. *Barbarians Inside the Gates and other controversial essays.* Hoover Press, 2020.

32. Marable, Manning. "Black Conservatives and Accommodation: Of Thomas Sowell and Others." *Negro History Bulletin* 45, no. 2 (1982): 32-35.

33. Aronoff, Kate, ed. *We Own the Future: Democratic Socialism—American Style*. The New Press, 2020.

34. Packer, George. "How America fractured into four parts." *The Atlantic* (2021).

35. Dorrien, Gary. *American Democratic Socialism: History, Politics, Religion, and Theory*. Yale University Press, 2021.

36. Cain, William E. "The End of Capitalism: Eugene V. Debs and the Argument for Socialism in America." *Society* 56 (2019): 466-480.

37. Accountable, Holding Utopia. "Bernie Sanders's Democratic Socialism."

38. Uetricht, Micah, and Meagan Day. *Bigger than Bernie: How we go from the Sanders campaign to democratic socialism*. Verso Books, 2020.

39. Daniels, Ronald J., Grant Shreve, and Phillip Spector. *What universities owe democracy*. JHU Press, 2021.

40. (Bonfield, Arthur E. "The Guarantee Clause of Article IV, Section 4: A study in constitutional desuetude." *Minn. L. Rev.* 46 (1961): 513.)

41. Tancredo, Thomas G. "Immigration, citizenship, and national security: The silent

invasion." *Mediterranean Quarterly* 15, no. 4 (2004): 4-15.

42. Longmire, Sylvia. *Cartel: the coming invasion of Mexico's drug wars*. St. Martin's Press, 2011.

43. Baumgartner, Alice, Beau D. Cleland, Susan-Mary Grant, Amy Greenberg, John Craig Hammond, John W. Quist, and Andrew L. Slap. *Continent in Crisis: The US Civil War in North America*. Fordham Univ Press, 2023.

44. Tarlow, Peter E. "The Mexican–US Border: Immigration, Corruption, Drugs, and Illegal Border Crossings." In *Challenges to US and Mexican Police and Tourism Stability*, pp. 241-271. Emerald Publishing Limited, 2023.

45. (U.S. Const. Art. IV, § 4)

46. Dunaway, Johanna, and Doris A. Graber. *Mass media and American politics*. Cq Press, 2022.

47. Clarke, Colin P. "Scenarios of Transnational Terrorism: Trends and Developments–A Fact-Based Threat Assessment." In *Routledge Handbook of Transnational Terrorism*, pp. 259-267. Routledge 2023.

48. Horne, Gerald. "Race Backward, Race Forward: Thomas Sowell, William Julius Wilson & Derrick Bell Considered." *Black Renaissance* 1, no. 2 (1997): 76.

49. Hansan, J.E. (2011). Origins of the state and federal public welfare programs (1932-1935).

50. Davies, Gareth, and Martha Derthick. "Race and social welfare policy: The Social Security Act of 1935." *Political Science Quarterly* 112, no. 2 (1997): 217-235.

51. Lopez, Mark Hugo, and Mohamad Moslimani. "Key facts about the nation's 47.2 million Black Americans." (2023).

52. Pirtle, Whitney N., Breanna Brock, Nonzenzele Aldonza, Kaline Leke, and Dallas Edge. "I didn't know what anti-blackness was until I got here": The unmet needs of Black students at Hispanic-serving institutions." *Urban Education* 59, no. 1 (2024): 330-357.

53. Gonzalez, Martín Alberto. "How Latino Anti-Blackness Upholds Racism In The United States: A Counterstory Book Review Of Tanya Katerí Hernández's Racial Innocence." *Journal Committed to Social Change on Race and Ethnicity* 9, no. 1 (2023): 206.

54. Vukelić, Tatjana. "Black Awakening in Obama's America: The End of an Illusion." *European Journal of Social Sciences* 6, no. 1 (2023): 62-71.

55. Hinton, Elizabeth, and DeAnza Cook. "The mass criminalization of Black Americans: A historical overview." *Annual Review of Criminology* 4 (2021): 261-286.

56. Green, Bernard Lee, Richard Maisiak, Min Qi Wang, Marcia F. Britt, and Nonie Ebeling. "Participation in health education, health promotion, and health research by African Americans: effects of the Tuskegee Syphilis Experiment." *Journal of Health Education* 28, no. 4 (1997): 196-201.

57. Mouser, Bruce L. "Baltimore's African experiment, 1822-1827." *The Journal of Negro History* 80, no. 3 (1995): 113-130.

58. Washington, Harriet A. *Medical apartheid: The dark history of medical experimentation on Black Americans from colonial times to the present.* Doubleday Books, 2006.

59. Dershowitz, Alan. *Get Trump: The Threat to Civil Liberties, Due Process, and Our Constitutional Rule of Law.* Simon and Schuster, 2023.

60. Lavalley, Ryan, and Khalilah Robinson Johnson. "Occupation, injustice, and anti-Black racism in the United States of America." *Journal of Occupational Science* 29, no. 4 (2022): 487-499.

61. Shindler, Colin. *A history of modern Israel.* Cambridge University Press, 2013.

62. Castaneda, Ernesto, Reilly Phelan, and Joseph Fournier. "The Backlash to the Backlash: The Moral and Electoral Failure of Anti-Immigrant Political Campaigns in the US 2018-2023." *Castañeda, Ernesto, Phelan, Reilly, Fournier, Joseph* (2024): 2018-2023.

63. FitzGerald, David Scott, and John D. Skrentny, eds. *Immigrant California: understanding the past, present, and future of US policy*. Stanford University Press, 2021.

64. Taylor, Max, and John Horgan. "The psychological and behavioral bases of Islamic fundamentalism." *Terrorism and Political Violence* 13, no. 4 (2001): 37-71.

65. Watt, William Montgomery. *Islamic Fundamentalism and Modernity (RLE Politics of Islam)*. Routledge, 2013.

66. Reeve, Zoey. "Islamist terrorism as parochial altruism." *Terrorism and political violence* 32, no. 1 (2020): 38-56.

67. Sterba, James P. "Completing Thomas Sowell's Study of Affirmative Action and Then Drawing Different Conclusions." (2004): 657-693.

68. Doleac, Jennifer L. "A Review of Thomas Sowell's Discrimination and Disparities." *Journal of Economic Literature* 59, no. 2 (2021): 574-589.

69. Woolley, Samuel C., and Philip N. Howard, eds. *Computational propaganda: Political parties, politicians, and political manipulation on social media*. Oxford University Press, 2018.

70. OSIPOVA, Nadezhda G., Sergey O. ELISHEV, and Gennadi B. PRONCHEV. "Mass Information Media and Propaganda Mouthpiece as a Tool for

Manipulating and Social Inequality Factor among the Young People." *Astra Salvensis* (2018).

71. Bartlett, Bruce. *Wrong on race: The Democratic Party's buried past.* Palgrave Macmillan, 2008.

72. Alexander, Gerard. "The myth of the racist Republicans." *Claremont Review of Books* 4, no. 2 (2004): 11-14.

73. Schiele, Jerome H. "Black Political Ideologies: Conceptions of African-American Subjugation and Social Welfare Policy Intervention." *Journal of Policy Practice* 8, no. 3 (2009).

74. Lofgren, Mike. *The deep state: The fall of the constitution and the rise of a shadow government.* Penguin, 2016.

75. Michaels, Jon D. "Trump and the deep state: The government strikes back." *Foreign Aff.* 96 (2017): 52.

76. Rosenfeld, Richard. "The 1994 Crime Bill: Legacy and Lessons-Overview and Reflections." *Fed. Sent'g Rep.* 32 (2019): 147.

77. Derfler, Leslie. *The Dreyfus Affair.* Bloomsbury Publishing USA, 2002.

78. Fitch, Nancy. "Mass culture, mass parliamentary politics, and modern anti-semitism: the Dreyfus Affair in rural France." *The American Historical Review* 97, no. 1 (1992): 55-95.

79. Shapira, Anita. *Israel: A history.* UPNE, 2012.

80. Cordesman, Anthony H. *Tracking the trends and numbers: Islam, Terrorism, stability and conflict in the Middle East.* Center for Strategic and International Studies (CSIS), 2022.

81. Cordesman, Anthony H. *Islam and the patterns in terrorism and violent extremism.* Center for Strategic and International Studies (CSIS), 2022.

82. Brachman, Jarret M. *Global jihadism: Theory and practice.* Routledge, 2008.

83. Tibi, Bassam. "The Islamist Venture of the Politicization of Islam to an Ideology of Islamism: A Critique of the Dominating Narrative in Western Islamic Studies." *Soundings: An Interdisciplinary Journal* 96, no. 4 (2013): 431-449.

84. Hacsek, Zsófia. "Global Jihadist Terrorism. Terrorist groups, Zones of Armed Conflict and National Counter-Terrorism strategies: edited by Paul Burke, Doaa'Elnakhala, & Seumas Miller, Northampton, MA, Edward Elgar Publishing, 2021, 338 pp.,£ 105, ISBN 9781800371293." (2022): 1-4.

85. Stivers, Richard. *The culture of cynicism: American morality in decline.* Wipf and Stock Publishers, 2023.

86. Dwinell, Erin, and Hannah Davis. "The Costs of Biden's Border Crisis: The First Two Years."

87. Bensman, Todd. "The Real Cost of an Open Border: How Americans are Paying the Price." (2023).

88. Kirkwood, R. Cort. "IMPEACH BIDEN ON HIS IMMIGRATION POLICIES." *The New American* 39, no. 17 (2023): 19-22.

89. Marche, Stephen. *The next civil war: Dispatches from the American future*. Simon and Schuster, 2023.

90. Smith, Candis Watts. "The Making of a Mantra: Americans' Racial Ideologies in the Era of Black, Blue, and All Lives Matter." *Journal of Race, Ethnicity, and Politics* 8, no. 3 (2023).

91. Hannase, Mulawarman. "The Dilemma Between Religious Doctrine and Political Pragmatism: Study of Hamas in Palestine." *Religió Jurnal Studi Agama-agama* 10, no. 1 (2020): 54-70.

92. Hammaduddin, Hafiz, Naseem Umer, and Zahid Hussain Dashti. "ANALYSING THE EFFORTS OF HAMAS FOR THE PALESTINIAN CAUSE." *Pakistan Journal of International Affairs* 4, no. 4 (2021).

93. Loewenthal, Amit, Sami H. Miaari, and Anke Hoeffler. "Aid and Radicalization: The Case of Hamas in the West Bank and Gaza." *The Journal of Development Studies* 59, no. 8 (2023): 1187-1212.

94. Johnson, Toni, and Mohammed Aly Sergie. "Islam: Governing under Sharia." *Council on Foreign Relations* 25 (2014).

95. https://www.researchomatic.com/multicultural-diversity-82756.html

96. Hamad, Ahmed Mohammed Adnan. "Legal Status of the President of the National Authority, the Council of Ministers and Legislative Council in Palestine." (2022). https://core.ac.uk/download/539341643.pdf.

97. Joint Subcommittee Hearing on Human Cost of Biden and Mayorkas' Border Crisis – Committee on Homeland Security. https://homeland.house.gov/2023/07/25/tomorrow-at-2pm-joint-subcommittee-hearing-on-human-cost-of-biden-and-mayorkas-border-crisis/

98. Review of Global Jihadist Terrorism. Terrorist groups, Zones of Armed Conflict and National Counter-Terrorism Strategies — Coventry University. https://pureportal.coventry.ac.uk/en/publications/global-jihadist-terrorism-terrorist-groups-zones-of-armed-conflic

ENDNOTES

---

[i] Military–industrial complex. (2024, February 9). In *Wikipedia*. https://en.wikipedia.org/wiki/Military%E2%80%93industrial_complex

[ii] The United States Was Energy Independent in 2019 for the First Time Since 1957 - IER (instituteforenergyresearch.org)

[iii] Serlin, Theo, and Dustin Swonder. "WHO WERE THE ISOLATIONISTS?." (2023).

[iv] Weldes, Jutta Eleonore. *Constructing national interests: The logic of United States national security in the post-war era.(Volumes I-III).* University of Minnesota, 1993.

[v] Groitl, Gerlinde. "Geopolitical Realities: The Case for Neo-Containment Against Russia and China." In *Russia, China and the Revisionist Assault on the Western Liberal International Order*, pp. 431-453. Cham: Springer International Publishing, 2023.

[vi] Siraj, Uzma, and Najimdeen Bakare. "Iran–USA Relations: From Exceptionalism to Containment Policy." *Journal of Asian Security and International Affairs* 9, no. 1 (2022): 99-121.

[vii] Hanhimäki, Jussi M. *The rise and fall of détente: American foreign policy and the transformation of the Cold War.* Potomac Books, Inc., 2012.

[viii] Khoo, Nicholas, and Zhang Qingmin. "'Mirror, mirror on the wall': China and the concept of multipolarity in the post Cold War era." In *National perspectives on a multipolar order*, pp. 21-41. Manchester University Press, 2021.

[ix] Haar, Roberta. "The Biden administration's incompatible views on multilateralism." *Atlantisch Perspectief* 45, no. 5 (2021): 20-24.

[x] *The Fraught Politics Facing Biden's Foreign Policy | Brookings*, 2017

[xi] Li, Wei. "Indo-Pacific Economic Framework: Biden's New Institutional Instrument in the Asia-Pacific Region." *East Asian Policy* 15, no. 03 (2023): 128-143.

[xii] Fitzgerald, Timothy, Kevin Hassett, Cody Kallen, and Casey B. Mulligan. "An Analysis of Vice President Biden's Economic Agenda: The Long Run Impacts of its Regulation, Taxes, and Spending." *University of Chicago, Becker Friedman Institute for Economics Working Paper* 2020-157 (2020).

[xiii] Sowell, Thomas. *Barbarians inside the gates and other controversial essays.* Hoover Press, 2020.

[xiv] Aronoff, Kate, ed. *We Own the Future: Democratic Socialism—American Style.* The New Press, 2020.

[xv] Reno, R. R. "Anger-Politics on the Right." *First Things* (2021): 1-17.

[xvi] Marable, Manning. "Black Conservatives and Accommodation: Of Thomas Sowell and Others." *Negro History Bulletin* 45, no. 2 (1982): 32-35.

[xvii] Di Martino, Daniel. "Biden's Immigration Parole Programs Are Working." The falsehood of the program.(2023).

[xviii] Uetricht, Micah, and Meagan Day. *Bigger than Bernie: How we go from the Sanders campaign to democratic socialism.* Verso Books, 2020.

[xix] Beermann, Jack M. "The Unhappy History of Civil Rights Legislation, Fifty Years Later." *Conn. L. Rev.* 34 (2001): 981.

[xx] Gilliam Jr, Franklin D. "The" welfare queen" experiment: How viewers react to images of African-American mothers on welfare." (1999).

[xxi] (https://homeland.house.gov/2023/10/26/factsheet-final-fy23-numbers-show-worst-year-at-americas-borders-ever/).

[xxii] Malik, Kenan. "The failure of multiculturalism: Community versus society in Europe." *Foreign Aff.* 94 (2015): 21.

[xxiii] Noury, Abdul, and Gerard Roland. "Identity politics and populism in

Europe." *Annual Review of Political Science* 23 (2020): 421-439.

xxiv Syzdykbekov, Y. S., G. M. Baigozhina, and N. K. Tutinova. "EUROPEAN EXPERIENCE IN THE FIELD OF MIGRATION POLICY: MULTICULTURAL ISSUES." 1 (2023): 204.

xxv Kaufmann, E. "How 'asymmetrical multiculturalism'generates populist blowback." *National Review* 6 (2019).

xxvi Tarlow, Peter E. "The Mexican–US Border: Immigration, Corruption, Drugs, and Illegal Border Crossings." In *Challenges to US and Mexican Police and Tourism Stability*, pp. 241-271. Emerald Publishing Limited, 2023.

xxvii Dunaway, Johanna, and Doris A. Graber. *Mass media and American politics.* Cq Press, 2022.

xxviii Fallows, James. *Breaking the news: How the media undermine American democracy.* Vintage, 1997.

xxix Littlefield, R. S. (2021). Controlling the Narrative. *Communicating Science in Times of Crisis: COVID-19 Pandemic*, 358.

xxx (Bonfield, Arthur E. "The Guarantee Clause of Article IV, Section 4: A study in constitutional desuetude." *Minn. L. Rev.* 46 (1961): 513.)

xxxi Agel, Jerome B. We, The People - Great Documents of the American Nation. New York, NY: Barnes & Noble Books, 2000

xxxii Marable, Manning. "Black Conservatives and Accommodation: Of Thomas Sowell and Others." *Negro History Bulletin* 45, no. 2 (1982): 32-35.

xxxiii Brooks, R., Michael A. Robinson, and Heidi Urben. "Speaking out: Why retired flag officers participate in political discourse." *Texas National Security Review* 7 (2023).

xxxiv Gonzalez, Martín Alberto. "How Latino Anti-Blackness Upholds Racism In The United States: A Counterstory Book Review Of Tanya Katerí Hernández's Racial Innocence." *Journal Committed to Social Change on Race and Ethnicity* 9, no. 1 (2023): 206.

xxxv Rahman, Fazlur. Islam. University of Chicago Press, 2020.

xxxvi Dadach, Zin-Eddine. "The Foundation of Islam." (2020).

xxxvii Nasr, Seyyed Hossein. "The meaning and concept of philosophy in Islam."

In History of Islamic Philosophy, pp. 21-26. Routledge, 2020.

xxxviii Ma'arif, Syamsul, Leonard C. Sebastian, and Sholihan Sholihan. "A Soft Approach to Counter Radicalism: The Role of Traditional Islamic Education." Walisongo: Jurnal Penelitian Sosial Keagamaan 28, no. 1 (2020).

xxxix Takfir | Counter Extremism Project. https://www.counterextremism.com/content/takfir

xl Amir, Shamaila, Ahmad Saeed, and Muhammad Akhtar Kang. "Explaining the main themes through the chiastic structure in Sura e Zukhruf, chapter 43 of Quran." *Praxis International Journal of Social Science and Literature* 3 (2020): 6-10.

xli Hanapi, Mohd Shukri. "From Jahiliyyah to Islamic worldview: In a search of an Islamic educational philosophy." *International Journal of Humanities and Social Science* 3, no. 2 (2013): 213-221

xlii Casewit, Daoud S. "HIJRA AS HISTORY AND METAPHOR: A SURVEY OF QUR'ANIC AND HADTH SOURCES." *The Muslim World* 88, no. 2 (1998): 105-128.

xliii Rushdi, Abraham. "The Selling of Islamic Martyrdom and Why Some Buy It." Eureka Street 16, no. 19 (2006): 31–33. https://search.informit.org/doi/10.3316/ielapa.314058137770126.

xliv Knapp, Michael G. *The concept and practice of jihad in Islam.* Army War Coll Carlisle Barracks PA, 2003.

xlv Andrea, Alfred J., and Andrew Holt. Sanctified Violence: Holy War in World History. Hackett Publishing, 2021.

xlvi *Nothing but failure?: the Arab League and the Gulf Cooperation Council as mediators in Middle Eastern conflicts.* Crisis States Research Centre, 2009.

xlvii Middle East Review of International Affairs, Vol. 5, No. 4 (December 2001)

xlviii Hamid, Shadi. Islamic exceptionalism: How the struggle over Islam is reshaping the world. St. Martin's Press, 2016.

xlix Muro, Hana Jalloul. *Sharia Law in the Twenty-first Century.* World Scientific, 2022.

l El-Jaichi, Saer, and Mona Kanwal Sheikh. "Explaining the Rise of Global

Jihad." Journal of Religion and Violence 8, no. 2 (2020): 196-208.

[li] Bisri, Hasan. "Khomeini's Concept of Wilâyat Al-Faqîh and Its Influence on the Contemporary Indonesian Islamic Thought." 33-52.

[lii] Agara, Tundre, Basheer Olalere Usamotu, and Olawale Olufemi Akinrinde. "Doctrinaire Schism and the Politics of Religious Sectarianism in Islam: Understanding the Root Cause of Sectarian and Religious Terrorism in the Middle-East and North Africa." De Securitate et Defensione. O Bezpieczeństwie i Obronności 1 (8) (2022): 179-201.

[liii] Gazali, Hatim, Dewi Anggraeni, and Mariam Eit Ahmed. "Salafi-Jihadist Movements and Ideology in Educational Institutions: Exploring the Nexus with Religious Moderation." Edukasia Islamika: Jurnal Pendidikan Islam 8, no. 1 (2023): 127-145.

[liv] Ayaz, Muhammad, and Hafiz Iftikhar Ahmad. "The Foundations of The Unity of Ummah in The Light of Holy Quran and Sunnah." Ar-Raniry: International Journal of Islamic Studies 5, no. 2 (2021): 225-238.

[lv] Al-Tarawneh, Alalddin. "The role of Quran translations in radicalizing Muslims in the west and misrepresenting Islam." Journal of Religion and Violence 9, no. 1 (2021): 101-122.

[lvi] AMERICA, IRAN IN LATIN. "Border wars: Iran's terror haven in Latin America."

[lvii] Spadiliero, Santiago. "Uninvited Guests in the Backyard: Dangers and Risks of Terrorist and Anti-American Activity in Latin America." (2023).

[lviii] Sageman, Marc. "Self-Categorization Theory." Routledge Handbook of Transnational Terrorism (2023): 6.

[lix] Mohamed, Yasien. "The Concept of Jihad in Qutb and Shari'ati." *Afkar: Jurnal Akidah & Pemikiran Islam* 10, no. 1 (2009): 109-128.

[lx] Liang, Christina Schori. "The Technology of Terror: From Dynamite to the Metaverse." Global Terrorism Index 2022. Institute for Economics and Peace, March 2022.

[lxi] Nirenstein, Fiamma. "Human Rights and Anti-Semitism."

[lxii] Maher, Shiraz. Salafi-Jihadism: The history of an idea. Oxford University Press, 2016.

[lxiii] Malakoutikhah, Zeynab. "Iran: Sponsoring or combating terrorism?." Studies in Conflict & Terrorism 43, no. 10 (2020): 913-939.

[lxiv] Dunning, Tristan, and Anas Iqtait. "Arming Palestine: Resistance, Evolution, and Institutionalisation." In The Arms Race in the Middle East: Contemporary Security Dynamics, pp. 171-193. Cham: Springer International Publishing, 2023.

[lxv] MacEoin, Denis. "The Babi concept of holy war." Religion 12, no. 2 (1982).

[lxvi] Firestone, Reuven. "Conceptions of Holy War in Biblical and Qur'ānic Tradition." The Journal of Religious Ethics (1996): 99-123.

[lxvii] Shahzad, Umer, Muhammad Umar Farooq, and Fengming Qin. "Impacts of USAID and development assistance toward counterterrorism efforts: Empirical evidence in context of Pakistan." *Asian Social Work and Policy Review* 13, no. 3 (2019): 320-333.

[lxviii] [lxviii] In fact, a federal audit reveals that for years the government has "lacked a framework to manage fraud risks in humanitarian responses," in Syria. The culprit is the United States Agency for International Development (USAID), the State Department offshoot with a $40 billion budget that annually doles out gigantic sums to foreign causes, including a multitude of leftist groups around the globe. (MAY 12, 2022. JUDICIAL WATCH, U.S. Gives Terrorist Nation $15 Billion in Humanitarian Aid Despite Fraud, Abuse)

[lxix] Wiarda, Howard J., and Esther M. Skelley. The crisis of American foreign policy: the effects of a divided America. Rowman & Littlefield, 2006.

[lxx] This annual report of worldwide threats to the national security of the United States responds to Section 617 of the FY21 Intelligence Authorization Act (Pub. L. No. 116-260). This report reflects the collective insights of the Intelligence Community (IC), which is committed every day to providing the nuanced, independent, and unvarnished intelligence that policymakers, warfighters, and domestic law enforcement personnel need to protect American lives and America's interests anywhere in the world.

www.ingramcontent.com/pod-product-compliance
Lightning Source LLC
Chambersburg PA
CBHW072106270326
41931CB00010B/1470